"With a powerful wit, intense attentiveness, and eloquent empathy, Jewly Hight is a dream come true for the songwriters to whom she pays careful and affectionate heed. By calling our attention to them, she lifts their voices, testifying concerning the ways their work uplifts, invigorates, and challenges our otherwise all-too-settled imaginations. Prepare to be enriched by this culturally crucial account."

—David Dark, author of *The Sacredness of Questioning Everything*

Right by Her Roots
Americana Women and Their Songs

Jewly Hight

BAYLOR UNIVERSITY PRESS

Cover Design by Jeremy Reiss
Cover image ©iStockphoto.com/mbbirdy

Library of Congress Cataloging-in-Publication Data

Hight, Jewly.
  Right by her roots : Americana women and their songs / Jewly Hight.
      p. cm.
  Includes bibliographical references and index.
  ISBN 978-1-60258-060-2 (pbk. : alk. paper)
  1. Women alternative country musicians--United States. 2.
Alternative country musicians--United States. 3. Alternative country
music--United States--History and criticism. I. Title.
  ML3524.H54 2011
  781.642082'0973--dc22
                         2010038798

Printed in the United States of America on acid-free paper with a
minimum of 30% pcw recycled content.

For Bob, who listened to every bit of it.

Table of Contents

Acknowledgments

I once worked in a bookstore. To a few of my colleagues there, I mentioned that I wanted to write a book someday. They thought that seemed well within the realm of possibility. And for the early vote of confidence I am grateful.

I am grateful, too, to Terry Mattingly for taking me seriously as a writer, putting me through my paces, and ultimately hooking me up with a publisher who was interested in what I had to offer.

The seeds of this book were planted while I was a student at Vanderbilt University Divinity School, engaged in weekly discussions with John McClure about how to distill the essence of a perspective within a song. He had much of worth to share on the subject. Ellen Armour was an invaluable guide,who helped me sharpen the theoretical tools I brought to this project and generously allowed me to test my ideas. Melissa Snarr, Robin Jensen, and Diane Sasson provided much-appreciated counsel. Dale Cockrell's investment in southern musical history was contagious. And Victor Judge was far and away the greatest advocate a writer could have.

There have been many important conversation partners along the way: Sarah Masen and David Dark, wise, kind souls who had walked the road before; Sherry Cothran-Woolsey, who was working her way from text to music at the same time that I was headed the other direction; Stephanie Fields, whose excitement about and intuitive understanding of where I was going, and why, meant a lot. Others chewed over ideas with me or took a look at what I was working on and offered the simple yet significant reassurance that it was actually turning into something. For that, I want to thank Aaron Hoke Doenges, Ann Coble, Ken Locke, Richard Lloyd, Jo Ellen Werking-Weedman, Dave Perkins, Zachary Gresham, Angela Cowser, Jessica Devaney, Elisabeth Dawson, Tamara Saviano, and Betsy Phillips.

I am appreciative to Bill Friskics-Warren for the inspiration I have found in his spiritually attuned writing about music, as well as for his input and feedback. My thanks also to Juli Thanki, a fine writer in her own right and a long-distance reader with good suggestions. And to Peter Cooper, my respect and gratitude for sharing his considerable expertise on all things related to country music.

None have been greater friends or greater help to me than Barry Mazor, a writer of high quality, intelligence, and style, and Nina Melechen, a history scholar with considerable music smarts to boot. I came away from each conversation with them thinking more clearly about whatever I happened to be writing at the time and, often, equipped with additional listening and reading resources. For their time, their ears, their thoughts—which made all the difference in the world—I am truly grateful.

It was a privilege talking with each of the songwriters in this book. I thank them for their thoughtfulness, the access they granted me, and the many hours they spent with me on the other end of the phone line. I would also like to express my gratitude to those without whom these interviews would not have happened: Fount Lynch, Kathi Whitley, Buddy Miller, Michael Nieves, Cary Baker, Mark Spector, Sue Schrader, Traci Thomas, David Macias, and Carla Parisi.

For shepherding this first-time author through the process with great kindness and patience I voice my appreciation to my editor, Nicole Murphy.

And I thank my parents, Ron and Jerri Hight, who never squandered an opportunity to ask how the book was coming along, or to offer support.

Trite as this may seem, it is also absolutely true: I could not have made it through this and emerged on the other side with a bona fide book if it had not been for all of these folks.

Last, but most certainly not least, I extend my eternal gratitude to my husband, Bob Nickerson, who was a partner to me throughout this long and winding journey in the truest sense of the word: a fellow shoulderer of the load. He offered insightful feedback, endless understanding, and caring company—the thing a writer glued to an inhuman computer screen for hours on end needs most.

Also, he really did let me read him the entire book aloud.

It helped.

Introduction
The Art of Digging

I t is May 2005. Twenty-five-year-old Abigail Washburn is flying on a plane to somewhere, quite possibly China, turning
over in her mind the debut album she has just recorded—*Song of
the Traveling Daughter*. She realizes there is still one more thing
she needs to add to its rejuvenation of American old-time and
Asian folk flavors, its lyrics in English and Chinese, its cosmo-
politan spirit: a little bit of background—*her* background, the
story of what this music is all about, and how it came to mean
something to her. So she writes a note. It will be the first thing
people see when they open up the CD booklet: "I was born in
Illinois. I've lived a lot of places since then, including China."[1]

Two sentences in, and already she has supplied both a point
of origin and the sense that her journey has ranged far from it.
"Living in China, immersed in a culture so different from my
own, became not only a voyage from home, but also a discovery
of home," she continues. "Many things took on new meaning to
me: biscuits and gravy, soda pop, stars and stripes, bluegrass,

rap, NASCAR, wide streets, suburbs, individual debt, and civil rights—all things seemingly uniquely American. When I returned to America, I wanted to continue the exploration, to delve deeper into the roots of things American—so I bought a banjo."[2]

As she writes these words, Washburn has a hunch: while the use to which she is putting that banjo may seem a little unorthodox, hearing how she arrived at her approach to music making will strike a chord with people. They will, she believes, understand her desire to grasp hold of sturdy roots as she makes sense of change in her life.

Shaken by the Roots

Washburn is hardly the first person for whom rootedness has intertwined with mutability. The United States is a nation of immigrants, people who thoroughly and completely uprooted themselves to get here when they did, and people willing to do the same to get here now. Those who were not immigrants were slaves or native peoples, and in their cases, the uprooting was certainly not by choice; even their memories of their roots were assailed with imperialistic, whitewashing force.

Americans ceased living rooted, rural lives close to their blood and cultural kin a few generations ago, when survival required migrating to not-so-rural places where there was work to be found. A great many baby boomers grew up in postwar suburbs without the sort of robust communities that had once done so much to shape how people saw the world and their places in it; folk music scholar Robert Cantwell has shown that this had more than a little to do with many of the middle class and college age among them seeking out folk music from before their time.[3] In this present time, we all but expect American youth to have to, or want to, leave the places where they grew up.

In all, life in our Internet age feels supremely fragmented. Social networking sites offer the chance to "reconnect" with some long-lost friend, lover, classmate, or third cousin, but

often, in the end, such sites just remind us how very *discon-*
nected we really are. And lots of people are intent on reaching
further back—well beyond the ranks of the living and online
profile-updating—through Web sites that will, for a monthly
fee, help them unearth generation after generation of their family roots. In 2010 alone there were two television shows that
did just that—albeit with a tad more glamour and editing—for
celebrities: network television's chipper *Who Do You Think You
Are?* and public television's serious-minded *Faces of America*."
With anxiety percolating nationwide over the subject of immi-
gration, the question of where people came from has become an
especially loaded one.

Popular music has also reached something of a conflicted
juncture. Since the '70s singer-songwriter era, performers have
emphasized the personalness of their material. The tendency has
escalated in recent years; Hugh Barker and Yuval Taylor, authors
of *Faking It: The Quest for Authenticity in Popular Music*, point out
that in 2004 three of the pop albums to hit number one bore the
artificially intimate titles of *Autobiography, Confessions,* and *The
Diary of Alicia Keys.*[4] Even so, the same songs that are portrayed
as the most personal, the most confessional often lack any real
sense of connection to the singer's larger personal narrative. On
the other hand, from the '90s on much music made by and for
Generations X and Y has been steeped in ironic distance; when
performers have revived an older musical style or sensibility,
they have frequently made clear that they do not mean it in the
same way that those who first played that same music meant it.[5]

Something Old, Something New

So it is a good time, indeed, to contemplate eight singers and
songwriters of contemporary American roots music—or, more
officially, Americana—who, in their music, and without the
shield of irony, work out their changing relationships to their
own roots; geographical, cultural, familial, or religious. Those
eight are Lucinda Williams, Julie Miller, Victoria Williams (no

relation to Lucinda), Michelle Shocked, Mary Gauthier, Ruthie Foster, Elizabeth Cook, and Abigail Washburn.

Though Americana began taking shape as a musical genre—a genre that would eventually have not just its own radio format but also trade organization and Grammy award category—only in the mid-'90s, several of these recording artists had already been making music for years by then. And the practice of drawing on older sounds in the creation of new ones had been around far longer. The call to get back to more traditional sensibilities cycles around with regular rhythm in country music, Protestant church music, and elsewhere. Sure, the neotraditional movement famously swept into country music in the early '80s with singers like George Strait and Ricky Skaggs, but, as pointed out by the late sociologist Richard A. Peterson, that was far from the first time the genre's momentum had swung from pop sounds to rootsier fare.[6] In the mid-'70s, cultural critic Greil Marcus described what the Band—country rockers who are now regarded as some of Americana's patron saints—gained from looking back in order to look forward: "Against a cult of youth they felt for a continuity of generations; against the instant America of the sixties they looked for the traditions that made new things not only possible, but valuable; against a flight from roots they set a sense of place."[7]

Americana is, ostensibly, home to all manner of American roots music styles (though it has notably little racial diversity in terms of performers): old-time, alt-country, hard country, country rock, roots rock, punkish string bands, bluegrass, southern soul, folksingers, singer-songwriters, indie folk singer-songwriters, blues, zydeco, sacred steel, gospel (so long as it is old enough), and so on. Some of these styles were once the popular music of their time and place, but none of them are ruling mainstream airwaves now. As popular music historian Diane Pecknold observes, what we are talking about when we talk about Americana is music that *is* commercial, just "not commercial enough to be played on mainstream radio."[8] On the other side of the coin, it is also music born of considerable artistic free-dom—though, when a major record label is involved, as we will see, the freedom may have to be fought for.

Having Their Druthers

These eight have all made choices about how to invest their cre-ative energies; chasing contemporary superstardom—with the trade-off it generally requires (less self-determination for more marketing muscle)—does not rank high on their lists. They would rather be able to make the music they want to make. In the forthright words of Elizabeth Cook, delivered with a know-ing laugh, "I get my way a lot. And I think I should. Because if I'm going to go out and do what I do, and spend Easter weekend touring the Rust Belt, then by God, you know . . . I need to get to have my druthers a little bit when it comes to what I'm doing."

The eight bodies of work before us present eight unmistak-able voices and vantage points; they are ripe for the consider-ation of what roots can mean to artistic, personal, and spiritual development. And if these women have not always gotten as much, or as serious, attention as they deserve, if they have been misinterpreted, underestimated, or oversimplified—like Cook, Julie Miller, and Victoria Williams, possessors of strikingly youthful-sounding female voices, and sometimes dismissed as innocent or girlish because of it—this is an effort to see, hear, and feel what is *really* there.

In this book, I consider the entirety of these singer-songwriters' recorded output—not just a few signature songs or a pivotal album; such abbreviated glimpses would hardly do justice to the full arcs of their journeys. Woven into the discus-sion is what each had to say, during hours of original interviews, about where she comes from, what she does, and why she does it. All eight proved generous conversation partners, willing to entertain big, demanding questions. Distill those questions to their essences, and they get to the heart of the book: Have these eight, indeed, stayed right by their roots? What does where they came from have to do with the music they make and what matters to them? How do they make sense of change? What do their bodies of work tell us they are about? How do they view the world? What do they give to and get from music making?

Eight Ways to Go

These kinds of questions matter deeply to me. I make my living asking questions of musicians, but, because of the nature of the job—generally speaking, reporting the newest and most newsworthy of stories—I am not always able to ask questions like these. When I studied theology as a master's student, I read constructive theologians, who apply new thinking to older traditions and bring their own creativity and experience to bear. And I take notice of the shape that ideas about spirituality, meaning, purpose, divinity, and humanity take in the work of a singer and songwriter who is given to writing about such things. Experience, I have found, is often a bigger influence than orthodoxy; I suspect that is just as true of a lot of people who have never written a song. Some of the newer theological approaches that I found compelling—feminist, womanist (which prioritizes black women's perspectives), and *mujerista* (which prioritizes Latinas')—emphasize that particular, on-the-ground voices, especially those that have not been listened to, ought to be; those voices can tell us what rings true in real lives.[9] And, since I have written songs and performed them myself, I know the challenge of trying to express an idea, emotion, or vignette in that way, then taking the risk of putting a song out there to find out whether or not it affects people at all the way I hoped it would.

This book treats as many different roots and routes as it does songwriters. At one end of the spectrum is Elizabeth Cook, who, in her own time and on her own terms, picked up where her mother's true-blue country singing aspirations left off. There is Ruthie Foster, too, whose mother and grandmother emboldened her to sing; she later turned to songwriting on her own. And there is Lucinda Williams; she studied the contrast between the two sides of her family and determined the kind of writer she did, and did not, want to be: one who integrated head and heart and was not pulled under by religious or emotional guilt. Mary Gauthier could not come from a more different place: she was an orphan, surrendered by her mother. And, in her songwriting, she turns the notion of belonging on its head; strangers who share her experience are family to her, and her family, strangers.

None of these eight are more sensitive to those on the receiving end of her music, however, than Julie Miller; she extends a heart acutely attuned to people's wounds and vulnerabilities. Victoria Williams' benevolent desire is that her music be "good for people"; she chooses to share with them her bracing, spontaneous freedom, so they can taste it for themselves. And Abigail Washburn shows that she takes to heart what speaks to her audiences—both Chinese and American—by her openness to reshaping her approach to music in ways big and small.

Personal change in the lives of some of these women has forever altered the way they make music. Miller used to feel as though she could not write songs at all, until she had a life-altering spiritual epiphany; now she writes them by the truckload. And Gauthier could not really conceive of whom she would write songs about—or for—until she worked through Alcoholics Anonymous' spiritually transformative twelve steps; then her perspective shifted, as she so efficiently puts it, "from I to we."

Shocked embodies a particularly vivid, and continual, example of change. She has kept things rather unpredictable by progressing through an array of musical styles; radical protest folksinger to subversive swing performer to writer of heartfelt dub-style spirituals and so on. The other thing about all that musical change is it profoundly changed *her*. She got interested in gospel music, probed what lay beneath its sound, and found herself primed for conversion.

Shocked has been at singing and songwriting for a quarter century, and Lucinda Williams' career has several years on hers. Cook, on the other hand, only recently reached the decade mark, and Washburn has been recording for half that long. That is no small range of age and experience. Williams can look back on her body of work with a different perspective—that is, a lot more of it. And it is with her that we begin our journey. Two decades she labored before having her breakthrough album, and, in that time, a good many people grew passionately attached to her songs. With the stakes at their highest, she did a bold thing: changed the way she wrote. What priorities drive a songwriter to do such a thing? What priorities drive any songwriter to go against the grain when it really counts? We are about to find out.

Lucinda Williams
Life-and-Death Matters

A Grammy-winning singer and songwriter of confessional force and the daughter of a respected poet, Lucinda Williams is one of her generation's most influential purveyors of literary folk, rock, and blues.

It is difficult to imagine a discussion of important Americana songwriting that does not consider the body of work of Lucinda Williams. Not only because she showed up early and stuck around, though she did and has—long enough to have already celebrated her thirtieth anniversary as a recording artist, making her the veteran of this group. Also, few performers in contemporary American roots music can claim as potent a mixture of audience devotion, musical influence, critical acclaim, and tangible success as her. To show for her time and effort, Williams has three Grammy Awards and, in the past decade, three Top 25 showings on the *Billboard* 200 chart. There is also her more lasting achievement, a thing that cannot be so easily captured on paper: she has set a high-water mark in roots music for raw, vigorously descriptive soul-baring.

Williams was born in Lake Charles, Louisiana, in 1953. When writers try to put their fingers on who or what she encountered early in life that inspired her to take her singing and songwriting in the directions she has, they may well bring up her literary father, Miller Williams, who was only the third poet to be selected to read at a U.S. presidential inauguration (in his case, President Clinton's second), and his literary circle of friends; or the revelatory experience she had at age twelve when somebody put on the turntable Bob Dylan's 1965 LP *Highway 61 Revisited*—the first album of his to fully merge substantial lyrics with electric rock and roll and blues; or her discovery at around age seventeen of the records her father owned by pre-war Delta bluesman Robert Johnson. Certainly, there are connections among all these points and the ways that Williams has fused passion and intellect in her own music. But there were other important catalysts, too.

She has also borne witness to destruction of the human spirit by inner darkness. Seldom do profilers make much of her developing a connection with the work of the viscerally confessional, Pulitzer Prize–winning poet Anne Sexton around the same time that Johnson's blues caught her ear. "I read the letters of Anne Sexton when I was a teenager," she recalls, appending this not insignificant fact to her thoughts on the subject of direct, unsentimental artistic expression. "I was real taken with her life and everything." Rarely, too, do they consider how her sensibilities were affected by her first experiences with people from her circle, writers particularly, committing suicide. Reading about such inner turmoil and witnessing its deadly results mattered to her. Not that they supplied her with a model for the artistic life; rather, they stoked the fires beneath her music and multiplied her desire for cathartic expression.

Anguished artists like Sexton, Sexton's poetic peer Sylvia Plath, and photographer of fringe dwellers Diane Arbus—all three of whom eventually took their own lives and were recurring, if incidental, topics during one of our interviews—capture Williams' attention to this day. She cannot shake the question their experiences raise for her: Why does a person, especially someone with a formidable expressive gift, let go of life? "I just want to know 'What went wrong? What happened? Who were they?'" she shares.

Within her own family, on her mother's side, Williams saw how easy it is to get swallowed up in dense shadows of debilitating emotion and religious guilt. And that seemed to her a terrifically unappealing path. In her father, who had been a professor of biology before switching his attentions to the writing and teaching of literature, she saw the possibility of living with questions and desires—and letting out what one needs to let out. She found that to be a better way to go.

From her influences and her roots, Williams drew insight about how to survive and even thrive, and she offers her response—strenuous, vital expression—in her music. There are a good many close-to-the-bone songs in her repertoire, songs weighted with the feeling that life and death hang in the balance, even if death is not their explicit subject matter. Hers are the songs of a soul who refuses to succumb.

Such intensity, particularly coming from a singer and songwriter who is a woman, may have something to do with her occasionally being pegged—rather unfairly—as a tortured soul. "I'm a very forward, positive person, actually," she rebuts. "People might not realize that about me. I mean, I'm not a Pollyanna, but, you know. . . ."

For a glimpse of Williams' particular kind of positivity, consider a pair of songs she wrote after the suicides of two writers she knew personally. Both are on her 1992 album *Sweet Old World* and are in their own ways life-affirming. "Pineola" is a rawboned country rock narrative, at once primal and literary, that captures the loss and grief people are thrown into when "Sonny" shoots himself. The way she tells the story gets across that his life and its promise meant something to those people. Says Williams, "The poet in 'Pineola,' he actually did take his own life. That was one of my earliest, earliest experiences seeing someone just completely throwing away a brilliant career. I mean, this guy, he was like the golden boy: Frank Stanford. Just rugged good looks and a charming personality. My dad and the other writers thought he was brilliant and he had a brilliant career as a writer ahead of him, and the rest of it. I was pretty young when that happened . . . I went to the funeral with my dad and some of the other writers. That experience, needless to say, made quite an impression on me."

The counterpart to "Pineola" is a gracefully wilted, Latin-tinged ballad called "Sweet Old World," inspired by the untimely death of another young poet, to whom Williams addresses the song. She asks if he felt worthless and unloved; she laments that he has given up the pleasures of sensual, bodily existence and human connection. Irreversible loss of life is the song's backdrop, but Williams overshadows it with affectionate descriptions of small moments that lend life meaning. "I don't look at that as a dark song," she explains. "At the end of it there's some joy there. Basically it's saying, you know, 'Life is worth it.'"

Happy as a Blueswoman

Williams' official catalog includes ten studio albums, plus a double-disc live set recorded at the Fillmore. The first two, 1979's *Ramblin'* and 1980's *Happy Woman Blues*, were released on Folkways, a label known historically for emphasizing the cultural worth of folk music that has since been purchased by the Smithsonian. The next two, 1988's *Lucinda Williams*—featuring "Passionate Kisses," which would earn her a songwriting Grammy when country-folk performer Mary Chapin Carpenter recorded it a few years later—and 1992's *Sweet Old World*, were also released by small, alternative labels (Rough Trade and Chameleon, respectively). Somewhere in there, one major label nearly took a chance on her but concluded she sounded a little too country for rock and too rock for country, and another let her make an album but not at all the way she wanted to make it, so she ended the relationship.

If there was one album that brought Williams significantly wider attention, it was 1998's *Car Wheels on a Gravel Road*, which passed through a few different incarnations and shifted hands before finally coming out on the major label Mercury—all of which paid off when it won a Grammy for Best Contemporary Folk Album. She stuck with Mercury—technically its rootsier imprint Lost Highway—for *Essence*, released in 2001, *World Without Tears*, in 2003, *West*, in 2007, *Little Honey*, a year later, and *Blessed*, in 2011.

Recording-wise, Williams presented herself as a blues singer before she showcased her songwriting. *Ramblin'* is all country blues and hillbilly covers—no originals whatsoever—and those covers are given rather sparse treatment; just her swooping vibrato singing and insistent acoustic guitar playing with some elemental, note-worrying licks laid overtop by a single accompanist. For this, her first album, she went with generations-old material, assuming that was what traditionally minded Folkways would want. Among the songs she chose were three by Robert Johnson, the most mythologized of pre-electric bluesmen— "Ramblin' on My Mind," "Malted Milk Blues," and "Stop Breakin' Down"—and one, "Me and My Chauffeur Blues," by Memphis Minnie, an exceptionally unique blueswomen for her time, who not only sang but wrote songs and played a mean guitar, too.

"I really got into Robert Johnson when I discovered him," Williams emphasizes. "I just really identified with him, with his lyrics. They were just so direct and so, you know, just overtly sexual and primal—*primal* is the word that comes to mind." In *Mystery Train*, Greil Marcus describes the same extremeness that Williams picked up on in Johnson's music: "It was a drama of sex, shot through with acts of violence and tenderness; with desires that no one could satisfy; with crimes that could not be explained; with punishments that could not be escaped."[1]

Williams has no problem summoning ferocious physicality herself. One wonders if the sheer bodiliness of those blues songs was what drew her to them in the first place. "Yeah," she confirms. "It's hard to explain in words. But that is what it is, I mean, which is why it's hard to explain in words. . . . It's the *feel* thing. Just the feeling of—I don't know—the tempo and the rhythm and the whole thing. But also the lyrics; the lyrics really grabbed me." As for those lyrics, "They got pretty down and dirty. . . . And I just thought it was brilliant, so honest. It made me feel good to listen to it and good to sing it. I mean, it was such a relief. It wasn't like blues was sad music; it was a celebration."

Blues certainly has a reputation for being sad—*blue*—music, but if that were the sum total of its emotional content, Williams would probably not have found so much in it that speaks to her. The "blues impulse," as defined by scholar of black music Craig Werner, may be survivalist, but it is anything but defeatist: "Singing the blues doesn't reaffirm the brutal experience, it reaffirms the value of life. The blues don't even pretend you're going to escape the cycle. You sing the blues so that you can live to sing the blues again."[2]

Even if Williams' performances on *Ramblin'* were not exactly revelatory, if she had not yet learned how to draw deep from her own well of visceral feeling, both that album and the title track of her next, *Happy Woman Blues*—a hard-driving original about pursuing satisfaction—strongly suggested that she would. "I had it in my head," she says in hindsight, "but I couldn't quite make it come out the way I really wanted it to until some years later." She almost never works in a straight-ahead, twelve-bar blues idiom, but her ability to write and sing with smoldering blues feeling is undeniable.

Williams recalls running into dismissive attitudes toward blues in the '70s when she played shows with other female singers and songwriters around Houston and Austin. Blues-pop singer-guitarist Bonnie Raitt was the subject of one backstage discussion: "Somebody said, 'Well, you know, we don't listen to her anymore, because she's singing those blues songs and that's just sexist stuff. It puts women down.'" Williams did not agree. "That was a big turning point for me," she says, "and I just went, 'Whatever. See ya. I'm going to go do my thing and embrace it and make it my own.'" And even though blues may today be frequently thought of as male-centric music—and, presumably, in the estimation of her peers backstage back then, not very empowering for a woman to sing—her attitude toward it was not without historical precedent. The first blues stars were the classic female blues divas of the 1920s and 1930s, like Bessie Smith, and, as scholar-activist Angela Y. Davis points out, women singing blues then—much like Williams singing it now—"had no qualms about announcing female desire."[3]

What Williams Wants

Williams vowed to herself, those years ago, that she would do her thing, embrace blues-style expression, and make it her own, and that is what she has done—and done in ways ultimately no less captivating and freeing to her numerous male listeners than the female members of her audience. She testifies forthrightly to the emotions roiled in relationships; she makes her desires known—sexual, spiritual, or otherwise—without beating around the bush and proves how satisfying it is for a woman, or any person, to freely and boldly express such things. With her lyrics, she has dug for bracing new language; with her singing, she has learned to let her gut lead.

All of those carnal elements are represented in "Hot Blood." The humid southern boogie on *Sweet Old World* lives up to its title. Williams sounds hot and bothered, alternately rising and plunging to the extremes of her vocal range as she describes intense physical sensation, with voice-like slide guitar licks echoing each line she sings. In this song, it does not take much to stoke her desire—nothing more than seeing the object of it doing workaday chores. She lowers her voice seductively at the end of each verse to describe the sightings: grocery shopping for casserole makings, doing laundry, changing a tire. Clearly it is not the mundane contexts that provide the heat—it is *her*.

Lest there be any question, considering Williams wrote "Hot Blood" nearly two decades ago, she has not felt the need to tone down her venting of desire as she has gotten older; she still seems absolutely in her element singing about it. In fact, some of her most recent albums boast her fiercest sexual declarations: "Come On," on *West*, and "Honey Bee," on *Little Honey*. She roars savagely over the carnal hard rock of "Come On." The wordplay of the title cuts several ways, each sharp as a knife's edge; the song is an agitated complaint, a well-aimed, dark-humored blow to the ego and a challenge that piles on pressure. She is not satisfied. Her lover, too busy being stuck on himself, has not made any effort to make her feel good. "When you're talking about something as serious as that, you're kind of angry and pissed off," she says, "but at the same time you're trying to be kind of tongue-in-cheek, I guess, a little bit."

"Honey Bee" is a rare instance of Williams working a traditional blues metaphor: the poked-with-a-stinger double entendre territory of classic blues numbers like Slim Harpo's "King Bee" or Memphis Minnie's "Bumble Bee." And her feelings are even less ambiguous than theirs, if such a thing is possible. As she bears down hard on the sledgehammering garage blues, twisting her voice into guttural contortions, she makes clear that she and her lover have a good, hot thing going, and she is not afraid to let herself get caught up in it.

Elsewhere, Williams sings not only about what she wants but also about actively going after it. There are two songs of that sort on *Essence*. During "Steal Your Love," she declares that she will claim the affections of her more bashful would-be lover. During "Essence"—the album's slinking, roots rock title track—she sings in a raw, hungry groan about pursuing her lover all over the place, seeking her spiritual and sexual fix. And if she cannot literally be at all places at once, surely her desire can be felt everywhere.

Exercising Free Will

Williams' embrace of the carnal bears no trace of religious guilt. There is none of the wrenching Saturday night–Sunday morning tension identified, rightly or wrongly, with the work of many church-influenced southern musicians; none of the compulsion to repent for having too good, too sensual, too intense a time. She has a fairly unique attitude toward religion for someone born during the '50s and raised in Lake Charles, Baton Rouge, and New Orleans, Louisiana; Jackson and Vicksburg, Mississippi; and other mostly southern towns (along with Mexico City and Santiago, Chile) where her father held teaching posts, and most especially for someone with grandfathers on both sides of her family who were Christian ministers. She describes growing up in close proximity to two markedly different interpretations of the Christian faith: one relatively at ease in the world and inclined to take on social problems, the other distrusting of the world and focused on people's need to be cleansed of its evils.

"My dad's father was a very progressive thinker, very open-minded," Williams recalls. "He was a Socialist Democrat, you know, very free thinker. I always say he was a Christian in the true sense of the word." She adds, "And then my mother's father was a . . . hellfire-and-brimstone fundamentalist. So I had that going on on that side of the family."

Williams resonated far less with the worldview of her mother than with that of her father, an agnostic. By the time she reached her teens, her dad was publishing collections of poetry: clear-eyed, sharp-humored verse, written in sensual yet scientific language and laced with playful, thoroughgoing skepticism. His "Notes in a Minister's Hymnbook," for instance, ends with the minister confined to earthy and earthly realities, confessing that the miracles in scripture are beyond him.[4]

When it came to religious grounding, then, Williams was presented with options, and she does not take that fact for granted: "Yeah, I think that I was real fortunate in that regard, because my dad . . . you know, he rebelled against it, but not in a guilty way. There wasn't any guilt involved. But my mother, on the other hand, struggled with intense guilt. . . . And I don't think she ever really recovered. She met my dad, who was the intellectual. Here is the poet guy who was totally different from the way she was raised. She just ran in his direction to get away. But she never really got away. She just had mental breakdowns and just struggled her whole life, my whole life."

Williams emerged from her upbringing with an active interest in religion, along with clear ideas about how she would and would not define her own relation to it. "I've often thought if I stayed in school I might've studied comparative religion," she muses. (For the record, her studies at the University of Arkansas, where her father was then employed, were cut three or so years short.) "I love the imagery, the art. I've got this collection of crosses. Why am I drawn, even though I'm not technically a Christian? I don't know. I love the symbolism. I like what it symbolizes. I don't believe in original sin, so I can't call myself a Christian. . . . I don't call myself agnostic. I don't call myself an atheist. If somebody asks me 'Do you believe in God?' I would say 'Yes.'"

On the rare occasions when Williams has taken up religion as a song subject, the result has packed a punch. In "Atonement" on *World Without Tears* she steps into the role of one of the most fascinating, feared, and dramatized figures in modern Protestant Christianity: the fire-and-brimstone preacher. The song draws a good bit of its inspiration from the novel *Wise Blood* by the southern, Catholic author Flannery O'Connor, who was a friend of Williams' father. It is by far one of the darkest and most sinister-sounding songs in her repertoire. "I'm always sort of struggling, you know, trying to find a way to explain that song to people before I sing it, so they'll understand it better," Williams says. "Sometimes I don't bother explaining. I just sing it and I think people get it. But that seems to be the best way to connect the song is to, you know, mention Flannery O'Connor, and *Wise Blood* particularly."

In *Wise Blood*, the protagonist Hazel Motes—a tortured spiritual seeker, in spite of himself—is flanked by preachers who are scheming shams at best and cruel manipulators at worst.[5] In the song "Atonement," Williams amplifies the worst impulses of those grotesquely flawed religious figures. Her preacher is a poor specimen indeed: violent with a false and power-hungry heart. He gleefully portrays people as vermin who need their noses rubbed in their own filth. What he is extending is clearly nothing like sacramental bread of communion—it is poison. The band lurches along in a depraved shuffle, the drums trashy and clanging, the bass overdriven to the point of sounding like a murderous mutant hornet, and the electric guitar solo mocking and dissonant. But Williams' singing is the most intimidating part, a taunting, jabbing attack, so thoroughly distorted by vocal effects as to obscure—or exorcise—any trace of humanity.

Though this song is laced with disgust for religious condemnation and corruption, religious passion, on the other hand, is something Williams admires. She made it a centerpiece of "Get Right with God," the 2001 Grammy winner for Best Female Rock Vocal Performance, on *Essence*. And to give that vocal performance, she put herself in what she imagined to be the mindset of a charismatic believer. Unlike "Atonement," the song is not meant to be ugly. It has a dogged country blues groove that you could dance to, a solid, energetic backbeat that practically begs for people to clap along. Williams' charismatic character is intent on making spirit-filled demonstrations of faith and self-flagellating sacrifice. Whatever it takes to satisfy God. "At the time I wrote it," Williams points out, "I was living in Nashville, and I'd been really intrigued by the Pentecostal serpent handlers." (She means those she read about in books like *Salvation on Sand Mountain: Snake Handling and Redemption in Southern Appalachia*. Such rare and extreme religious practices as snake handling are hardly common within Nashville's city limits.)

There is real verve to Williams' singing of "Get Right with God," but she is also just distanced enough from the words that the song would never be confused with autobiography; it is more like an admiring, immersive character study. "I mean, because anyone who's that passionate, you know, I admire the passion," she says. She is quite aware, though, that even the most heartfelt appreciation of the words she sings is not the same thing as meaning them to be directly applied to her life. "Well, like when Charlie Louvin [of the legendary country and gospel brother duo the Louvin Brothers] was opening up for us on this tour," she offers by way of example. "He started coming out and singing that song with me. I mean, now when he sings it, he's coming from a whole other perspective."

One of Williams' most recent divine addresses is "Unsuffer Me" on *West*, and it seems nearer to where she is coming from herself. Listening only to the music and her vocal delivery, one could be forgiven for assuming the song is aimed at a lover—a human lover. She drawls and groans lustfully over rock that is not only slow as molasses but heavy, thick and dark as it, too, with wailing, drawn-out guitar licks and sinuous strings. But as soon as the lyrics register, you hear something else: a string of petitions both prayerful and erotic, with wordplay that draws on, yet stands out from, the familiar language of both. She explains of her intentions, "I look at a song like 'Unsuffer Me' . . . as a song of spiritual redemption, spiritual cleansing, and opening myself up to a higher power and kind of saying, 'Look, I'm kind of letting go; I'm giving myself over to whatever that spiritual higher power is,' kind of thing." She asks that higher power to touch her, to loose her bonds, salve her pain, tap her capacity to love, and bring her ecstasy. And the simple act of voicing her spiritual yearnings itself seems to bring her some relief.

Bold Language Arts

Unvarnished expression, of this or any other sort, fulfills a primal need for Williams. "It's satisfying . . . to write about anything that's been on my mind, that I've been thinking about," she offers. "Once I get it down on paper, it's very therapeutic and kind of cathartic almost, just the act of completing a song. Because everything I write, it's something that I'm looking at or I'm experiencing firsthand or I'm observing or I've been through or something. It's like my journal almost. That's why I write in the first place."

Williams describes her relationship with expression in a song on *West* called, quite simply, "Words." It is rich in imagery and thoroughly alliterative—really more a poem than a song—and glides with bossa nova-like sophistication accented by pearlescent guitar arpeggios. She personifies her words, describing them as active, resilient, trustworthy beings. Her words are her companions, defenders, and healers, even when she faces a force as potentially dampening as verbal abuse—an experience that inspired the song: "That's what that song is coming from, actually a place of 'You can say whatever you want to say, but you'll never take this away from me. You'll never be able to own that part of me.'" What Williams fears most is *not* using her words.

For a long time, her poet father served as a sounding board for her lyric writing, challenging her to not settle for anything less than potent, original, evocative language. She relates, "When I very first started writing, my dad said, 'Okay, songwriting . . . rule number one: stay away from overused clichés, like "the moon in June" and "stars in your eyes." And don't overuse the same words all the time.'" Until *Car Wheels on a Gravel Road*, she would send him her songs to critique before she recorded them; by that time, she had learned her lessons well and developed her own lean yet robust approach to lyric writing.

However, Williams has not always had a very easy time realizing her visions for her songs. No period in her career was more difficult in that regard than the making of *Car Wheels*. She recorded the album—most of it, anyway—three separate times with three separate producers: first her former lead guitarist and producer Gurf Morlix, then country rock and folk agitator Steve Earle, and finally Roy Bittan, longtime keyboardist for Bruce Springsteen's E Street Band. The by-product, of course, was that the time, money, and effort it took to get the album made multiplied. And Williams got plenty of grief for it, a notorious example being a 1997 *New York Times Magazine* feature than ran under the derisive headline "Lucinda Williams Is in Pain." The writer of it sat in on some of her under-the-gun recording sessions with Bittan, then proceeded to describe them in a way that made her sound completely irrational, and even a little crazy.[6] If Williams' record making process was scrutinized, the final version of *Car Wheels* won her fervent praise, a larger audience, and a Grammy. It also raised the stakes substantially where her songwriting was concerned. "It was the first time that I'd been . . . discovered, quote unquote, and people were looking at my songs more closely," Williams recalls. "And I found myself trapped almost with this idea that I had to somehow create all these new narrative songs, which . . . don't all come that quickly and easily."

Williams does have a way with narrative. There were songs on *Car Wheels* that captured the feel and power of places in her youthful southern geography. In the appealingly sturdy country rock title track, she wove together clear-eyed memories from a young child's perspective: shacks and cotton fields on the other side of the car window, the unsettling tones of adult voices issuing gruff orders one minute and keeping secrets the next. The very next track, "2 Kool 2 Be 4-Gotten," is a hip, humid reverie that lazes just behind the beat, and one of the most detail-rich songs in Williams' catalog. She describes indelible moments, like hearing the music of Mississippi native Robert Johnson playing in a Clarksdale, Mississippi, juke joint, encountering a zealous, aspiring snake handler, and saying "no" to jumping off a bridge with a lover.

Even with Williams' established reputation for narrative songs and people's expectations that she try to outdo herself with more and better of the same, she took a risk and followed her creative instincts in a very different direction. "I started messing around with some ideas and ended up with . . . what

I call kind of 'small' songs, like 'Steal Your Love' and 'Are You Down?'" she says, referring to two lyrically minimalistic songs on her subsequent album, *Essence*. "At first I thought, 'Well, this is a nice idea for a song, but it has to go further than this. It's not enough.' . . . And then something in me just went, 'You know what? What the hell? Let's see what happens.'"

The so-called "small" songs—small only in terms of word count—are lean, chorus-less compositions pried out of familiar song structure. She dared to follow the success of *Car Wheels* with a good many of those hypnotic, groove-riding meditations, first on *Essence*, next on *World Without Tears*, then on *West*. She ventures, "If I'd done *Car Wheels II*, I would have been criticized for doing just another *Car Wheels*. You can't really win for losing, because if you keep doing the same record over and over, then that's going to become kind of boring. But if you try to do something different, then people criticize you for doing something different. So you really just have to just stand your ground and do what you feel like the right thing to do is to keep yourself interested first and then hope that everybody else catches up."[7]

For a songwriter who had finally "arrived," it was no small risk. "There was a little backlash from [*Essence*], because it didn't have as many narrative songs on it and [was] just a different kind of thing. Then with *World Without Tears*, there was a little backlash from that, especially on 'Righteously.' I got 'Oh, she's trying to do hip-hop.'" Williams, you see, had not given "Righteously" a proper chorus. Nor had she sung it, per se; instead she had done a seductive sung-spoken slurring—not exactly rapping—over the seamless churn-and-flow of the drums and bass and heated streaks of slide guitar.

The Gift That Should Never Be Given Up

That Williams has at times struggled with record labels, producers, and critics in order to expand her range of expression and to make real the ideas she hears in her head lends a song like "Drunken Angel" the authority of experience. It is a jangling country rock eulogy with teeth on *Car Wheels on a Gravel Road*. She had a gifted writer in mind—this time of songs rather than poems—whose career and life were cut short not by suicide but by chosen lifestyle; the "drunken angel" was deceased Texas singer-songwriter and hard-living bohemian Blaze Foley. She gushes about the power his songs had over people, and it is on that same point that she takes him to task. There is disgust in her voice as she digs at blunt questions; she wants to know why he squandered the chance to pour his soul into songs that stirred people to devotion. Williams says of Foley, "I saw him playing and being around, you know, when I was in Houston and Austin. He was just one of these wild, wooly characters who'd try to keep up with [legendary, now also deceased, singer-songwriter] Townes Van Zandt, which no one could do. Of course, there was Townes, and then how many other ones have there been who just kind of drove themselves down? Even with what they had, they just couldn't seem to stay above ground."

There is, however, real-time urgency to "Little Rock Star" on *Little Honey*. Williams' musician addressee is in the thick of danger, not beyond it, being still alive and capable of making music. The track gradually swells into a rock anthem of towering, U2-like proportions with a clamorous wall of guitars. Propelled by this dramatic accompaniment, she runs down the troubling facts: this musician has a volatile self-destructive streak to go with his considerable talent. As the irony-laced title suggests, she has little patience for his out-of-control, exhibitionist antics. But it is clear she also feels genuine concern and empathy and a strong desire to not see this person crash and burn. "'Little Rock Star' was inspired partly from my friendship with Ryan Adams," Williams offers. And considering that Adams—a country-spiked rock and roller—has a history of drug and alcohol abuse and sometimes unpredictable behavior, the song's sentiments make sense. "I knew him when he first moved to Nashville, his genius and brilliance, which I was just blown away by," she says. "But then he struggled with the self-destructive nature. I saw people just kind of standing back going, 'Oh, god. What is he going to do?'"

Williams is quick to praise musicians she feels are deserving, and just as quick to shoot down excuses people might make for those who seem to doom themselves, and their artistry, with their destructive behavior; the two reactions are not unrelated. "I could have been like that if I'd chosen that path," she insists, referring to a ruinous path taken by a multitude of performers, not any particular one. "You talk about somebody and people go 'Oh, well, he or she had such a difficult childhood,' or whatever. It's like 'You want to talk about difficult childhoods? Where do you want to start?' I'm very empathetic. I'm able to understand it because my mother suffered from severe mental illness and alcoholism. So I sort of look at it like it's a cop-out, to tell you the honest truth. It pisses me off."

Little Honey is also home to another song about an artist in peril, "Rarity," though the sound and spirit of it could hardly be more different from those of "Little Rock Star," or, for that matter, "Drunken Angel." It is tranquil, reverent, and the album's longest track by a margin of nearly three minutes, a drifting soundscape of glassy guitars, burnished horns, and faintly pulsing percussion. Williams has said elsewhere that she wrote the song with the experimental, and fairly obscure, singer and songwriter Mia Doi Todd in mind.[8] She savors her superlative, poetic words of praise for this musician, releasing them slowly with gently drawled vibrato, and mourns the incongruity between Todd's artistic gifts and character and the unappreciative reception they have gotten. Williams' lyrics are enflamed with a righteous indignation that is also deeply mournful.

What's Inside Must Come Out

There is nothing at all casual about the relationships Williams envisions between musicians and their creative outlets, no doubt because songwriting is not at all a casual thing for her. "It probably keeps me from going crazy," she says. And what if she could not write? "I think I would just die," she answers, playing along with the hypothetical question but not seeming to be completely exaggerating. If her answer sounds dramatic, consider that Williams is an emotionally perceptive artist, and she has known intimately, and known of, plenty of people eaten up by inner pain, even within her own family; she took note of what happens when they let their voices go silent and shut down. The catharsis of songwriting is essential to Williams, giving her a way to acknowledge the reality of suffering—hers or others'—to maintain emotional sensation, to celebrate desire, passion, and pleasure, to expel venom and get air to wounds, and to beat back feelings of isolation, futility, or despair. If some singer-songwriters do their purging in ways that come off as self-indulgent oversharing, there is no denying Williams' gifts—both that she possesses uncommon ability and that she offers her audience something of worth—or the fact that her audience responds to them so passionately and personally.

The title track of *World Without Tears*, a willowy country soul ballad, is a sort of companion piece to "Sweet Old World," only, in this case, focused on the not-so-sweet features of human experience. The song is a meditation on the idea that suffering is sewn into the fabric of human existence. Williams personifies the pain, imagining scars, fractures, and bruises searching out their human targets. She is aware not only of what suffering does to people but also that people can inflict it on themselves and each other.

The wounds that can be caused by others receive every bit as frequent and intense attention in her body of work as the theme of desire—maybe even more. "Wrap My Head Around That," on *West*, is a song that gives voice to raw hurt and frustration; a nine-minute mashup of jazz, blues, and hip-hop, peppered with electronic whirs, whooshes, and samples of her voice. The barbed rhythms of her spoken delivery could draw blood, as could the lyrics. Elaborating her lover's wrongs—chief among them duplicity and taking her for a fool—she grinds them between her teeth and spits them out until it seems she is about to explode. At the chorus, her voice cracks and pleads as she retraces her lover's words, which have turned out to mean worse than nothing.

During "Those Three Days," a country rock ballad on *World Without Tears*, Williams drives home feelings of being used and discarded with exceptionally forceful imagery and sarcasm. To be the subject and reciprocator of such passion, then to have it abruptly ripped away, is, she stresses, like having her body colonized and tormented by scorpions. Her description is so visceral and so far from broken-hearted clichés that it shocks the system. Then she jabs with questions, wanting to know whether her lover got all he could possibly need and want from her in three days; whether their brief affair was the closest he could get to loving her forever.

Never has Williams articulated the desire to purge the memory of a person more vividly than she does three tracks later during "Minneapolis"; never has she sounded more numbed by pain, singing in a slackened vibrato over a lulling, liquid bed of guitar and organ. There is a chilling undercurrent of violence that would rival an Appalachian murder ballad and a setting nearly as desolate as a murder ballad's graveyard: a frigid, gray northern winter. Left wounded by her lover, and poisoned by the memory, she wants—needs—to get it all out, to spit it out of her mouth, to bleed it out of her wound if she is to ever recover.

Elsewhere, Williams focuses on how others have been affected by things done to them. *Sweet Old World* has a melancholic country rock song called "He Never Got Enough Love" that tells the story of a boy abandoned by his mother, beaten by his father, and told he was worthless enough times that he came to believe it. The ending is a tragic one, set up by his tragic life: he got a gun and shot someone, as a sort of twisted fulfillment of paternal prophecy. It is a senseless act, but Williams points to a cause, plain as day, in the song title.

"Your Sweet Side," recorded several years later on *World Without Tears*, is a more nuanced portrait of the aftermath of an abusive childhood. Oscillating between two chords, the band maintains an insouciant groove, while Williams' vocal attack is anything but laidback; she talks the verses with punchy syncopation, launching into a bluesy roar as she delivers the chorus' melody. The lyrics veer from her lover's early traumas to his emotional maimedness in adulthood. Her anger is reserved for the way he was treated; for him, she has only tenderness and understanding.

Keeping in Touch

Though Williams describes the pain people cause each other in no uncertain terms, there is, in her oeuvre, the sense that isolation is a much worse state—perhaps even *the* worst, dangerous as it can be to emotional survival. Recall "Sweet Old World" and its reminder that human connection is a lot to gain, and to lose.

"Out of Touch," on *Essence*, could be interpreted as a description of postmodern alienation, but Williams' original intentions were more personal: "[T]hat was my attempt at trying to connect. In this case it was my sister. . . . It's about just, you know, feeling out of touch, not connecting; wanting to and not being able to." Sounding sad and a little lost, Williams sings bluesy, descending lines, each cracked right down the middle by a single-beat pause. She relates encounters that leave her cold: when small-talk feels halting and desperate, when honking on the freeway is the only form of contact. Living out of touch, she seems to say, is it not really *living*.

"Are You Alright?" the languorous lead track on *West*, is also rife with anxiety about relational distance. Williams shares, "I wrote that about my brother. . . . He just chooses to not connect." Line after line, the lyrics reach out, laden with worry and longing for a response. She needs to know that he is okay, that he is not alone.

Williams also recognizes another aspect of relationships, an aspect that makes a song like "Are You Alright?" all the more urgent: their potential to be redemptive. In country music, many a songwriter has cast a loving woman—and occasionally a loving man—in the role of a loving savior of a soul who is otherwise headed nowhere good. Historian Curt W. Ellison identifies a tradition in mainstream country songwriting in which the way salvation is portrayed "replaces the love of Jesus with the love of women."[9] Williams does not go in for the notion of one person saving another exactly; her hope takes a different form. Her pleading ballad "Sidewalks of the City," on *Sweet Old World*, holds up a romantic relationship as a source of comfort in a strange city. Hemmed in by the realities of poverty, homelessness, and violence, she asks her lover for reassurance that she is not facing it on her own—that there is someone there she can actually touch and feel, who loves her.

Two songs on *Little Honey* explore the substantial good that can come from romantic love. In "Knowing," a lissome soul ballad swathed in lyrical guitar and luminous organ and horns, she marvels in meditational language at the enlightenment she has found in a relationship. "Plan to Marry," on the other hand, is a spare folk song with a message. "It's kind of almost a sociological look at why, even though there are all these tragedies and devastations going on all around us, war and poverty . . . people still kind of forge on," Williams explains. "People still get married; people still have babies. . . . We still look to the future. . . . I think human nature just needs to feel that we've got some kind of future ahead of us." She sings four verses back to back, rife with oblique references to troubling social and political events of the previous decade. In light of all the wrongness in the world, she is driven to ask why people marry. The answer she gives? Because love holds a power and promise of a different sort.

Her choice—and that it is a choice is something that should not be forgotten—is to throw her lot in with the hopers and lovers.

Pondering the difference the choice makes, Williams reflects, "My dad used to talk about a big dark well and we're all standing on the edge looking into the well. And he said some of us fall in and the rest of us don't. But we're all kind of standing on the edge, you know. And at any given moment based on. . . . It's just our own strength. I don't know. I guess I'm always questioning what makes someone not have that, lose that strength."

More Than a Feeling

It was no secret when Williams took a personal chance on love— not her first—and got married in 2009. She and her husband, Tom Overby, exchanged vows onstage immediately follow- ing her show at the Minneapolis rock club First Avenue. There are videos of the ceremony captured by audience members on YouTube; the audio is drowned out at moments by celebratory whoops from the people flanking the stage.[10] It was *that* public of an event, and for a reason. Williams' audience wants to know what is going on in her life; wants to know whether she is happy.

Hugh Barker and Yuval Taylor note that soul-baring has practically become expected of the modern singer-songwriter. And if anything, this late twentieth-century musical develop- ment has added new wrinkles to the question of what makes for good music: "Art has to be evaluated by some criteria—some artists have always aimed to please their audience, while others have aimed to satisfy their own need to project their inner selves outward. The latter urge is no less valid than the former, but it cannot be successful unless it connects with an audience."[11]

Williams specializes in songs that spill her guts. But it is also clear her audience responds strongly when she puts herself out there and seems to hold nothing back; by doing it for so long, and with such vivifying force, she has earned their trust, their interest, and their emotional commitment. She acknowledges their stake in her songwriting; she writes *for* herself, *to* particu- lar people in her life, and *with* everybody in mind: "I mean, it's definitely about me dealing with the angst of something and just kind of getting it out of my system. And then it's also kind of like sending a little message, but nobody knows who it's about or anything. But I also like to make my songs universal."

When Williams was preparing for her string of thirtieth-anniversary shows and relearning songs from her Folkways albums that she had not sung in years—even decades—she was tempted to omit some, like "Lafayette," that she had come to see as too simplistic or obvious, the work of a younger, less experienced Lucinda Williams: "When I first started singing it, I was a little embarrassed by some of the lines. . . . Then I just kind of had to transcend that. . . . A lot of people still love those older songs. I kind of had to look at it like it wasn't my song almost, like I was just singing an early old song, you know, like an old folk song or something." A song, in other words, that belongs to everybody.

The kind of devotion Williams gets from her listeners is not something to be taken for granted. But because they care so much about her music, and watch closely for indications of her inner state, assumptions can be made, and nuances missed. A case in point: She released *Little Honey* after she and Overby were engaged; the album opens with "Real Love," a rock 'n' roll number declaring her delight at finding real, rare love with someone. The thing was, she wrote the song *before* she and Overby fell in love. Plus, its sentiment is by no means representative of every song on the album. "So everybody's going 'This is your happy album,'" Williams recalls of the interviews she gave when *Little Honey* came out. "And I go 'You know what? Wait a minute. Slow down. Let me tell you what these songs are about.' And then I have to dissect the whole album. Because they hear 'Real Love' right off the bat and they're like 'Yay!'"

It is as though Williams almost considers her happiness incidental, a quality bound to ebb and flow throughout the course of her life and work. At the heart of the matter, and at the heart of the songs, is this: she is glad to be alive, glad to be creating, glad she has sharpened her singing and writing over the years, and has the chance to continue doing so. Life and artistry, she well knows, thanks to her roots, are fragile, unpredictable things. "It's a gift—I mean, life is a gift," she says. "God knows I certainly have my down days. A lot of us do. . . . At least I have an outlet."

Williams' most strong-willed and primal "yes" to life may well be a song called "Joy" on *Car Wheels on a Gravel Road*, a wiry, downhome blues number, powered by an insistent groove and heated by feral bottleneck and resonator guitar. Someone has stolen away her joy, her lifeblood; she is not about to let it stand. "'Joy' was actually written about an ex-lover, believe it or not," offers Williams. "Now it's become something else." Now life and death are at stake. She vows to go to West Memphis and Slidell to get her joy back; the fierceness in her voice suggests she is prepared to go a whole lot further than that—all over God's green earth if she has to. Each time she gets to the song's defiant hook, she swings high and wrings four smoldering syllables out of the word "joy," then she sinks an octave below, as though she is proving her expressive reach and drinking in the fullness of human experience.

Williams is a woman who will not be denied. She *will* have her joy.

2

Julie Miller
Heart to Heart

A profoundly empathetic songwriter who extends her heart to wounded and vulnerable people, Julie Miller and her singer-guitarist-producer husband Buddy are regarded as the first couple of Americana, though she began her recording career in a different genre: contemporary Christian music.

This possessor of a petite, inconsolable voice ventures the offer of her heart tentatively, sighing in small downward arcs above delicately finger-picked acoustic guitar chords. Her offer is really more of a plea: that her heart be received, handled tenderly, and healed, by God, who remains unnamed, but on whose power and compassionate willingness to do such things she leans. That plea is also an apology: for her heart's woefully wounded condition and the helplessness she feels to make it better on her own. By the song's end, she is flanked by lyrical backing: piano, accordion, percussion, keening cello, and a stately, yet sympathetic harmonizing female vibrato. But none of it assuages her need to be healed.

"Broken Things" by Julie Miller is, in many ways, the antithesis of Lucinda Williams' "Joy." Our ears are unaccustomed to hearing a singer and songwriter sound as profoundly vulnerable as Miller does singing this song—profoundly vulnerable toward God; exposed before people. I have seen a highly educated person respond to it with disbelief that her performance could be anything but a display of manipulative, put-on emotion. But Miller is someone who can always be trusted to mean and feel what she sings. The point of music making, for her, is to let her heart through.

"It's like my goal now isn't to make it sound impressive in any way, because that would certainly be a very futile energy," she says, acknowledging the unimposing—though striking—character of her voice. "My goal is just to make it as truthful and connecting to another person as I can. . . . The satisfaction of doing it is in the true-heartedness of it."

She holds her musical partner and husband, Buddy Miller, to the same standard of true-hearted singing—and he happens to be one of the most soulful roots-country singers alive.[1] She laughs, "It is so unbelievable the things I have the nerve to say to him. I mean, a time or two another musician might overhear it or something and they'll just look at me like, 'Wow! I can't believe she said that to Buddy!' It's like I'll really more and more hold his nose to the grindstone about being inside the words he's [singing], especially if it's that kind of song; to not be thinking 'Here's what I sound like' or 'What are people thinking?' To do nothing but think about the meaning of what he's singing."

There is something else, besides meaning what she is singing, that you can count on with Julie Miller: she always has other people in mind. She cares less about their feelings toward her music, their critical appraisals or accolades, than about their *feelings*. She never makes it seem as though her emotions are the only ones that matter. And wounded people have her special attention; she inhabits their woundedness with them, unwilling to watch a person suffer alone. Nor can she abide dehumanizing messages embedded in the spirits of people who have been preyed upon in their vulnerability. "It's just like my heart is just feeling with them and for them and yearning and just wanting them to know that they're not as alone as they think they are," she says. "The awfulest thing is to be without hope."

That is not to say that Miller limits herself to heavyhearted-ness. Elsewhere her singing can sound sunny, silly, exultant—even tough. Conversation reveals her to be not only sensitive, warmly empathetic, and spiritually attuned but also gravely confiding, hilariously zany, and aware. She has been known to take great, goofy liberties onstage, teasing Buddy (her straight man) or grabbing silverware off the front tables in a club to use as percussion instruments. But she is far too seldom given credit for being experienced in life—despite the fact that she has been through a great many painful things, and that she broke with her roots in just about every way that a person can, with good reason, and negotiated a new, more complicated relationship with them as her life changed.

"[People] put you in a box, because they hear one song—'Oh, she's a happy little munchkin,' you know, or something," reflects Miller. "To bring even further meaning to the happier or sweeter other songs, I want the full picture of the true person to be seen, so that . . . the height and depth and width of it all is one . . . truly heartfelt message. And if I just sound like a sweet, little, quote unquote Christian girl, you know, because Christians have to sound like this or something. . . ." Without finish-ing her sentence, she makes clear that she is no fan of superficial conformity, religious or otherwise.

A Time for Everything

Miller was born in 1956. Now in her mid-fifties, she is several decades removed from her first backup-singing gigs in her native Texas. Over the course of a recording career that began twenty years ago, she has not spent much energy trying to sound like anyone doing any particular thing is supposed to sound, not even during her early '90s stint in the contemporary Christian music industry, a world with fairly well-defined parameters for aesthetics and content[2]—and a world that would ultimately prove not to be such a good fit for her.

Truth be told, Miller has a difficult time with the idea of *having* to be creative, and that goes for writing songs on a deadline. "There was one point years back when one of the publishing companies offered me, according to Buddy, a big advance to sign with them," she recalls amusedly. "'You mean I would sign with them and they'd give me money and then I had to promise to write—whatever it was—ten songs in ten months?' I mean, I thought 'That would be the death of all songwriting—to owe a song.'. . . Because coming at songs from that pressure of owing or having to or should . . . I mean, it would be impossible for me to get to a free place of creativity."

Partly—but only partly—because of her resistance to working on a schedule, Miller's output has arrived at a fairly erratic pace. It began with four Christian solo albums in rapid succession: *Meet Julie Miller* in 1990, *He Walks Through Walls* in 1991, *Orphans and Angels* in 1993, and *Invisible Girl* in 1994. Then, with longer gaps between them, came two solo Americana albums— 1997's *Blue Pony* and 1999's *Broken Things*—and two duo albums with Buddy (who is always a very involved partner in her solo efforts, too)—2001's *Buddy & Julie Miller* and *Written in Chalk* in 2009. Besides the albums, Miller's songs have been recorded by numerous other performers; by Buddy, of course, and by a host of top-tier mainstream country acts, like the Dixie Chicks, Lee Ann Womack, Miranda Lambert, and Brooks & Dunn.

As coveted as Miller's songs have become, she was, at first, a singer only. More specifically, she was a self-critical singer who could not stomach anything she came up with in the way of songwriting. Only after a spiritual transformation—her conversion experience in the '80s—did she find herself able to write. "For years I'd been singing in bars and in bands and stuff, and I'd always wanted to write a song, so earnestly, deeply, and never been able to," she recounts. "I'd try to write a few lines and it would make me sick and I'd just tear it up. And as soon as I experienced the love and acceptance of God in this miraculous way, it was just like this overflow wouldn't *not* come out. And it was like all thoughts of 'Oh, it should be like this' were irrelevant. I was just letting out this expression that was an overflow to him."

In form, structure, and flair—or, rather, lack thereof—those early songs were a far cry from the ones she writes now. But the spirit of them, their unvarnished expression and sense of divine–human connection, was not so different from the songs for which she has become known. "They were so free," she recalls fondly. "They were like 'I don't care how songs go. I'm not doing, quote, *that*. I'm by myself . . . with God, in the darkness, releasing my spirit, and this is how it's coming out.' . . . I love the trueness of what that was, the honestness, the pureness of what that was."

Moved by the memory, she continues, "I finally knew God loved me so much, it didn't matter what anybody thought of me, not even what I thought of me. So it didn't matter if I was a bad songwriter, or if I *was* a songwriter. And it was like God set me free to be, you know, an inexperienced songwriter. And that's how you learn how to write songs, usually. You have to start out with songs that aren't as good as the songs that you usually are able to write later on. . . . And I used to, before I had him, I couldn't bear to have to start at such a place and show anybody . . . a bad song or anything like that." For someone who would go on to a career centered on her songwriting, that liberation could hardly have been more significant.

Getting Off Script

The way Miller talks about receiving divine reassurance that anything she did from the heart—songwriting included— would be valued is almost reminiscent of a nurturing parent–child relationship. But the loving parent–God image was not a big feature of her religious roots. Not in her family, nor in the

Southern Baptist churches they attended. "I don't know if a lot of dysfunctional families [are] like that, where you go to church but don't say 'God' or 'Jesus' at home," she says. Hers was; no one was supposed to disclose what they *really* thought or felt. "The one thing we did do, though, is when we were in the car—my parents sang and they sang in church a lot, and did duets and stuff—they'd be singing their songs in the front seat going to church, and I would sing; I was singing the third harmony. . . . We could sing about Jesus in the car, but we could not just talk about Jesus. . . . It was like, to my family, going to church was like a stamp of [approval]; 'Hold out your hand so God can give you this "good" stamp.'"

People's images of God can profoundly shape how they experience the world. Feminist Christian theologian Sallie McFague has shown compellingly that divine metaphors—historically, those like God as an almighty, ruling king, or a stern, distant patriarch—have real-world consequences that can help or harm.[3] McFague offered, as one theoretical alternative, an image of a caring divine mother or father: "[P]arental love nurtures what it has brought into existence, wanting growth and fulfillment for all. . . . [I]t loves the weak and vulnerable as well as the strong and beautiful."[4] With Miller, the image transcends theory; that is, she wholeheartedly lives it. In God, she found a longed-for parent who met her neglected needs and made her feel loved, cared for, and completely accepted.

That epiphany, which altered the course of her life *and* her music, came while she and Buddy were living and gigging in New York City, part of a roots music scene well stocked with rising talent. "We were unloading to play in some bar," she begins, "and I was just sitting in the front of the van and the guys were taking stuff in, and I just heard the voice of God. . . . [I]t was like he thumbed through these awful, sad, dreadful pictures of my life . . . and he said, 'I never wanted it to be like this.' And he said, 'I always wanted us to be together.' . . . [I]t wasn't like, you know, you think of Christians or religious people with their rules and their this or their that. It was God's heart longing for me. I mean, it was a revelation."

This supplanted impressions of God Miller had picked up from the religious tradition she was born into, but it was by no means the beginning of her split from her roots. Halfway through high school, rock 'n' roll and progressive country music stole her attention away from cheerleading, something she had pursued mostly for her mother's sake anyhow. She gave college a try and very quickly concluded that it was not where she ought to be—news she dreaded breaking to her high-achieving, high-expecting mom. It was then that Miller stopped, once and for all, trying to do and be all the things she had been told she ought to. She broke with the perfectionism she had come to see as empty, pointless, and false and adopted a freewheeling, decidedly non-Baptist lifestyle ("I was the most leaf-in-the-wind thing there ever, ever was"), plunging into the heady, mid-'70s progressive country scene in Austin.

"It was," she recalls, "like my mind had been what mommy and the church had said all that time, and now I'd seen that that didn't mean anything. And they wanted me to be perfect and what were they doing? So how real was this? . . . I guess, too, the music was such a relief and a release. . . . I was always troubled within, but didn't know how to get help. And so I just jumped off this far cliff. . . . 'What'd those hippies say? Yeah! Sex, drugs and rock 'n' roll!' . . . It really was like I just became someone else." Someone who no longer cared about trying to be a "good girl" and just wanted to sing with progressive country singer-songwriter Jerry Jeff Walker.

In Austin, there was plenty to get caught up in. Just a couple of years before, Willie Nelson—then in the midst of his transformation into Texas' quintessential longhaired, country-singing out-law—a DJ named Joe Gracey, and few other people had decided the countercultural blend of country and rock percolating in the local scene deserved its own radio station, and KOKE-FM was born.[5] In high school, Miller listened to the station religiously,

and, on top of listening, called in almost daily to find out everything she could from Gracey about the records he was playing.
"Until I would bug them so much . . . I'd bake cookies and take
them to them," she laughs. That was how she discovered her first
vocal idol: '70s country, rock, and pop singer Linda Ronstadt.

Miller may not have landed a gig with Walker, but she sang
with her share of bar bands, and eventually met Buddy in one
of them. The chief requirements of her backup-singing role—to
blend with the lead singer and look good while doing it—were
quite different from those of a singer and songwriter who bares
her heart center stage. "I never wanted to be *the* singer," Miller
clarifies lightheartedly. "That required way too much responsibility and thinking and trying to get it together. I loved just
having no responsibility—'la, la, la'—and be the girl singer and
wear sexy clothes. But, actually, I didn't feel like that sexy girl
onstage I was so desperately trying to pull off. . . . They'd always
send you up a drink or two, you know, to get you through."

Besides the powerful dissonance between that persona and
how she felt on the inside, Miller wished she had a different
voice, one that could project like Ronstadt's, or like that of her
next vocal idol, early R&B singer Etta James. "I had this little
voice," she says, "and I loved all these girls with these gigantic
voices, because I think I wanted to sound tough or something."

In the '80s, after she and Buddy left New York, they returned
to Texas and joined up with an intensive, evangelistic Christian community called Agape Force. She describes it as offering
some good spiritual teaching but exerting fairly heavy-handed
control over its members. "Clothes short to long hung in the
closet," she offers dryly. There she pushed her voice in a very different direction in order to connect with an audience she would
never have found in a club: children. Given the assignment by
the leader of Agape Force to write and record demos of Christian songs for kids, she wanted to make sure she was feeling the
music the way its young audience would. "To write the songs, for
some reason, unintentionally, I would sing in a child's voice," she

recalls. "It was like I'd have to get in character, you know, get in the thoughts of a child and make the songs relate that way. . . . But after that—it was so funny—I never sang the same again. It changed the way I sang."

Out of the Abundance of the Heart

Considering that Miller had once needed liquid courage in order to get onstage at all, it is no small thing that she reached a point where she wanted to put herself, her feelings, and her voice out there in the world for people to hear—in songs of hers, and beyond the auspices of somebody else's kids' project. She devoted a good portion of her first two albums—*Meet Julie Miller* and *He Walks Through Walls*, recorded when she was in her mid-thirties for the Christian pop and rock label Myrrh—to earnest, exuberant retellings of her story of coming to know a personal God. These are her most evangelistic collections of songs; she had found a source of comfort and wanted to share it. In some songs, she sings of God, or Jesus, pursuing her like a lover would. "You Knew the Way to My Heart," on *Meet Julie Miller*, is one of them, a bright, jangly, New Wave pop expression of gratitude to Jesus, who knew it took compassion to touch the heart she was trying so desperately to protect. In her enthusiasm, or songwriterly inexperience, she crammed the verses with more words than she could easily sing. The very next track, "Mystery Love," ponders the relationship from a more sober angle; she regrets having ever kept her divine lover at a distance. The feeling turns to awe at the chorus, as she trains her attention on a love so faithful that she cannot wrap her head around it. The rock ballad title track of *He Walks Through Walls* proclaims divine love that knows no barriers, a comforting notion for an emotionally imprisoned soul.

On *Orphans and Angels* and *Invisible Girl*—the latter her final and most robust effort for the contemporary Christian market, released on a fledgling independent label after Myrrh lost interest—the romantic metaphor gave way to a parental one. Miller sings "In My Eyes," a slow-burning ballad given a hint of urgency by her beat-anticipating delivery, from the perspective of God, a doting parent who speaks tender, salving words to a little girl with a battered self-image.

Of all of the vulnerable people who find their ways into Miller's songs, none appear more frequently than these: children, usually girls, who have been abused and women who carry psychic and spiritual wounds of abuse into adulthood. Socially and religiously, these kinds of traumatic stories are often shrouded in shame, hidden away, considered untouchable. And they certainly do not make for easy, breezy song subjects. Miller, though, applies great care in bringing these wounds to light with deep understanding and radical empathy. She has been there.

She recounts a story of the abuse she suffered from her late father with the clarity of someone who has, in years since, faced the source of her pain: "We were watching *Titanic*, the old version. So it's this little boy in it crying for his mommy. And you've gotten to know this little boy, so you cared about him. And I started crying and crying. I was seven. . . . [My dad] said, 'Don't you cry!' And he grabbed me and he whipped me and he said, 'I'm going to whip you until you stop crying!' And I couldn't stop crying for a little bit and I finally was able to stop and I remember thinking, 'He's crazy. Poor crazy man.' . . . I just didn't know how he could do that to somebody for that. He had whipped me till I learned to ride my bicycle, stuff like that."

It would be too easy, and terribly dismissive, to say Miller's songs redeem her suffering, or to suggest they are the inevitable outgrowth of what she has been through. If we interpret her life merely as a case of cause and effect, we do so unjustly. Cultural critic Bill Friskics-Warren, one of the Millers' most thoughtful interpreters, resists the notion that "Miller had to go through hell to become the profoundly empathetic soul that she is."[6] Not only that, but she could have grown bitter; could have closed herself off; could have let her heart be hardened.

Instead, Miller cultivated empathy. When she gave concerts in churches, singing songs from her first two albums, people who had been abused sensed she was someone in whom they could confide. "After I did the first Christian record or two," she says, "every time I would do a show, I would spend more time . . . just with wounded people. I mean, it was, like, unbelievable everywhere. This was in the Christian groups, in the churches; people coming up to me. I am not kidding. There was at one point—I don't even remember the town—but a girl who asked me 'Could you ask the preacher to ask the fathers not to molest their children?' I mean, just as simple and straightforward as that."

"It was everywhere," she continues. "I mean, it was so awful and so blowing my mind. It was just things I can't even repeat that people would ask me to pray for them [about] things I couldn't believe people could even be caught up in. And I was humbled . . . that they would come to me and trust that they could tell me and I would have no judgment but compassion, and that I could pray for them and everything."

Miller was so moved by the people she met that she wrote songs about them—or perhaps more accurately, for them. It was then that she turned her songwriting focus from what God had done for her toward others' pain and what God could do for them. The songs she has written since that time are less explicitly evangelistic, but her desire to share God's comfort and healing with people has not waned one bit. (Talk with her for any amount of time, and you will get a sense of just how deep that desire is; it seems never to leave her mind.) "There was," she recalls, "a particular girl [and] she had a story like many people. But she just moved my heart in such a deep and sympathetic, yearning way. I met her in England, and her father was a minister and he had molested her all her life. She'd been abused so much and she was in a terrible situation." Thinking of her, Miller wrote "Nobody's Child," a crisp, Byrdsian folk-rock number that opens *Invisible Girl*. In the song, she promises, with been-there, felt-that empathy, that there is a loving, permanent, and safe home to be found in divine connection.

"Angelina," on *He Walks Through Walls*—a minor-key, Appa-lachian-flavored rock number that gains much from Buddy's chiming, incisive guitar figures—comes at abuse from a differ-ent angle. The woman's experience is not the focus of Miller's emotion; instead, she worries for the woman's would-be lover, warning that the woman is a troubled romantic predator, prone to play out her desire for revenge on her father upon other men. Empathetic this song is not—at least not toward this woman, Angelina. But it shows considerable awareness of the relational aftermath of abuse.

"Precious to God," on *Orphans and Angels*, is a devastatingly sad song in subdued 6/8 time. Miller sounds crestfallen at the thought of a girl who puts up a brave front for the outside world when, at night, in the very place where she is supposed to be safe, she faces her father's twisted sexual urges. "Emily's Eyes," the title track of a 1992 multiartist benefit album for abused children, also speaks for a preyed-on young girl who cannot speak for herself and reassures her that the worthlessness she feels does not reflect how God sees her.

In songs like these, Miller does more than acknowledge the pain of abused people and salve it with her empathy; she quietly yet firmly combats what the abuse has made them believe about themselves—that they are less than human. A reaffirmation of their humanity will not make everything all right, but it may be the thing they need to hear most.

When Miller left contemporary Christian music and landed, along with Buddy, in Americana, she did not stop writing com-passionate songs about suffering people. On *Blue Pony*—the first album she made for the now-defunct independent roots label Hightone—there is a song called "Dancing Girl" that shows a side of her that does not hesitate to take off the gloves and take up for the vulnerable; that is deeply stirred yet not the least bit sentimental. With the hint of a sneer, she describes how the dancing girl lives, driving home the perverseness of a daddy exploiting his daughter one minute and acting affectionately toward her the next.

Many a time Miller has written an emotionally heavy song and given it to her preternaturally matched duet partner-husband to sing. And that is what she did with "That's Just How She Cries," a lilting ballad on their self-titled duo album. To hear a male voice sing the song, and sing it so reverently, is affecting. He grieves at the fact that a woman in pain cannot make herself heard and longs to understand and share in what she is feeling. The particulars of the woman's history are not given, but the song is a close-up portrait of the sort of wounded soul that often captures Miller's attention: someone silenced by what has been done to her and how powerless she has been to stop it, or to even get anyone to believe her story.

"All the Pieces of Mary," another song on *Blue Pony*, also takes as its subject a scarred woman with a mysterious past. Against pensive, organ-laced alt-pop, Miller captures the essence of Mary, a fragmented woman whose mental illness is her only shield against traumatic memories. The way Miller's voice is softened by concern and the way she phrases the chorus—one line slipping into the next in a seemingly endless circle, evoking Mary's dizzying psychological merry-go-round ride—make it feel like she has drawn as near to Mary, and Mary's brokenness, as a person could. Nearer, even, than most would be willing to go.

"Maggie" is a melancholic folk tune on *Broken Things*, poignantly colored by mandolin and accordion. The song is another example of Miller feeling for a woman who is haunted by a childhood she would rather keep hidden; once more she dwells on how this living, breathing person has been affected by suffering. It is rarely the abstract concept of pain that grabs her. "You know, I'm not very theoretical," she offers. "Usually, everything I write about has a literal, specific person or incident story that is really what it's about. I mean, nothing can move me as much as hearing the stories of what real people have suffered and experienced."

There is a danger, though, when a person is moved as powerfully by those stories as Miller is. Her wholehearted empathy is a rare and wonderful quality, but, stretched to extremes, it can also become incapacitating. She describes what those times are like for her: "[Y]ou're overwhelmed . . . and you take everybody else's pain in that's around you, because there's so much of that, too. I'm one of those, you know, I feel everybody's pain, and that's a lot. It's really paralyzing the way I allow it to not process, I guess, through; it just sort of comes in and sits a while."

And when it comes and sits a while, Miller can find herself beneath such a heavy emotional burden that it is hard to do anything. She had endured a period like that not long before our first interview, and in an exceedingly generous effort to help me understand what she had been going through, she began our conversation with the story of the daughter of a close female friend taking her own life; Miller had been very invested in both mother and daughter. As if that were not enough, around that same time Miller's brother perished in a Texas lightning storm. She shares, "The shock and grief of such a traumatic scenario, with the horrendous, tragic scenario of my brother in the street struck by lightning; those two things together . . . it's like my mind broke."

"Thank goodness for Buddy," she adds, "or nothing would get from [point] A to B. It was like I could spend all day on A, but that would be all."

Across the Distance

For someone who inhabits the world of roots music, Miller has done precious little writing about *her* roots. By her own count, the sum total of the songs about where she came from—at least those that have been released—is four: "Blue Pony," a sweet tribute to a grandmother she spent a lot of time with when she was young; "Baby Don't Let Me Down," a country rocker on Buddy's 1997 album *Poison Love* that draws on the stories of her uncle's farming and her teenaged cousin's accidental death;

and a pair of songs on *Written in Chalk*—"Ellis County," inspired by her mother's downhome upbringing, and "Chalk," about her relationship with her father. She sings lead on just one of the four; Buddy carries the rest. For Miller, this remains tender territory. "There's still tears to be cried there," she says. "There's so much love and there's all this pain."

"Chalk" feels especially bruised, from the bent, blue melody to the lyrics. In the lyrics, she unburdens her heart to her father with a devastating sense of regret, making the wrenching confession that she has hidden her pain all her life trying to protect him, only to find it has harmed them both. "You know, we try to help our parents; we think that our parents need us to pretend this thing that they're pretending, like, to save their feelings," she reflects. "And it's deep. We'll kill ourselves, whatever it takes. And then to find, if you live long enough, that you weren't helping them at all." That was one song she could not bring herself to sing; Buddy, doing it for her, cuts to the bone of the words.

Miller has come to believe that no matter how impenetrable they may appear, all people—even her father—are vulnerable. She used to wonder why so many people seemed to give no indication of feeling that way, while she often felt like she was unable *not* to broadcast the feeling. "'When will I be able to feel like everybody else acts like they're feeling: invulnerable, knowing what they're doing, not fearful, confident?' It blew my mind . . . just as I've lived, how everyone is a child, and if they don't accept that and allow that, they're just going to stumble in their efforts at being so big; because everyone is a little child inside."

There is a certain egalitarianism to Miller's perspective; it applies to everyone, just as she has empathy for everyone. She—and perhaps only she—could look at the CEO of a global oil corporation and see a spiritual orphan. This view of humanity comes through loud and clear in her song "Orphan Train" on *Broken Things*—not to be confused with a historical ballad of the same title by the political folkie Utah Phillips. (Miller's is, however, the same "Orphan Train" that country-singing women like Lee Ann Womack and Allison Moorer have covered.) Over a primal Appalachian rock attack, laced with Buddy's sinewy guitar figures, Miller and her kindred spirit Victoria Williams—there is no match for the disarming sound they produce singing together—deliver verse after verse, beckoning people in positions of power, wealth, and influence or of marginalization, abandonment, and poverty to join them in their journey toward spiritual home. It is an invitation for everybody and recognizes no hierarchy.

Too Ancient to Be Pop

Behind an Appalachian modal melody like that of "Orphan Train"—which may well strike our ears as primitive—there is plenty of history and theory as to the origins of the sound. But Miller's attraction to it was not that of a folklorist's—for her, it was far more instinctual. "There was a natural thing in me," she explains, "that I was always drawn to what I know now to be a Celtic-type, or Appalachian-type yearning melody." The all-important thing was the music's emotional quality; and those melodies *can* feel like some of the world's oldest vehicles for desperation and mourning. Such has been the image popularly associated with Appalachian music. A century ago it was already seen as ancient folk fare: Anglo-Celtic sounds, the folklorists theorized, had been passed down by the isolated, mountain-dwelling descendants of English and Scots-Irish settlers and had, therefore, been kept uncorrupted.[7] Really, the music came from much more racially and ethnically diverse sources than that; even so, there *is* something about the leanness of the melodies that seems to conjure hardship and sorrow. Miller has certainly felt those things in the music.

However, she gets overcome with laughter recalling the day in the late '80s that she was told that she had been writing Anglo-Celtic songs without knowing it. The person who informed her was none other than in-demand producer T Bone

Burnett, who would go on to excel at the rarer-than-rare feat of creating platinum-selling roots music juggernauts—the *O Brother, Where Art Thou* soundtrack, for one—but was not so well known to the Millers when they met with him that first time:[8] "He listened to our [demo] tape and he goes, 'You know, you guys are, like, Celtic.' And after that, when we left—we didn't end up taking him up on his offer or anything, because 'Who is he?'— 'But he says we're Celtic?' [This time, for storytelling purposes, she pronounces the musical descriptor just like the name of Boston's professional basketball team.] . . . Isn't that hilarious? And this was me and Buddy both calling it 'Celtic.' We'd never heard the word."[9]

Clearly, by Miller's third album, *Orphans and Angels*, she had caught on to what that word meant; the title of one song, a song that has the sound, includes a parenthetical definition of sorts: "Praise to the Lord, Amen (Appalachian Praise)." The song blends the qualities of a Protestant hymn and a contemporary praise chorus—partially formal yet also simple, repetitive lyrics declaring God's healing and liberating attributes and an austere melody stretched over a resolute 6/8 march, flanked by the reedy textures of penny whistle and hurdy-gurdy. She had, she says, found the rather inexperienced hurdy-gurdy player that she and Buddy used on the recording busking on a street corner. But she was first taken with the sound of the European folk instrument—a sort of mechanically cranked fiddle—when she happened upon a couple of members of the Irish punk band the Pogues rehearsing with one backstage and felt compelled to interrupt and find out more about this exotic instrument. "It was like I was captured by it," she giggles. "It was like 'I can't help it; I must be totally rude. I must follow the sound of the hurdy-gurdy.'"

As goofy as Miller's discoveries of the proper name and instrumentation for Anglo-Celtic and Appalachian music may have been, in her repertoire, the music can be laden with sorrow. When she was mourning the death of a friend—Christian folksinger-songwriter Mark Heard—that was the sort of music that streamed out of her: "All My Tears (Be Washed Away)," one of her most indelible Appalachian-tinged originals. "When he died and [Buddy and I] sang at his memorial in L.A. and I came back home . . . I just let pour out what was in there," she remembers. "And instantly came out 'All My Tears.'" The song is also significant because it foreshadowed where her music was headed—namely, outside the sectarian contemporary Christian pop world. First she recorded it with country rock matriarch Emmylou Harris' harmonies for *Orphans and Angels*; then Harris put it on her own influential *Wrecking Ball* album; and Miller later revisited it on *Broken Things*. By then, her music was reaching an Americana audience who welcomed a contemporary take on a traditional sound.

Contemporary Christian music is a niche genre because of its positioning as music with an expressly religious message and purpose—as opposed to secular music; so, in order to be relevant and accessible, the music is more or less supposed to sound like current mainstream pop. And "All My Tears" certainly did not. "It wasn't like anything contemporary Christian *at all*," she emphasizes. "That song really had come from my internalization—I'm sure of some Emmylou stuff—but even more so of Ralph Stanley, who is my Elvis."

Ralph Stanley is a first-generation bluegrass pioneer who favors old-timey mountain sounds and is known for singing—with a voice that sounds as old as anything in the world—in mournful, raw-boned, Primitive Baptist–style a capella. As it happens, Miller's maternal grandparents met while doing a bit of a capella singing of their own at a shape note singing school (a communal gathering, especially popular in the South, where people learned a more accessible form of musical notation and did a day's worth of strenuous, unaccompanied singing).[10] However, since they were not of a religious tradition that prohibited the use of musical instruments, she has vivid memories of her grandfather leading the family in hymn singing at the piano.

Says Miller, "[W]hen I heard Ralph Stanley . . . it just was like it just got to some deep, deep part of me for my grandfather. . . . And something in my grandparents' singing was so old, I guess. And my grandfather . . . he lived in Tennessee and then his family rode in a covered wagon to Texas. . . . [T]here's such a line of the music where, you know, it comes down through the mountains down through Tennessee, Arkansas, down to Texas. You can follow and you can hear it."

Authority of Experience

Miller also feels a visceral connection to other, more bodily styles of music; her tastes defy oversimplified characterizations of her as a sweet and pious person who likes her music to be the same way. She is fond of joking that, were it not for Buddy's attachment to stone-cold country music, she would have been a rock 'n' roller. And there is something to that. Miller *has* recorded a full-blown punk song, for *Invisible Girl*, "The Back of Your Head," written by a Christian Celtic punk band called the Electrics. The band members, bagpiper included, provide her pummeling, three-chord backing on the track. Her agitated, rapid-fire delivery of the lyrics is more about attitude than enunciation. Even though the performance is not the sort of thing people are used to hearing from her, she does not sound out of her element.

Far more frequent than Miller's forays into punk are her gritty rock and blues numbers. There are songs in her repertoire that show another side of her, tough-sounding songs that tell off would-be deceivers. "The Devil Is an Angel" on *Blue Pony* is one of them. As a sly, downhome combo marks the backbeat with a ragged boom-thwack-boom, she challenges a smooth seducer. She applies bluesy note bending to the savvy lyrics without shedding her girlish vocal timbre. If the devil is a silver-tongued fallen angel, this character is no more trustworthy. In fact, he might *be* the devil.

So might the shady character she takes on and tells off in "Dirty Water," a biting country blues cowritten by Buddy on their first duo album. She is not buying what this character is selling, attractive as it may seem; she has heard this one before, and she knows better. Miller fends off a different sort of threat during "Strange Lover," a boozy, depraved-sounding blues on *Broken Things*. With a swaggering slur, distorted by a vocal effect, she takes aim at a cocaine-addicted lover; she will not put up with his destructive behavior for a moment more.

Miller comes off as experienced in these songs; someone not to be messed with; someone talking about things she has tangled with up close. And she *has*. There is a sense in which she is revisiting her past, channeling her wilder days in Austin and New York, and measuring the distance between the old and new her. She describes singing those songs in the language of spiritual warfare against a real, prowling devil: "I feel like I'm going from focusing on love and kindness and the sweet dear things to what I still know and will always remember of the depths of the lies and schemes and aims, cruelty of the Enemy . . . ," she shares. "The Devil, I mean, he is really, really, really out to cause as much horror and suffering to mankind as he can trick us into, with lies. . . . Yeah, when I sing those songs, I'm looking to those who would be naïve and unaware, and with authority of having had been there, just trying to, from one fellow traveler to another, just let them know 'Wait I've been down there. Don't go that way.'"

She adds, "It's almost like I want to get their attention with 'Look, you think . . . I've been at vacation Bible school and I'm saying all these nice Christian things because that's what Christians say. . . . [B]ut I want you to know that I'm not just saying this, and it's not just words, and I've been to some dark, dark, dark, dark, *dark* places.'" If she chooses to spare us the gory details of some of the traumas she has endured, she can surely feel them when she sings those songs. "I'm *not* kidding," she emphasizes. "I mean, I'm not *trying* to sound like I mean something; it's like

I'm there and I don't have to try. I have to try, you know, to just keep it down a little."

There are times, though, when Miller's blues are not so much about warning as pleasure. Usually the devil does not make an appearance in those songs, but Buddy does, as her partner in a hot and playful back-and-forth. "You Make My Heart Beat Too Fast," on the first Buddy and Julie album, is a primal expression of attraction, her entry in a long line of pop songs about love's irrational, physical symptoms. She tugs each phrase into a carnal downward arc, issuing the demands of a woman who knows what she wants, her vocal motion amplified by Buddy's feral guitar attack and low, raw harmony. "Gasoline and Matches," a cowrite by the couple on *Written in Chalk*, treads similarly classic territory, working the metaphor of highly combustible mutual attraction. The song rides a sinewy, proto-electric blues groove, and the singing partners sound both experienced in the sensation and caught up in it.

Can Miller recall a particular time when she threw off people's perceptions of her innocence by singing blues? "Almost every time. If it was a new place that hadn't heard us before, and I would get to a blues song, everybody would do a double-take, like 'Wait, is that the same girl that sang with him a while ago?' . . . I think people like to quickly sum up people. It's just our nature or something, I guess. And I've experienced that all my life. If I couldn't do [the blues] with the other part, I wouldn't be happy; I wouldn't be satisfied. I would feel like part of the story was left out, if they thought, you know, I was only that. Because that's the whole truth."

She can, however, put her finger on a time when she scrambled the assumptions of church people. "I mean, there was a point when we were in a ministry and I had pink hair," she says. "The whole church was like '(gasp) Julie's not saved!' People would come up to me to witness to me, because they thought I was somebody right off the street."

The Spirit Is Willing

There is another significant part of Miller's experience that is felt more than directly addressed in her songs: her physical pain. She has lived with the chronic pain, tiredness, heightened environmental sensitivity, and muscle spasms of fibromyalgia for more than three decades; which means, as she points out with well-earned exasperation, she was suffering from the condition well before doctors acknowledged it existed. Her symptoms have reached such a point that touring is pretty much out of the question. And how she feels physically has also had plenty to do with the greatly slowed pace of her recorded output in the last decade. It would be understandable, then, if Miller's own physical suffering were all she ever thought or wrote about; and yet she hardly ever explicitly writes about it.

"I guess pain of the body is a little harder to sound poetic," she chuckles. "But pain of the body equals pain of the heart, I can tell you that. You know, people go 'Oh, I'd rather have physical pain than emotional pain.' But physical pain *is* emotional pain." Indeed, it is not hard to hear a uniting of the two in a song like "Broken Things."

Besides "My Psychiatrist"—a silly keyboard-and-drum machine number on her debut album that casts God as her mental health specialist—another rare example of a song speaking to what is going on in her body is "I Need You," a dogged rock 'n' roll cut on *Broken Things*. It was born of her maddening experiences over the years with doctors who either did not really listen to her or did not really help. She relates, "I went to a doctor once and he said, 'Well, we only give pain pills for people who are in acute pain. But if you're in chronic pain, then we don't.'. . . And that's actually the beginnings of that song. And then I thought, 'But they don't want to give this medicine to you, because you'll become addicted.' And then I was thinking, you know, 'I need something; I need something that is a pain reliever, but that isn't addictive, and that heals everything. And that's God.'" Miller gives one of her more urgent and aggressive vocal performances on the track, and Buddy matches it with a squalling, dissonant fit of a guitar solo.

When a person sings, her entire body becomes a musical instrument; and when her body is wracked with fibromyalgia symptoms, singing is considerably more difficult. "Actually, fibromyalgia, when you tense a muscle—and you just tense it not to lift a weight and then let it down, but to just hold some-thing steady that's not necessarily heavy—that kind of muscle tension is what with fibromyalgia starts triggering all kinds of muscle spasms. And singing actually is that kind of [muscle tension]. . . . You know, how you have to hold your mouth open slightly."

"Without fibromyalgia affecting my whole body, including my jaw and my throat, I think that I would probably sound a whole lot like Etta James." She bursts into laughter at the absur-dity of the thought. "I would be trying still, probably. I think I would be at least aiming to sing more like 'Okay, you're supposed to *sing* if you're singing.'"

It is true that the soft, breathy way Miller releases a note is nothing at all like James' full-throated attack. But, despite her diffidence, the smallness of her voice harbors something bigger than its sound. There, where physicality and emotion meet, we hear her confront her vulnerability, and share it, as a visceral tes-tament to the fullness of her humanity; we hear her resistance to being silenced by all that she has endured, and still endures; we hear her lift her heart, laden as it is, and extend it out, reach-ing into isolated corners where hurting people live.

Singing can be hard with Miller's condition. But that in itself is not her foremost concern; there is something that strikes even deeper. "You know what the worst thing about pain and suffer-ing is for me? The most torturous thing about it is the lack of control, of being able—or not being able—to help others. It tor-tures me just to sit, not to [be able to] do some of the things that would be in my heart to do."

3

Victoria Williams
Seriously Free

Victoria Williams is a Louisiana-born, California desert–dwelling jazzy, alternative folk-rock pioneer. Her unfettered approach to singing and songwriting has a way of confronting and dissolving even the strongest inhibitions.

In 1993 Victoria Williams' songs met with a fate that is rare for a recording artist so early in her career and lacking any radio hits to speak of. Big names in the then-ubiquitous genre of alternative rock, and its roots and grunge tributaries, recorded them for a tribute and benefit album—a tribute to and benefit for *her*—titled *Sweet Relief.* Thanks in no small part to the participation of acts like Pearl Jam, Lou Reed, and Soul Asylum (and, incidentally, Lucinda Williams and Michelle Shocked), the album raised funds to pay off medical bills for Williams' multiple sclerosis treatment—and gave her music a deserved boost in visibility, making a convincing argument that she belonged in and mattered to the alternative music scene.

More than a decade and a half after the fact, none of this is on Williams' mind when she brings up *Sweet Relief* in our interviews. She does not talk about how it had helped her financially or professionally, nor how it had taken her songs and her name to new audiences. Instead, she remembers how it had helped banish the nagging suspicion that maybe, just maybe, she was not a *real* songwriter: "That's why it was so nice when they did that *Sweet Relief* record and I heard all these people singing my songs. I was so happy. I was like, 'Wow, I never thought anybody could sing my songs.' Then I was like, 'They really are songs.'"

It was really not so outlandish that Williams would wonder whether her music was taken seriously: she intends her songs for adult listeners—and welcomes it when kids respond, too—but has never conformed to a lot of the conventions of music aimed at adults, like emotionally heavy or personally revealing songwriting.[1] That is not how Williams writes; with her, there is no brooding, no explicit confession. What she does do often is wriggle out of linear song structure or delight in celebrating things that might, on the surface, seem small or silly. As for her singing, her voice has a tender, wobbly, unconventional timbre, and she puts it to wild, fanciful, equally unconventional use. As for her outlook on life, songwriting, and performing, she welcomes gusts of spiritual inspiration, wherever she might be when they hit, and seldom falls in line with mainstream attitudes.

Altogether, Williams has accomplished a rare feat: staring the priorities of contemporary, capitalistic, American adulthood in the eye and declining to play along with its rules and priorities, instead favoring the sort of blessedly, brazenly truthful intuition that is not often preserved after youth and a countercultural freedom that is not skeptical of age.

It's Different Out Here

That Williams has not had a problem trusting anyone over thirty is a good thing, since she is now in her fifties herself; she was born in 1958 and began her recording career nearly a quarter-century ago. She and her music seemed, and still seem, so free both because and in spite of her roots in Louisiana. The first words she grabs for to describe her upbringing in the modest-sized river city of Shreveport, Louisiana—"in the country, south of town," to be exact—are "conservative" and "Methodist," two things nobody would have accused her of being later on. Still, it was not as though creativity was frowned upon in her family. "My folks," she points out, "were conservative, yet artists, too; mother a painter, and dad a photographer and wood craftsman." She can recall her mother getting so absorbed in painting that she would lose all track of time and still be at it, in her pajamas no less, when her father got home from work. So there was that.

There was also this: Williams took full advantage of the freedoms she was afforded as a six-year-old living outside of town in 1964. She was an imaginative kid and plenty happy to roam around on her own. She muses, "It was a much more trusting time, I think. . . . [T]hey didn't lock their doors. I would ride my bike—it was a few miles away—to my best friend, like, when I was six, seven years old." In her repertoire, there are songs that recall just how exhilarating an experience that was.

Before there were Victoria Williams albums, there was Victoria Williams the Louisiana musician. Her mother listened to a lot of classical music, and her father, a clarinet player, to big band jazz; in the roots musical melting pot that is Louisiana, she eventually joined up with a country band called G. W. Korners and backed an aging, Flying V–playing blues guitarist. "Well," she begins, "when I was in Louisiana, when I first started playing with this band [G. W. Korners], we'd play out in East Texas. I also played guitar with this old black man in this blues band: Raymond Blakes."

The time came, though, when Williams needed to leave— partly to escape a bad relationship and partly to make her own way, and her own music. California was her far-off destination. "I felt like I couldn't stay in Louisiana," she explains. "It was a dead-end street, me staying in Louisiana. It was bad news. It was better for me to leave. So, yeah, it definitely was a big deal. What my mother said about me going to California is that her friends all said, 'Oh, that's good. She'll do real good. They'll like her out there.'" The memory sparks laughter, followed by an admission: "Maybe I was a little not-as-accepted in Louisiana."

Just as her mom's friends predicted, Williams made quite the impression in Los Angeles, playing street corners and listening rooms. "When I had arrived in California the punk scene was really big," she says. "I remember there were ads in the newspaper. . . . I knew too much to play in their band. They didn't want anybody that knew how to play the guitar. I also studied [music] in college and stuff. So that was odd. But I didn't play around the punk scene. I was 'Louisiana Williams,' but I was just playing solo with guitar."

By 1987 there was a Victoria Williams album, *Happy Come Home*, followed three years later by another, *Swing the Statue!* It was during this period, while opening for veteran country rocker Neil Young, that her multiple sclerosis first appeared; onstage, her hands simply refused to play the guitar. *Sweet Relief* brought a boost in 1993. The next year she released *Loose*, the only album of hers to chart; it reached number forty on *Billboard*'s Heatseekers chart. Her 1995 live album *This Moment in Toronto with the Loose Band* documented that tour. In 1998, she put out *Musings of a Creek Dipper*; in 2000, *Water to Drink*; and in 2002, *Sings Some Ol' Songs*. The ol' songs were not Williams' originals, though up until then she had mostly recorded material she had written; they were pop and jazz standards. Even at a decade old, at the time of this writing the covers set is her most recent solo album.

Throughout her recordings, you can hear the freest parts of her Louisiana roots—free-ranging childhood adventures; memorable, outsider characters; swampy, loose-limbed sounds. She amplified the freedom by venturing even further outside the mainstream, discarding everything that had never resonated with her about it, and finding countercultural kindred spirits in California desert country rock. She may have been a little young—ten, say—when hippies proliferated in the late '60s, but Williams was a kid given to questioning the status quo: "I believe the time I grew up in, with the news on the TV of all the riots and protests and the Kennedys and [Martin Luther] King's [Jr.] death, with Vietnam, [was] not making sense to me; the My Lai massacre, the children's beautiful faces. I asked a lot of questions about that war as a child and could see from my folks that it didn't make sense to them either. It still doesn't make sense to me, war."

Ever since the Neil Young tour, multiple sclerosis has impacted what Williams can do and how much of it and when—much like how fibromyalgia affects her friend, Julie Miller. MS is not lethal, but it is also not curable. It attacks the immune system, disrupts communication between the brain and spinal cord, and generally wreaks neurological havoc, which, for Williams, sometimes takes the form of muscle spasms and energy-sapping spells of numbness. It is no easy thing to live with, but she is defiantly optimistic. "It's a bona fide drag," she admits. "I have to keep saying, 'Okay, well, Vic, you say God doesn't give you anything more than you can handle.' It's like, 'Okay, here goes.'" And as if MS were not enough, a hepatitis C diagnosis a few years back introduced yet another set of symptoms and treatments. Partly because of the prohibitive cost of the latter and partly because she cultivates a harmonious relationship with the natural world, she has become something of an amateur expert in natural health remedies—things like rigorous herbal tea regiments, the healing properties of olives, and ozone therapy.

Though they would be plenty, health problems are not all Williams has weathered. Her marriage to fellow singer-songwriter Peter Case ended shortly after her recording career began. In the mid-'90s, she married another kindred singer-songwriterly sort, Mark Olson—who had, up until that point, co-led the influential alt-country band the Jayhawks. They made a home together in the California desert of Joshua Tree; more of a small farm, really, complete with animals, dust, more than two hundred fruit-bearing trees, and their own humble recording studio. There they fashioned several charmingly stripped-down albums; under Olson's name, as the trio the Original Harmony Ridge Creekdippers, or a combination of both. Williams and Olson toured and sang together a lot; his musical and practical support made a big difference for her on the road. But a few years ago they split, too. Now she tends to the flora and fauna of the remote desert haven—apricot, plum, apple, and almond trees, among them—on her own.

Just as out of the mainstream as Williams' choice to live in the desert—off the beaten path and away from the pollution and pace of the city—is the religious tradition to which she has found herself drawn. She grew up mainline Protestant—Methodist, to be exact—but went her own wild way for a time, before having a conversion experience in Los Angeles. She tells the story this way: "I only 'took the walk' years later watching Jimmy Swaggart alone in an apartment in Los Feliz." The next day, she responded to materials she had gotten in the mail from Seventh Day Adventists, "wanting to know if I wanted to enroll in a Bible study," and was surprised—though not unpleasantly so—when an older man representing that church showed up at her at home and prayed with her. She has since attended at least a couple of charismatic churches—"speaking-in-tongues" churches, in her words (though she does not go to one right now)—and has engaged in ecstatic speech, she says, plenty of times herself. All this makes her a sometime participant in the modern-day incarnation of a once profoundly countercultural, anything-but-elitist Pentecostal movement.

Life, Liberty, and the Pursuit of Everyone's Happiness

Williams has not shaped her music according to the harsher realities of her life so much as her desire—determination, really—to live at peace with them and to make things better any way she can. She has, over the years, repeatedly mentioned an altruistic aim for her music.[2] As she put it to me, "I've always said that I felt so fortunate to be asked to even make a record. And I thought, 'If I'm going to make a record, I always prayed that it would be good for people.' . . . Because I don't want to do anything that's not good for people." Or, articulated slightly differently, "If I'm going to make a noise, I do want it to be a joyful noise[3] . . . something that's good for people. I definitely don't want to add to the mayhem of this world that we're in."

How can Williams tell when a song meets that criterion? "I can't really ever judge. But I know if a song makes me feel good. If I sing it and it feels good, it makes me feel, like, in some way a relief from something, then I think it's probably, hopefully good for other people, so they could relate to it, too. That's what you hope."

Strikingly, considering all that Williams endures physically, there are few, if any, songs in her oeuvre that dissect her own sadness or pain; those emotions in general are less apparent in her singing and songwriting than in Miller's empathy-centered work. "Sometimes I don't tell real personal things," Williams says. "I can really throw a big pity party. . . . When I get really pitiful I'm just like 'Do I really want to go around singing this? No.' Then I think, 'Okay, well, there are some things for my own personal get-through-this part.'" If she wanted to, she could write wrenching songs about what she has suffered emotionally and physically, songs that would command the authority of experience. But if she has any songs like that, she has kept them to herself over the years.

To borrow Williams' phrase, what is good for people in her songs, and the way she performs them, is her freedom; that palpable, potent, youthful, inviting quality. People listening to her albums, attending her shows, or sharing the stage with her can sense that the voice and imagination they are encountering are those of a willfully unfettered, against-the-grain person. What is more, they can tell that she has no interest in keeping that freedom for herself.

"Century Plant," an easygoing country rock number on *Loose*—which Williams recorded during her mid-thirties—is an invitation to defy constricting social scripts at any age. Like a lot of her songs, it was sparked by something she noticed that most people would pass right by without a second thought. "You know, it happened that there was a century plant in my yard, and it did make that giant magnificent bloom that they only make once, once every hundred years," she explains. "I started thinking about, 'Wow, a man's life is a hundred years. And you never know when you're going to bloom.'" Verse by verse, she tells stories of late bloomers—elderly folks, that is—going back to school; joining the Peace Corps; taking up painting, cycling, and white water rafting; and finding fulfillment in the process. During the chorus, she invites everyone within earshot out to play, just as one neighborhood kid would another.

Madeleine L'Engle, writer of such age-transcending science fiction as *A Wrinkle in Time*, described what a marvelous achievement it is for a person to embody several ages at once: "[T]o retain our childlike openness does not mean to be childish. Only the most mature of us are able to be childlike. And to be able to be childlike involves memory; we must never forget any part of ourselves."[4] Southern fiction author Eudora Welty, too, noted how rare it is to find an unspoiled artistic connection to youth: "Children, like animals, use all their senses to discover the world. Then artists come along and discover it the same way, all over again. Here and there, it's the same world. Or now and then we'll hear from an artist who's never lost it."[5]

Williams is just such an artist. When she sings, her voice can sound like it bears the spirit of a seven-year-old girl or a seventy-seven-year-old woman. That breadth, she muses, may be what people have connected with in her music: "Maybe the sense of growing; maybe the sense of childhood and . . . learning to accept all ages and all walks, all stages of life." An open-armed embrace of every season of life, from early childhood to old age, is a rare thing indeed in twenty-first-century Western, and particularly American, culture.

Just Think of the Alternatives

So, then, does Williams find anything troubling about the way adulthood is *really* lived? To this question, she gives her most indignant response of all: "Well, *yeah*. I feel like man has become disengaged from the land. . . . I feel like it's a shame that people have wasted so much time in front of the TV. There's . . . some worthless fodder going into people's [minds]. . . . There's, you know, not much edifying things [on television]. People, they've grown lazy and don't even know where things come from. They don't even know where certain plants come from. You know what I mean? I feel sad that this nation has somehow tried to create this consumerism. . . . The honest truth is, I feel like it's gone after the almighty buck. And you know what it says in the Good Word; it says you can't serve money and God. And I think this is the big problem with America, is that it's really chosen money, you know . . . over everything. And greed is the ruination of mankind, I think."

Williams' worldview is thoroughly countercultural: youthful (but not superficially so, and not at all ageist); antimaterialistic; thoroughly in tune with nature; and skeptical of numbing mass culture, capitalism, and the endless supply of products to buy (not to mention the urge to buy them) from far-removed sources. Those sentiments surface in some of her songs; but being as free-spirited as she is aware, she treats them in playful ways, the better to deflate the buttoned-down seriousness of such mainstream priorities. It is more a matter of writing from the way she sees the world than it is protest. Though she has not thought of what she does in this way, she is pleased by the notion that she may have caused people to rethink some things. "I hadn't meant to challenge anyone," she says. "I like that. I think that's beautiful."

In "Big Fish," on *Happy Come Home*, Williams pokes fun at the human urge to dominate everyone and everything. It is a clowning, mandolin-driven tune, a comedy of nature, and the joke is on people who try to manipulate others with their power. She spends verses describing birds, frogs, hippopotami, bees, and— of course—a big fish, all contentedly occupying their natural spots, and contrasts them with young human bullies defending their territory. With playful blues talk, she cuts egos down to size. As the music lopes on with droll improvisation on soprano sax, she vamps wryly about things like land development and dam building, as though not at all impressed with such displays of engineering mastery.

From the start of Williams' career, all manner of animals, wild and domestic, have shown up in her songwriting as objects of whimsical affection. Her debut *Happy Come Home* and its waggish title track, "Happy," both take their names from a dog. But her focus on the natural world took on new intensity after the multiple sclerosis spells began; some believe the disease to have environmental causes, and some—like her—seek natural treatments. From *Loose* forward, she may not have written about what was going on with her body per se, but she *has* written about the relationship between a person's well-being and her surroundings; she has pondered, in song, how pollutants affect the human body, and worried over people's alienation from the natural world, their obliviousness to what might harm and what might heal. All this started surfacing in her repertoire a good dozen years before Al Gore stirred the environmentalist pot with his climate change documentary *An Inconvenient Truth*.

On the first album with multiple sclerosis in the picture, *Loose*, Williams covered "Nature's Way," which the psychedelic folk-rock band Spirit recorded in 1970. The idea of the song is that changes in the environment are really nature's desperate cries for help. Even though she did not write it and hews close to the original version, it feels personal and urgent, like a truth that she knows by instinct—which, in a way, it is.

By Williams' next album, *Musings of a Creek Dipper*, she was telling a similar story in her own way, in the form of a funny-sad jazz original called "Allergic Boy." She wrote it with her asthmatic childhood neighbor in mind, suspecting—in light of her new environmental awareness—that the chemicals used by his crop-dusting father might have been the reason he was sick all the time. The boy she sings of cannot even attend a birthday party without breaking out in a severe allergic reaction.

Williams migrated to the desert to put distance between her body and its sources of stress—that is, except for the sweltering summer heat—and she has written about the move and its benefits. In a pair of songs on *Musings of a Creek Dipper*, she juxtaposes life in the city with life far away from it. The album opens with "Periwinkle Sky," a free-flowing, wonder-filled piano ballad brimming with reasons why she would rather stay out there than head into town. "Tree Song (Eucalyptus Lullaby)," a woozy, surreal R&B song, comes several tracks later. With loosey-goosey vocal delivery, she catalogs the properties of various trees and plants, meditating on the good of living among such flora. The song takes a primal turn when she sings of not just wanting to, but *having* to get out of the city.

Greed is another of Williams' songwriting targets. The psychedelic rock song "Junk," on *Water to Drink*, makes the love of possessions sound like a self-defeating, even primitive, curiosity. During a spoken interlude, she takes on the role of a future documentarian, attempting to explain the by-then-extinct phenomenon of materialism. The implication—her hope, really—is that things will not always be this way. In the shape-shifting song "Get Away" on *Loose*, escape is the aim—escape from materialism's pusherman. On *Swing the Statue!* the off-kilter blues boogie "On Time" advocates for escape of a related sort—from rigid schedules and relentless striving for success.

Appreciating the Little Things

Williams calls it like she sees it, sanguinely and imaginatively poking at the weaknesses in mainstream social patterns. But that is certainly not all she does; nor is it necessarily the most important thing. She expends more creative and childlike energy shining a light on underappreciated and overlooked people, animals, and things. Delighting in the functional beauty of, say, a gift bag or a plain old pair of shoes can even be an antidote to greed. "I know kids can get so much incredible joy out of the darnedest little things," Williams says. "Sometimes, you know, you give a kid this big old expensive gift and everything, and they want to play with the bag, the bag that it came in."

The very first track on her very first album, *Happy Come Home*, is "Shoes," a frolicsome paean to exactly that—footwear. Half of the song is even addressed *to* shoes—as opposed to people. The reason for the praise is simple: wearing shoes gives a girl freedom to go places and do things, to run, dance, and stamp out a fire. She also acknowledges how readily shoes, for all their utility, are worn out, resoled, and replaced, making them things worth enjoying but not obsessing over.

As for the natural world, there are, in Williams' body of work, a number of funny little songs written in tribute to trifling creatures. During "Wobbling," a courtly waltz on *Swing the Statue!*, her theatrical delivery mirrors the silly, unsteady gait of a baby bird. Claude, a friendly squirrel with a bad eye and a club paw, merits his own jazzy pop number—titled "Claude," of course on *Water to Drink*. The central character of "Little Bird," which appears on the same album, is, indeed, a little bird; one who has alighted in search of crumbs from a party spread. A lot of songwriters—for that matter, a lot of people over the age of ten—would miss these kinds of details. Williams does not.

That attentiveness applies equally to the way she sees people. Their unsavory reputations or social invisibility are of no concern to her; she sees them differently and sets the records about them straight. "Boogieman," on *Swing the Statue!* is about a shady but apparently compassionate hermit who took in and raised an abandoned baby. "Crazy Mary," on *Loose*—one of her better-known songs, thanks, in part, to Pearl Jam's performance of it—is about an alcoholic, mentally unstable woman who died in a freak accident. There is Hank, too, a homeless man in "Statue of a Bum" on *Happy Come Home* who gives his sizable inheritance to an orphanage, and Harry, a notorious musician memorialized in "Harry Went to Heaven," on *Loose*.

Says Williams of the real-life inspiration behind "Crazy Mary," "Well, I didn't know her. But I know she was this woman that had a big fear of automobiles. She would never ever get in an automobile. She would walk all the way into town. . . . [A] car had a wreck and wrecked right into her house. . . . I've always thought of it that she had this great faith in God in the other part of her life. Maybe she didn't have faith in automobiles, but . . . And that she went to a better place when she left. That was the dream sequence; that's what it told me in the dream." The bridge captures the dream sequence; the rest of the song—meaty, minor-key alt-rock laced with serpentine strings—feels like it is under a heavy haunting. But for that brief moment in the bridge, everything shifts to a luminous major key, and she envisions Mary transcending the squalor of her shack. With one small stroke—and readiness to see more to Mary than craziness—she transforms the story.

The subject of "Harry Went to Heaven" was a guitar-playing friend of Williams' who taught her jazz chords; she wrote the song feeling that he was not remembered in a way that did him justice after he died. "I went down to the musician's union and they had a wake for him there," she says. "They were all talking about, 'Oh, Harry, you know, he had a drinking problem,' and all this. 'That's how come he didn't make it big,' and all this stuff. I think that's why I went home and I wrote this. I called it 'Harry Went to Heaven' because I thought, 'Well, I think Harry went to heaven, because look at all the good just from him playing the music; the good feelings people got from the music.'" In songs like these, Williams entertains the possibility that there is good to be found even in spurned lives.

Beyond the age of innocence, past the discovery that there are lots of people who operate in sinister, or at least self-serving, ways, maintaining an optimistic view of human beings is a choice. And if it were an easy one, more people would probably make it. "I believe that as a child we have trust, and trust has been betrayed when trusting man," Williams reasons. "But then, I suppose you have to just realize that all men have fallen. Then you really have to put your trust in God and hope for the best in every man, that they would [heed] . . . their better side, you know."

As simplistic as it may sound, she believes everyone is in need of love, and seems to stand ready to offer it; she has so many songs that feature "love" in the title or take it up as a central theme that she gets a little sheepish at the mention of them all. Romantic love is a favorite theme—*the* theme, really—of popular music, but most of her love songs do not go *there*. Mostly, she has other emotional and spiritual needs in mind. She means loved by God when she sings "You R Loved." An anthemic roots rock number stoked by B-3 organ and the horn section of the funk band Tower of Power, it is the second track on *Loose* and one of her more beloved songs. The lyrics of the song "Love," also on *Loose*, get no more specific than its wide-open title suggests. What is worth noting about it is the fact that she spends a few lines of the bridge voicing her wish that her audience be, like children, unguarded enough to receive love, an idea in harmony with the spirit she projects. "Joy of Love," a welcoming, horn-brightened number on *Water to Drink*, offers a child as an example of what it is to love freely. That same album concludes with "A Little Bit of Love," a sing-along-friendly message song set to a sort of stately march; her rousing, action-oriented language casts love as an answer to human suffering and injustice.

Where They Stop Nobody Knows

Despite where the emphasis is often placed in dissecting the work of a singer-songwriter—the lyrics—the words Williams writes are not the only meaningful thing about what she does; the way she sings them and the wild, whimsical feel of the music itself merit equal attention. The shapes her songs take can be fantastically unpredictable. Of some of her more meandering songs, she says matter-of-factly, "They just come out like that." That comment underscores just how far her approach is from meticulous, revision-heavy song craft, and it is a pretty fair description of what goes on; sometimes she simply sings and says absolutely anything that comes to mind into a tape recorder. Whatever she captures in those moments is the song, as it will be. She admits, "There have been songs that are on my records that I only learned from going back and painstakingly listening to the tapes and learn[ing] what I did."

Two on *Happy Come Home* came about in that way, and they are nothing short of vividly nonlinear, narrative musical adventures: "TC" and "Main Road." "Luckily I had a tape player . . . because I just sat down at the piano and just started telling the story about TC, and that's how that song came out," she recounts. Both songs bear lavish arrangements, courtesy of pop composer and Brian Wilson collaborator Van Dyke Parks, and both have the potential to temporarily scrub one's memory of standard verse-chorus-verse song structure.

This version of "TC"—unlike the live one on *This Moment*— is carried by orchestral accompaniment. After a sweeping intro, Williams' singing, the storyline, and the strings and harp all signal that a carefree frolic is afoot. The speaker—a young Victoria, perhaps—whistles for her dogs (one of many sound effects Williams performs during the course of the song) and sets off to find her friend TC. She alternates between singing in a high, quavering voice and narrating with zany, theatrical exuberance. The music pauses when her speaker arrives at TC's house and raps on the door. After it picks up again, the short, crisp bow strokes and string plucking soften, as Williams steps outside of the unfolding story to offer a bit of background on this TC character; we learn he served in the military, worked construction, gigged in bars, and did plenty more besides, before retiring to a life of strumming ukulele for animals in his backyard. She even acts out his uke performances, flitting between snippets of "You Are My Sunshine" and "Oh My Darlin'." Soon the strings sink and settle, as Williams' narrator contemplates with awe how little need TC has for anything like aspirations to upward mobility at this point in his life.

In the live version of the song, Williams accompanies herself solo on piano, stopping and starting and skipping between octaves for mischievous dramatic effect. It is evident on the recording that her off-kilter sound effects and fanciful improvisation draw audible laughter from the crowd. Even in a stripped-down performance like this one, listening to the song is a journey well off the beaten path.

"Main Road" is something of a companion piece to "TC"; besides appearing on the same album and featuring similarly grandiose instrumentation, it, too, depicts a young girl's footloose and fancy-free wanderings. This time, she ventures out on her little red bicycle to run errands for her mother and satisfy her own imagination. As idyllic as the scene is, the melody's dips into a minor key and the rumbling timpani signal that there are fearful things lurking along her path. Williams' voice darts around, cataloging encroaching dangers, real and imagined; then swoops high and freefalls, floating this adventuresome fantasy—or memory—all the way into the realm of grown-up life.

By Williams' own account, she has always been a tomboy. There is something about the way she carries and expresses herself that evokes the stage of childhood before a kid feels the pressure bearing down to commit to either a feminine or masculine role. But in adulthood—and, especially, in the entertainment industry—that she has retained her tomboyish spirit is no insignificant thing. Even when she was on the roster of major record labels, whose artist and repertoire personnel often see it as part of their job to manage their artists' public personas, she never appeared particularly done-up, sexed-up, or glamorized. In her photos and videos, you see her in baggy pants and brogans, plain, loose-fitting dresses, oversized sweaters, muddied sneakers, and the like; hers is the wardrobe of a bohemian soul who likes to be free to move around, as the spirit moves. Williams dresses, she says, "in a loose, comfortable way." "I can't understand how people can walk in some of these shoes," she observes, no doubt thinking of something along the lines of stiletto heels. "I mean, I don't understand, but they do. Maybe that's the whole thing, just being able to . . . balance like that. It must take a lot." In the final scene of *Happy Come Home*—a short documentary that filmmaker D. A. Pennebaker made about her around the time she released her debut album—she launches into a goofy, improvised ballet wearing one of those characteristically unrestricting skirts.[6] And that right there—that unselfconscious embrace of the moment—is a way we encounter her freedom.

Songs like "Main Road" and "TC" are, Williams confirms, inspired by her childhood memories, her solo adventures on bicycle. TC was somebody she actually knew and visited: "He lived out there in the woods in a trailer with his wife and those animals." Those early tastes of freedom are a robust presence in her songs. But so is the sense that she was headed down her own path. "Summer of Drugs," a darkly mellow, psychedelic rock song on *Swing the Statue!* that was covered by Soul Asylum, tells the story of her developing very different interests during her teenage years than her parents had during theirs; the title ought to offer a pretty good clue as to what those might have been.

Sounds Unfamiliar

Williams does not need lavish orchestration—the sort she had in spades on *Happy Come Home*—in order to bring her songs to life. In fact, when many of the layers are peeled away—as they are on her live album and the homemade Creekdippers records, or to a lesser degree on studio albums, like *Swing the Statue!* (on which "Tarbelly and Featherfoot" evokes the winding feeling of "Main Road" and "TC" without the instrumental embellishment)—we hear a capricious and imaginative musician who is all about being in the moment; one who thrives when she keeps it loose.

Her electric guitar playing is underappreciated—and, of course, with multiple sclerosis she cannot always count on being physically able to play. But she has a loose, rhythmically original feel for the instrument, a result, in part, of the sensibilities she developed in Louisiana playing country and blues. Witness her touch on *Swing the Statue!*: she comes at "Boogieman" with slyly angled licks, pushing out triplets against an otherwise straight time signature; during "On Time," it is her, rather than a drummer, anchoring the groove on rhythm guitar. Neither performance is pristine—there are errant notes and irregularities aplenty; but the small mistakes are welcomed as part of the living, breathing, unfettered spirit she cultivates in her music making.

There is something else that is bound to grab you during any performance of Williams': her singing. She has been known to leap into a sky-high register in bursts of contagious joy. The timbre of her voice—small and quavering, frequently cheerful, and often betraying a hint of a Louisiana drawl—was, and is, unlike much else out there in the roots, pop, and rock music of her lifetime. She can sound like a wise old crone, as she does during "Boogieman," or an excited little girl, as during "Shoes." Then there are times, as during her rendition of "Moon River" on *Sings Some Ol' Songs*, when she slips in a single breath from sounding strikingly young to sultry and mature. Sometimes she acts out the lyrics, exaggerates the storyline; other times, she bends words in odd ways, doing things that sound both fun and funny. Her singing is a true, offbeat pleasure that can melt self-serious inhibitions and reunite our grave adult selves with the parts of us we could have sworn we had lost.

But when it comes to the world of popular music, sounding too idiosyncratic, too countercultural, too unlike anyone else out there can—as Williams has seen—make a singer feel, well, *out there*. "Well, you know, writers—I don't know if it's because they on their own or they just read somebody else's review—but I do hear a lot of times that my voice is hard to handle . . . [that it's] hard to listen to my voice," Williams confesses. "I don't read reviews very much because . . . I just don't read reviews very much. But that, I have seen that."

Williams is not immune to those critiques. What performer who wants to connect with an audience would be? She is as intelligent as she is creative. After she had been writing, recording, and performing for a decade and a half—and gained some perspective on how her voice and songs were received—she collected recordings of pop and jazz standards she had made over the years and released them as an album called *Sings Some Ol' Songs*. Several of the songs were sunny, romantic numbers straight out of the genre- and generation-transcending Great American Songbook, like George and Ira Gershwin's "Someone to Watch over Me," Rodgers and Hart's "My Funny Valentine," and Irving Berlin's "Blue Skies." "Well," Williams starts to explain, "I know that when I put out the covers record, I was thinking, 'Maybe something that people know would make it easier for people to understand my voice.' I thought it would make it easier. . . . If it's something you don't know *and* a different kind of voice, then you've got two strikes against you. But, then, if you had songs that you know and then a different voice, you can hear [the voice]. It's easier to identify with, I would think." And did it accomplish what she had hoped it would? "Actually there was this girl that . . . told me that the first record that she ever bought of mine was *Sing Some Ol' Songs*. She didn't know my stuff. So that actually did sort of work, I guess."

Williams has not released an album of her own in about a decade, but she has been working on a recording project—which she would very much like to finish up and put out—and performing as much as she is able, which is not always a lot: "I mean, because it's pretty much a full-time job taking care of this place." Responsibilities on the farm can encroach at any moment—even during phone interviews. "Like, right now I'm looking at things and, oh, it's 7:20 and I haven't fed the horses. And those poor horses are out there and I haven't fed them and I'm sitting here talking on the phone, and I should be feeding those horses. There's always stuff to do." Exactly what her new album will sound like when it comes and how she will apply the perspective she has gained on her work are open questions.

There are, Williams points out, things she has changed about her singing: "I don't sing things in that high a key anymore, because that can hurt your ears." And she has changed her mind about her old practice of not listing her lyrics in liner notes or anywhere else; it was meant to give fans a sort of choose-your-own-adventure freedom with her songs, but now she wonders if it left her intentions a little *too* wide open. "I, growing up, listening to songs, a lot of times learned completely different lyrics because I didn't know what they were saying; I was singing something different," she recalls. "Then I was thinking, 'Well, somebody might . . . hear something that might be a lot better than this, so I'm just going to not put it down what it is, so that people can make up whatever they want.' But that was not right. I think it's better to write down the lyrics because otherwise . . . nobody's going to know what it says exactly."

Loose Tongues

Even if Williams has determined in hindsight that she ought to temper certain aspects of it, expressive freedom is still at the heart of what she does; that such awareness is present alongside the freedom is admirable. Perhaps paradoxically, her renditions of popular material also accent her readiness to get caught up in the moment. The malleable melody and structure of some of the jazz and pop standards she has done, as well as some songs she has written in those styles, present her with the perfect opportunities to improvise vocally.

She closes her guitar-and-piano reading of the Jerome Kern/Johnny Mercer number "I'm Old Fashioned" with scatting that approximates—among other things—chirps, whines, and gulps. She murmurs and coos through the middle portion of Rodgers and Hart's "My Funny Valentine." "Claude"—already an ode to a silly subject: a squirrel—takes a turn toward the sublime when her affection for the creature melts her "doobie-doos" into puddles of delight. During "Happy to Have Known Pappy"—a vaudevillian number on *Loose* commemorating the beloved late proprietor of a desert honky-tonk—she launches into the lyric with such pleasure and playful energy that her delivery takes on a wild, galloping rhythm. What she is feeling and unable to express through words alone emerges in the freedom of her singing, and there is an inherently spiritual element to it; with her, creative freedom and spiritual freedom are often intertwined.

Williams says she has "always spoken in tongues." And that is no coincidence; her singing takes a similarly ecstatic turn when she scats and breaks into all manner of word-transcending, spontaneous vocalization. "Yeah, there's kind of a freedom in jazz," she muses. "Now, there you go back to your tongues. Jazz singing and speaking in tongues, well, they're different but . . . When people scat, sometimes they do that, but I don't know what they're saying."

Williams is not the only one to make the comparison between scatting and tongues. Scholars of African American culture Stephen J. Casmier and Donald H. Matthews classify both as "non-mimetic" discourse, meaning it goes beyond the bounds of the literal and realistic. With specifically African American expression in mind, they explain that the non-mimetic "involves its beholder, overcomes alienating conventions and human banality, undermines hegemonies, and invokes creativity, the sublime, presence and spirituality."[7] Harvey Cox, in his apology for the vitality and relevance of contemporary Pentecostalism, suggests tongues speaking is "primal speech" that breaks free from the constrictions of middle-class, mainline Protestant Western Christianity: "In an age of bombast, hype, and doublespeak . . . the first Pentecostals learned to speak—and their successors still speak—with another voice, a language of the heart."[8] Sounds a bit like where Williams is coming from.

Cox is describing tongues speaking that happens where it is expected, even encouraged, to happen—that is, at charismatic churches and revival meetings. Williams says she has experienced it in those sorts of settings, sure—and even that is a significant departure from the more formal worship style of her noncharismatic, Methodist upbringing. But she also talks—and sings—about witnessing ecstatic speech in decidedly nonreligious spaces. Say, drinking establishments and subway platforms.

During the intro of "Holy Spirit," on *Swing the Statue!* entranced voices circle in a chorus of "Kumbaya" to the hypnotic beat of a hand drum; it is the unmistakable sound of a campfire gathering. The communal singing and warmth of the flames are meant to stoke feelings of love and goodwill toward God and nature and everyone else and, ultimately, to usher in a spiritual experience. During the chorus of "Holy Spirit," which is every bit as simple and singable as the archetypal campfire song Williams references at the start, she gives a name to what she is experiencing at such moments: the Holy Spirit, tangibly, actively present. After the utopian campfire image, she describes coming upon a stranger whistling to the rhythms of the subway trains and joining in the off-key music; the kind of rare, shared moment that happens only when you are open to it. She clarifies what is really going on here, too; the Spirit—big "S"—is moving. During the bridge, she expands the list of places and ways she has felt the Spirit; on mountaintops and beneath open skies; in churches and bars; laughing and crying, shouting and singing, feeling a touch to the heart.

And Williams sees no reason at all to confine a spontaneous spiritual experience to a designated religious space. Witness her account of what happened one night when she unleashed that song in a honky-tonk not far from where she lives—Pappy and Harriet's Pioneertown Palace, of "Happy to Have Known Pappy" fame: "We played 'Holy Spirit' and the Holy Spirit just totally fell on the entire place. It was glorious. I was just praising God. 'This is, like, amazing.'"

Clearly Williams cares a great deal about how her music affects listeners, which is a different thing than whether people like it, respect it, or buy it (though she, no doubt, would prefer that they do all of the above). She wants to feel free, to just go with it—which can be challenging, with her physical limitations and her responsibilities on the farm, and risky, because there is always the possibility that she might lose people. But what she wants most to do in her freest moments is take the audience with her. Because that—not comfortable conformity—would be good for them. This the Louisiana-bred desert dweller knows from experience. Says Williams, "I totally don't wanna, you know, exclude anybody." And we have every reason to believe she means it.

4

Michelle Shocked
True to Conscience

An intrepid roots music sojourner and activist, Michelle Shocked has fought against the currents of the popular music industry to follow her convictions, in the process starting her own independent record label and becoming a devoted white member of a black church.

If there are any other contemporary musicians on the planet besides Michelle Shocked who have twice recorded commercial albums without knowing it, surely nobody else's unplanned albums bookend a greater period of change than hers do. Her musical journey has been nothing if not exhilaratingly, and at times bewilderingly, distinctive. The first of Shocked's inadvertent albums, 1986's *The Texas Campfire Tapes*, documents a young, bitingly witty, politically pointed solo picker and singer of folk ballads and jump blues, who is a good deal more well traveled and knowing than her liberty-taking British "discoverer," Pete Lawrence, would have people think. Lawrence had gotten Shocked's permission to tape her on his Sony Walkman by identifying himself as a journalist—as opposed to who he really was: somebody in the business of selling music. He nonetheless put out the field recordings on his independent label Cooking Vinyl and dubbed them *The Texas Campfire Tapes*, since he had captured her picking and singing by the fire at Texas' Kerrville Folk Festival. Before she even knew an album existed, she had become something of an overnight folk sensation in the United Kingdom. Major labels got interested in signing her. And sign she did, with Mercury/PolyGram, shrewdly bargaining for ownership of her master recordings rather than taking a big payday up front. The label's promotional muscle helped boost her next few albums to MTV, *Late Night with David Letterman*, and *Rolling Stone* levels of visibility.

Shocked's next unintended album, *ToHeavenURide*, was captured two decades later: an unauthorized recording by sound personnel at Colorado's Telluride Bluegrass Festival. After discovering its existence, she released it in 2007 on her own small, independent label Mighty Sound. By then, her circumstances were different; *she* was different. *ToHeavenURide* reveals Shocked coleading an electrified black church band through a Sunday morning festival set with African American music minister Sean Dancy. She is still attuned to matters of social justice, but now also intent on giving extemporaneous praise to God, her fellow musicians, and others whose faith or talent or both she admires. The group vamps joyously from the hip on spirituals, hymns, gospel, and spiritual roots-pop. Compare the two albums, and you hear impulses that seem worlds apart; they might as well have been released during two different careers. And they were—sort of. By the time Shocked's gospel-infused live recording came out, much of the mainstream media buzz that stirred when she released new music on Mercury had abated. To chalk that up only to popular culture's short attention span or its ageism—though neither are irrelevant—would be to overlook the defining, intentional choices Shocked has made over the course of her career, and, really, to miss her point.

She is the first to acknowledge that things have changed. "I don't really have a recording career, per se, at this point," she observes wryly. "The SoundScan [sales tracking] figures would belie the fact that I've had hit videos and radio airplay and stuff." She can point to her commercially counterintuitive moves dating back to the albums that came on the heels of *The Texas Campfire Tapes*: 1988's *Short Sharp Shocked* and 1989's *Captain Swing*. As she puts it, "[P]eople [were told] by a major label to come hear kind of a folk-rock—I don't know—Bob Dylan, if that's not too presumptuous. Then they got served a heaping helping of big band swing on the second album [*Captain Swing*]: 'We didn't come here for that.' So I always assumed that I was my own worst enemy in terms of attracting an audience . . . that it was going to be all the people who would raise their hand and say [their tastes were] 'none of the above.' I was the only person who would satisfy that requirement." Shocked's posture of steeling herself for the possibility that she might, in the course of doing what she does, put off some less devoted listeners could hardly be more different from Victoria Williams holding back songs she worries would not be uplifting for her audience.

That folk-to-swing shift is just one of many creative and professional decisions of Shocked's that have run the risk of complicating the performer–audience relationship. If people thought they knew her musical style, and liked what they thought they knew, what were they to make of hearing very different things from her? Frequently and significantly altering what you put out there is not the safest way to amass a fan base and sell records. But, throughout her career, Shocked has been admirably committed to priorities other than commercial success.

She is the rare musician who was primed for a dramatic spiritual epiphany by sampling a certain style of music, for politically conscious reasons; and if the musical journey had found a starting point in her roots, the consciousness had not. Many a performer has been attracted to gospel's fervency—dipped a toe in and emerged inspired to add churchly organ, a choir, a hopeful message, or emotional singing to their music. But most are not so affected by the meaning and feeling in religious music that they convert to the religion. Shocked was, and she did.

Quite an Introduction

Shocked's body of work unfurls a striking narrative of change on several levels, and the best place to begin is at the beginning of it. *The Texas Campfire Tapes* were hardly a suitable introduction to Shocked as a recording artist. She had no say in which songs were included or in what order or how they were framed; that was all Lawrence's doing. Only much later, in 2003, did she rerelease those tape recordings in their entirety, with the sound quality enhanced, all songs in their proper order, and her extemporaneous commentary restored. She christened the new-old version *Texas Campfire Takes*.

Lawrence shaped first impressions of this Michelle Shocked character by shrouding her in pastoral myth in his liner notes. He wrote, "These songs tell the life story of a girl from Gilmer, Texas who spends a lot of time on the road. She has a gift for words and a unique turn of phrase. Sit back and lose your heart to the hills of Texas."[1]

Of course, this was no favor to Shocked, the real-life person. She had indeed been born in Dallas, Texas, in 1962, with the given name of Karen Michelle Johnston, and raised in Gilmer, Texas, by her Mormon fundamentalist mother and stepfather, but, in truth, she had grown dissatisfied enough with almost everything about the place, save its variegated musical heritage, to run away in her teens. Her ideological and religious roots she wanted nothing to do with—her musical roots were worth holding onto. There would be much nomadic roaming and squatting, in different area codes and time zones, during her pre-music career, activist years.

"If you heard the way they told my story . . . it sounded really hokey," she says. "And that was because the guy had recorded me on the Sony Walkman and had a few photos but really was just going back with his impressions. And [as] with a lot of those cultural anthropologists, completely overlooking every cultural prejudice they had brought with them that were forming those impressions. . . . You know, he wrote those liner notes without ever bothering to contact me and say, 'Do you mind if I write these liner [notes]?' It was all to his own glory at what a clever, clever scout he had been to come back with this curiosity that no one had seen." Shocked, of course, was the curiosity. And with her piquant command of language and readiness to offer her two savvy cents on an array of cultural and political topics, it is hard to imagine how anyone could have thought of her as a tabula rasa.

Based on Lawrence's pseudo-biographical fragments, plus the twelve songs of Shocked's that he selected, listeners might have expected her to play strictly rustic folk ballads and blues, with her acoustic guitar as her only accompaniment. And yet that was not what they found on Shocked's first premeditated album, *Short Sharp Shocked*. To begin with, the cover featured a black-and-white photo of Shocked in a decidedly nonrustic setting: caught in the chokehold of a San Francisco policeman as she protested during the 1984 Democratic National Convention. And her feeling that the rural Texas of her roots is a suffocating environment for an adventurous young soul comes through loud and clear in songs like "Memories of East Texas," "(Making the Run to) Gladewater," and "VxFxDx." Bare acoustic folk moments are in the minority. Shocked's highest-charting song, "Anchorage," would have been one of them, had the finger-picked guitar figure not been anchored by a minimalist roots rhythm section. Elsewhere, there is more muscular, plugged-in instrumentation, and more groove; some of it uptown, like the sly jazz-pop of "When I Grow Up," some downhome, like the country blues "Graffiti Limbo," and some in between, like the Texas blues-rock shuffle "If Love Was a Train" and the rockabilly boogie of "(Making the Run to) Gladewater." Shocked used her voice in strikingly different ways than she had on *Texas Campfire*, too. She sounded nimble, animated, all over the place, loosing her live-wire vibrato, throwing herself into characters with abandon, and telling stories with streetwise humor.

Even as Shocked was drawing on the musical sensibilities of her native state, she was also engaged in a process of distancing herself from her roots there; of supplanting her geographical home with more, and more colorful, places; of self-reinvention. "[A] lot of people were like, 'Boy, for a rootless girl you sure do sing about your roots, your home a lot,'" she remembers. "But I think I really did manage to embrace . . . the pride of the vagabond and the itinerant. Being a runaway, I really felt like my memory of home was the only home that I had. And so I figured, 'I better start making up some geographical homes for myself, or I'm not going to be any different than anybody else out there who is from a place that is not that interesting.' And, you know, I cobbled it together." "Fogtown," a punk song about San Francisco street life that unofficially ended *Short Sharp Shocked*, is but one example of the cobbling.

The following year, Shocked again gave people something they had not heard from her: an album of rootsy dance music in 1989's *Captain Swing*. It is hardly strictly "swing." "Silent Ways" is a foray into Western swing, but she also draws on Dixieland jazz with "Must Be Luff" and dips into a number of blues and R&B tributaries. Beneath the danceability, a lot of the songs are laced with subversive, cleverly coded political messages. The perky, playful samba-pop number "On the Greener Side" is a self-assured woman's brush-off of her subpar suitor; she knows there is something, or someone, better out there. But there is more to it than that: Shocked was not just talking up the proverbial greener side but the political Green *Party*. Then there is "(Don't You Mess Around with) My Little Sister," a tough-talking rockabilly song ratcheted up from its earlier incarnation on *The Texas Campfire Tapes*. The song works perfectly well as the threat of an overprotective "big brother," but Shocked also has another, more Orwellian "Big Brother" in mind—as well as another "little sister" (the United States' neighbors to the south).

Other songs are more straightforward, like "Streetcorner Ambassador," a bebop number with a cabaret-style, half-time chorus. The theme is an infrequent one for jazz: portraying homeless people as important and influential citizens. The swanky urban blues number "God Is a Real Estate Developer" has all the sardonic bite its title implies. With cynical humor, Shocked portrays God as uninvolved and God's followers as greedy and self-righteous. If the idea is not novel, the treatment certainly is. She recalls, with amusement, "My audience was so reassured by that song: 'She's one of us. She's one of us. She knows that the mega-church TV evangelists are just treating us like dupes and pawns. And she didn't fall for it. Even though she's a hick from east Texas, she somehow was too smart for that.'" The song says a great deal about her feelings toward religion at the time.

The Groove Is the Message

Unlike the vast majority of modern singer-songwriters, Shocked was not terribly interested in writing about the joys and travails of romantic love—any she had lived or could imagine—unless such a topic might make an interesting vehicle for a subversive social or political message. "I said, 'I don't do love songs,'" she recalls. "I really felt like that was really a cheap way to look for inspiration. I mean, not just because of my own political consciousness, but because I saw it as a dead end. . . . If you wrote love songs it would basically doom you to dysfunctional and unhappy personal relationships, because you would run out of material otherwise. . . . I honestly made a conscious decision. I was like, 'My personal life is my personal life; It's not the subject of my songwriting.'"

As for the actual subjects and styles of Shocked's songwriting, she has never drawn lines between message and groove. In fact, she makes it a point to blend the two, a sensibility she attributes to growing up in a region that was home to a thriving, diverse dance music culture and—believe it or not—to being under the thumb of Mormon fundamentalism. The way she tells it, she and her young Mormon peers were denied most all pleasures—all, that is, but music and dancing.

"That link on my website, 'Her Neck of the Woods,'[2] it talks about me having this in common with so many of my east Texas kin, musical kin, because music serves a utilitarian purpose," she explains. "After work you don't go sit in a concert hall and listen to some strummy, strummy guy sing through his nose. You gather up the family . . . you go down to the meeting hall and the band's playing and you're waltzing your sweetheart around the dance floor, and the girls and boys are all flirting, you know, the first chance they have to interact: 'Do you want do dance? Okay, sure.' So it just, it didn't feel mutually exclusive to me, you know, music that had a rhythm and a swing to it and had clever lyrics."

Cleverness, humor, and wit play a central, and pleasing, role in Shocked's repertoire. "They are for storytelling what groove is for dance music," she says. Witness how persuasively she argues that the black jump bluesman Louis Jordan deserves to be known as a "great protest singer": "My favorite version of subversion is that Louis Jordan song 'Ain't Nobody Here but Us Chickens.' I love that. To me, that is, like, the Malcolm X of addressing racism. . . . [The song] is, like, going 'You stupid fool. You thought you were going to catch us congregating in the barnyard.' . . . I just think that's like telling Charlie 'Go stuff yourself, man, because we are more clever by acting like we are fools, you know, like we're just ignorant old Negroes who don't knows no betters.' I just think it's brilliant. It's so subversive."

Shocked's marriage of the political with the entertaining and rhythmically upbeat is not insignificant. She came of age a generation after the urban folk revival of the 1960s. Like her, the urban folkies had guitars and voices, songs and progressive political principles; but even at the height of the civil rights movement, their musical movement had fairly narrow racial appeal and tended to neglect more bodily and groove-centric styles. Craig Werner notes, "Part of the problem with the folk revival was that it failed to attract the black listeners who preferred Motown, Sam Cooke, or even less 'historically correct' versions of gospel or the blues. . . . What the folkies *didn't* want in their blues was electricity, drums, any tinge of the fallen modern world."[3] Oftentimes, electricity, drums, and modern sounds are *exactly* what Shocked wants. On this point, her earlier half-apologetic self-comparison to Bob Dylan is an apt one; not only was he representative of the folkies who prioritized writing new songs rather than leaning only on old ones—which is her preference, too—but before the '60s were out, he was plugging in and chasing a forward-thinking roots aesthetic. Her interests clearly also include contemporary sounds.

Shocked's protest songs are, as a rule, more pointed than utopian. The reissued versions of *Short Sharp Shocked* and *Captain Swing*—not on Mercury, but Mighty Sound, where Shocked enjoys complete control of her entire catalog—include live versions of scathing, never-before-released songs like "Campus Crusade," a brutal caricature of campus evangelists, and "Garden Salad Diplomacy," a punning, a capella critique of the United States quashing foreign rebellions. The radical postures she adopts in protest songs say much about her intentions. "I feel like I write from an antagonistic point of view," she reflects. "I always write from the premise that people are going to be turned off by it; that they're not going to accept or embrace the unorthodox point of view. So even when you have people who are like, 'I've been inspired by it' or 'I've been influenced by it,' I always think of them as the weirdoes as the, you know, exceptions to the rule. Most of the time when I think of the audience, it's not that I'm trying to piss people off, it's not that I'm trying to offend anybody, but I just assume if I'm telling my truth and I'm, you know, being just idiosyncratic that most people are going to be like 'Huh? We don't get it.'"

Blackface Minstrel with a Message

Racism has often been the target of Shocked's antagonistic point of view. After *Captain Swing*, she attempted quite an ambitious undertaking on the subject of race, music, and roots, informed in part by the work of her then-husband, music journalist and historian Bart Bull. The 1991 album was called *Arkansas Traveler*, and it would be the last one she would make for Mercury. The *O Brother, Where Art Thou?* soundtrack—a project that, like *Arkansas Traveler*, pooled roots-minded musicians and shone a spotlight on American roots music, yet, unlike *Arkansas Traveler*, sold millions of copies—was still nine years off when Shocked decided to take to the road and record old-timey original songs and remade traditional numbers with an impressive cross-section of roots musicians.

In Chicago, she enlisted Pops Staples, the Staples Singers' patriarch and master of sinewy, downhome, gospel-soul guitar; in Woodstock, Levon Helm and Garth Hudson of roots rock godfathers the Band; in Los Angeles, the globally minded modern bluesman Taj Mahal; in St. Charles, Missouri, Uncle Tupelo, a band that helped jumpstart the '90s alt-country fad; in Memphis, Clarence "Gatemouth" Brown, a fiddling, guitar-slinging bridge between jazzy country and blues; in Wilkesboro, North Carolina, Doc Watson, masterful, flat-picking folk and country guitarist; in Franklin, Tennessee, Alison Krauss and Union Station, the most famous of contemporary bluegrass-pop groups; and even her mandolin-playing biological father—who had *not* been the source of her strict upbringing—billed as Dollar Bill Johnston, in both Mountain View, Arkansas, and Mineola, Texas.

More than just making an expensive album on the label's dime, Shocked was reveling in preservation of and innovation in American roots music traditions in which she shared. Having her self-taught dad play a part in the project was a nod to his role in introducing her to rootsy musical horizons—by way of old-time music festivals and the albums of Texas country-folk songwriting veteran Guy Clark—and making the music seem well within her reach. She is adamant that "American musicians have the richest heritage and birthright of any country on earth." "Why on earth," she asks indignantly, "would we sell it for a bowl of porridge? Why would we give that rich diversity away for the sake of having a marketing niche or a branding opportunity, when you could at the end of the day call yourself an American musician?" So what if doing a little bit of all of it scrambles her genre identity? She would rather be known for having consciously embraced a wide variety of American roots musical styles, from Texas and beyond, with open arms.

Being a songwriter first and foremost, Shocked found her way into the traditional material on *Arkansas Traveler* by keeping snippets of familiar melodies and themes and turning the spirits of the songs on their heads. She did it with "Cotton-Eyed Joe," a rag about a rambler who seduced women and left them in his wake. "Prodigal Daughter" is her answer; it is considerably slower than its rollicking predecessor—that is, until Krauss and Union Station take it for a spin late in the track—and emotionally heavier, too, with its focus on the predicament of the shamed young women. No longer is this Cotton-Eyed Joe the subject of lighthearted admiration.

Shocked made another mighty shift in the musical mood of "Soldier's Joy," her variation on another frolicsome old fiddle tune. She lays the melody against desperate-sounding, minor-key verses and employs the image of "soldier's joy"—a nineteenth-century euphemism for morphine—to depict the gruesome fatalism of war. Uncle Tupelo's raw, blunted attack powers the song.

"Jump Jim Crow" is one of her bolder subversions on the album, and an indication of her deeper intent. She took as inspiration a song by the seminal blackface minstrel Thomas "Daddy" Rice that caricatured a black man as a shiftless, dim-witted joke. Only, in her hands, played as jaunty ragtime laced with Mahal's guttural humming and grunting, the black man no longer plays the fool in the story; now the white man does, outsmarted by a character who puts on an elaborate, subversive act.

Then there is the album's cover to consider. Shocked is seated on a stump by a shack, a hobo's bindle across her lap, her feet soaking in a pan and a dirt road snaking off into the distance. It was not what she had *really* wanted, but it was what Mercury would allow. In the liner notes, she explains, "My earliest intention was to present this record with a cover photo of myself wearing blackface. Aside from providing controversy for hatemongers or offending the delicate sensibilities of the politically correct, my sincere intention was that it would provide a genuine focus on the real 'roots' of many of the tunes included; blackface minstrelsy. It's my contention that a blackface tradition is alive and well hidden behind the modern mask. I believe that 'blacking up' should be done correctly; as an exploration for the source of that hollow ring we mistakenly believe was immaculately conceived in Las Vegas, and in a context of true respect for the cultures we ape."[4]

Mercury's representatives inserted their own comments just below hers: "The views and opinions expressed on this recording are solely those of Michelle Shocked and do not necessarily represent those of the musicians who have generously contributed their time and talent to this project."[5]

What Shocked was advocating for was educated and morally responsible roots-borrowing—particularly when it comes to recognizing black musical contributions. On *Arkansas Traveler* and elsewhere, she strives to call out the fraught, tangled racial history of American music; to see to it credit is given where credit is due; to put more of her energy into desegregating the music than maintaining the status quo.

Historically aware chroniclers of music, from Tony Russell—and his abbreviated but influential 1970 book *Blacks, Whites and Blues*—forward,[6] have made known that American folk music is not nearly as lily white in origin as we might think; that early racial cross-pollination in music has too often been ignored;

that actually varied black and white musical repertoires have been pointedly oversimplified. In *Segregating Sound*, Karl Hagstrom Miller explains how southern music came, by enterprising and frequently prejudiced commercial and academic forces, to be divided along lines of race, his point being that what now seems like a neat and self-evident arrangement did not at all begin that way.[7]

There's Been a Change

Shocked was taking a risk by bringing up a subject that was, and still is, likely to foster confusion or disagreement—and by doing it in such a provocative way. *Arkansas Traveler* marked the beginning of the end for her relationship with Mercury. But there was bigger change than that afoot; the same woman who had gotten a kick out of singing "God Is a Real Estate Developer" was on her way to a big-time spiritual awakening, and music was the catalyst.

"I was at the top of my game," she says matter-of-factly and without a trace of regret. "You know, *Arkansas Traveler* had been released and nominated for a Grammy. I was touring, I was headlining a tour with Taj Mahal, the Band and [Uncle Tupelo]. . . . I had just gotten married that summer. And my career was well established. But I had an instinct that if this was . . . the height, if this was the pinnacle, if this was the top, there was a long way to fall. And, you know, the timing of it was quite miraculous, because you hear a lot of times of people kind of turning to God when they've hit bottom. My instincts—and I don't think it's because I'm a pessimist; I'm an idealist—but my instincts told me, you know, 'You've got a long way to fall.' And it [wasn't] long after that . . . everything fell apart."

The disintegration prompted by the direction that Shocked wanted to pursue—which included a gospel-influenced recording project—was, indeed, spectacular. Mercury refused to put out an album like *that* by *her*, reportedly citing "stylistic inconsistency."[8] When you think about it, that is really not such an irrational complaint from a company whose priority—in stark contrast to hers—was first and foremost to get an easily place-able, brandable, marketable product to sell. But neither would the label let her out of her contract. So, a model of empowerment for performers everywhere, she took up for herself in a way no recording artist ever had, appealing to the Thirteenth Amend-ment of the Constitution to argue that she was being held by her label in involuntary servitude. Eventually Mercury settled, and she was released from the label.

Shocked attributes the fact that she was ever on a major label at all, and ended the relationship when she did, to activist's resourcefulness. "I was ambivalent going into the whole enter-prise," she says. "I felt like as long as I could be effective working inside the system, I would continue to do so. But I really hoped that if I was no longer effective working inside the system, that I would have the courage of my convictions to remove myself from the privileges and the . . . perks, I guess . . . of being, you know, a name brand or something like that. . . . [T]hanks to my prescience with the contract that I negotiated, I had kind of cre-ated a future for myself no matter what by owning those master [recording]s."

That Shocked was in career limbo during this period did not mean she was altogether artistically inactive. She recorded small-scale projects and sold them only at her shows and by mail order. The first version of *Kind Hearted Woman*, appearing in 1994, featured just her voice and Stratocaster electric gui-tar; for the 1996 version, she rerecorded the songs with a lean three-piece band. In 1996 *Artists Make Lousy Slaves* was written in two days and recorded in one with guitarist Fiachna Ó Bra-onáin of the Irish band the Hothouse Flowers (just in time for him and Shocked to hit the road as a duo). The album indeed sounds like the fruits of quick basement sessions. The point was that Shocked's desire and ability to create—unlike, perhaps, the then-tangled business side of her career—were not subject to anyone else's control.

There is something raw and special about the second version of *Kind Hearted Woman* and the project that followed it in 1998, *Good News*. Too often overlooked as placeholders between the bigger works in her catalog, they reveal the inner stirrings she felt as she transitioned from Mercury to independence, and from criticizing religion at a distance to plunging herself into it within a religious community. *Kind Hearted Woman* pointed subtly to changes afoot. "Eddie," jazzy talking blues, portrays a protagonist taking God very seriously, even if that seriousness comes in the form of anger. Several other songs, like the freeform narrative "Stillborn," zoom in on people at poignant moments of vulnerability.

Shocked reaches for spiritual language to describe what she was experiencing when she wrote those songs. "You spend every waking moment trying to be strong, trying to be infallible, trying to protect yourself and insulate yourself from any exposure of maybe you don't know what you're doing or why you're doing it," she says. "And then when you reach that point of humility where you just say, 'I can't do it anymore. Just break me.' And then you've now faced your worst fear, which is to be broken, only to discover that . . . [God] loves you more than you can ever love yourself and He's gonna therefore protect you far better than you can ever protect yourself. . . . So you let go and it does, in fact, make you soft and malleable. . . . And *Kind Hearted Woman* was that watershed."

Read the album's liner notes carefully and you find a curious first-time inclusion alongside the more obvious contributors to Shocked's career, like accounting firms and music publishing companies. There is one Charles E. Blake, minister of West Angeles Church of God in Christ (COGIC)—a megachurch in the African American Holiness-Pentecostal denomination—listed among the "thank yous."[9] It may have seemed a mystery at the time, but it was certainly no fluke.

From a commercial standpoint, Shocked treated her next release, 1998's *Good News*, as though it was really no big deal.

Even by independent standards, the number of CDs she had pressed was tiny: just twenty-five hundred. But that scrappy, spirited album serves as an essential hinge between earlier and later periods of her career, and it shows her attempting to merge her disparate passions. In that way, *Good News* was a very big deal. The album's title track is a forceful mashup of gospel and garage rock. Shocked testifies with righteous agitation, and the guitar and organ give their jabbing answer. But the lyrics are the real revelation. They are laced with bluesy, earthy imagery, calling out profit-driven corporate manufacturers for devastating Louisiana swampland; but they also make a declaration of prophetic faith, invoking Matthew 18:20—Christ's promise of presence wherever three or more are gathered—and Thomas A. Dorsey's comforting gospel hymn "Peace in the Valley." Together, both elements convey that the people prayerfully uniting themselves against this injustice are empowered by an engaged God.

Here in "Good News," a song commissioned by the environmental organization Greenpeace, Shocked's activist concerns and newfound respect for religion met for the very first time. She was powerfully relieved: "Yeah, that was like a godsend to say 'It's okay, Michelle. You're way out of your depth, but I can make this comprehensible to you. I can give you a foothold, I can show you a connection, a way to connect to this.' And it was that Greenpeace campaign to Cancer Alley where I saw an African American community using their traditions, their church traditions, to gather their community together to fight oppression. And I was like, literally, 'Thank God. This I know.'"

"Can't Take My Joy," a crisply syncopated a capella spiritual, also brings spiritual and political realms into contact. Shocked sings it in multipart harmony with her then-band the Anointed Earls and spreads the lead vocal parts around. The first verse takes up such undesirable human qualities as greed. It is hardly a stretch to imagine that she has corporate and political perpetrators in the back of her mind. Still, she concludes with the confident declaration that those realities cannot rob her of her spiritual vitality, her joy. The emotional quality coloring the subdued R&B number "Forgive to Forget" was a new one for Shocked the singer and songwriter: penitence. Hearing her sing, with a softened, vulnerable quality and a touch of self-deprecating humor, about letting go of bitterness was a new listening experience; she must have been *having* a new experience to write that way.

To launch her label, Mighty Sound—"sound" referring to sturdiness, rather than to noise—in 2002, Shocked put out a radically souped-up and expanded version of *Good News* called *Deep Natural*. To the songs from *Good News*, she added her first attempts at devotional songwriting. "That's So Amazing," a blissful pop-R&B number, expresses the newness and wonder a fresh convert feels; the acoustic confession "If Not Here" seems to capture her in the act of yielding to the divine; "Moanin' Dove" has the guitar-strumming simplicity, zeal, and directness of the Jesus People's early '70s folk hymns; and the anthem "Psalm," as its title suggests, is steeped in Hebrew Bible imagery, rendered in King James English, marveling at divine miracles in the natural world, and counting God's stirring in her once-hardened heart as one of them. "Peachfuzz," bouncy, storytelling funk, was another addition, religious only in its playful, though not unserious, take on the Eden myth: that a gay teen-aged boy is oblivious to girls his age (who are not necessarily oblivious to him) and wants instead to flirt with someone of his own sex is proof that Adam and Eve were not the only model for relationships.

Shocked's most dizzying, all-at-once display of stylistic variety—at least so far—came when she released *Threesome* in 2005, three albums that arrived simultaneously: *Got No Strings*, *Mexican Standoff*, and *Don't Ask, Don't Tell*. They were, respectively, a collection of classic Disney songs reinterpreted Western swing–style; a Tex-Mex set split between Latin flavors and roadhouse blues, referencing the culture-blending border states of her native Texas and her current home of California; and a jazz- and blues-informed storytelling showcase, tackling romantic dissolution from her wry, witty, and never *too* personally revealing angle. She framed it both as her divorce trilogy—no strings, get it?—and a follow-up to her first American roots music trilogy, which had encompassed *Short Sharp Shocked*, *Captain Swing*, and *Arkansas Traveler*. The big picture is more striking than each of the three albums themselves; Shocked is still finding pockets of musical culture to explore.

Strange Things, Indeed

The next entry in Shocked's discography was the second of those live albums she had not meant to make. *ToHeavenURide* was recorded during her set at the Telluride Bluegrass Festival—unbeknownst to her, of course—in 2003, though four more years would pass before she released it. Her aim in that performance was to bring the music she had been getting more and more interested in—gospel—to a music festival where hot acoustic picking is highly valued, and to stir things up. She explains her motivations with a mixture of musical and scriptural references: "It's like it says in the Bible, Christ says, 'I'm the living vine. If you don't partake of the living vine the branches wither.'[10]. . . So the problem with most music styles is they may have at one point been inspired or gotten their inspiration from those sources, but they strayed farther and farther from the roots of it and they get very technical, they get very dry. It's impressive, it's mathematically satisfying, but it's not spiritually nourishing. So I felt like it was a good thing to contribute to the festival overall."

Bluegrass is, in actuality, a fairly modern music, predating rockabilly by only a handful of years, and home today to both staunch traditionalists and innovators who work in often virtuosic, sometimes highly technical, elements of rock, jazz, or other styles. Some of it maintains close ties to white, harmony-singing southern gospel music. What it does not have is racial diversity. So it is no small point that Shocked strategically shared her spotlight role at a bluegrass festival with Sean Dancy, a black church music minister, and his musically gifted family.

"When I'm working in that realm [Sean Dancy] has the authority," she says matter-of-factly. "To a great degree, I'm borrowing his authority when I speak, so it makes very much sense to me to open up the possibility that it's not owned by any one of us, but we're all up there invoking and inviting the spirit together. I'm respectful of the conventions of being a marquee act. The people have heard of me—they haven't heard of Sean. But that doesn't mean that the gifts of the spirit that he's blessed with can't be shared among everybody. . . . So I performed the function of an interlocutor. It was like I was saying, 'I'm one of y'all, but I've also had some insight into this other world. Let's go exploring it together.'"

For a gospel set, the material on *ToHeavenURide* is pretty varied. It includes four Shocked originals; three from her existing repertoire, "Good News," "Psalm," and "Can't Take My Joy," plus the slow-stuttering funk song "Quality of Mercy," a reminder that mercy is, by definition, undeserved, which she wrote for Tim Robbins' big-screen exploration of capital punishment, *Dead Man Walking*. There are also a couple of spirituals, "Wade in the Water" and "Study War No More," as well as "Uncloudy Day," a gospel song dating to the late eighteenth century, "We're Blessed," a praise chorus by contemporary urban gospel singer Fred Hammond, and a World War II–era gospel composition by sanctified singer-guitarist Sister Rosetta Tharpe called "Strange Things Happening Every Day."[11]

Shocked was offering some strong clues as to the spiritual-musical headspace she was in. She had found common ground between the activism that people had long associated with her and the interest in spiritual uplift that they were not at all used to hearing from her. After an especially caught-up performance of "Good News," she sensed that she might be going too far too fast for some folks and tried to bring the audience up to speed by recounting what a revelation it was for her to see poor black citizens in Louisiana making prayer a central part of their community organizing.

The spirituals Shocked sang that day had in the time of slavery offered not only a soul salve but also veiled political strategies for liberation. "['Wade in the Water'] was written to accompany the rite of baptism, but Harriet Tubman also used it to communicate to fugitives escaping to the North that they should be sure to 'wade in the water' in order to throw bloodhounds off their scent."[12] "Study War No More" favored nonviolent resistance.[13] "Uncloudy Day" is part of a significant body of gospel songs and spirituals that looked forward to the relief heaven would offer from the hardships of life. The eminent black theologian James H. Cone sees active resistance in slaves' singing of heaven-themed spirituals: "[T]hey had to disobey all values that hindered their obedience to the coming Kingdom. Heaven then did not mean passivity but revolution against the present order."[14]

As committed as Shocked is to advocating for change in the here and now, she, too, argues that songs with otherworldly orientations can be politically challenging—to privileged listeners. "You should come to understand much better how privileged a life you have if things look better in this life than the next one, because there is ninety percent of this earth's population that can't say that," she says with conviction. "You haven't had food for a week or you've been imprisoned for speaking your mind or you don't have a home or your country is torn up by war that you have no control over—you start walking in those shoes and this life doesn't look quite so good anymore. Even the hope of trying to make a difference or make a change when you don't have those basic necessities . . . I wish people would use it more as a barometer for how privileged and blessed they actually are rather than for how unrealistic or pie-in-the-sky some folks might wish things were."

On the Telluride stage, Shocked also demonstrated an awareness of more contemporary gospel music; with her was the sort of keyboard- and electric guitar–driven band that you might hear in a black church now. And the set list featured a song by current African American worship leader Fred Hammond, a name that would likely be familiar to any urban gospel fan.

Shocked's most recent album, 2009's *Soul of My Soul*, is comparatively light on gospel material, with the exception of "Liquid Prayer," a soul-pop original about entrusting her fractured heart to God. There is, however, no shortage of piss and vinegar in the political selections. "Other People" begins as a straight-ahead break-up ballad, addressed to an insensitive, bullying partner. Then, in a signature Shocked twist, it becomes clear that the relationship in question is not romantic at all but with the United States and its policies.

The message of "Ballad of the Battle of the Ballot and the Bullet Part I: Ugly Americans" is not veiled even for a moment. The agitated country rock number quickly progresses into full-contact confrontation. First Shocked pleads with her audience, almost apologetically, to do some political soul-searching; to take inventory of the motivations behind military decisions being made here and abroad. By the song's bridge, she has taken up a combative posture, challenging everyone who disagrees with her to say so and direct their venom at her instead of staying silent, although her aggrieved vocal performance sounds deeper emotional notes than those of righteous anger alone. Her delivery does not convey much hope that people will get on board with her but seems steeled for the opposite reaction.

Indeed, says Shocked, "I've never been afraid of antagonizing my audience with my forthrightness about my political convictions. I've always felt like if you don't like them you really should not be at a Michelle Shocked show." She adds, "They turned the tables on me" ("they" meaning her audience). "These last eight years I have not ceased to be shocked, dismayed, surprised to find that my very progressive audience had somewhere along the line become very, very reactionary, very easily manipulated by political tactics of fear and xenophobia, to the point that . . . they were trying to tell me that I had really gone too far and that I needed to tone it down. And I wasn't getting the encouragement and the cheers and the 'you go girl' kind of thing that I had taken for granted."

The relationship Shocked has with her audience is a complex one to be sure, and it can sometimes be intense. She has always spoken her mind, according to her political consciousness and her conscience. As the fact that she was accustomed to being cheered for doing so suggests, her refusal to tone down her social and political commentary and her willingness to antagonize had also gotten her the respect and attachment of an audience who valued such sharp, uncompromising edges in an artist, perhaps even regarding them as markers of integrity. Shocked can always be counted on to be truthful about what injustices in the world she feels deserve attention; that is among the valuable things she offers in her music. But it can be a treacherous road for an artist to travel. Popular opinion is not always kind to a woman of such strong convictions in her field; record labels can lose patience; audiences can turn.

Shocked admits that aspects of the course she has chosen have complicated things for her: "I've been given this really, deeply intrinsic insecurity, and the way that I have addressed it is not to . . . try to do all the things that make me seem normal, that make me seem acceptable, that would earn me the status or respect, but rather to learn how to be comfortable with being considered odd, or different, or weird. Instead of trying to fit in, I've really put a lot of effort into learning how to be comfortable with *not* fitting in."

Integrating the Choir Loft

As for not fitting in, Shocked's convictions about music would eventually take her well beyond a major label album critiquing blackface minstrelsy. She recounts, "I guess by *Arkansas Traveler* I could already tell that what had started as a politically motivated commitment to social justice and cultural politics of racism left me very open-handed and willing to go down a road that I would have never . . . predicted for myself. So that's why I say I don't know where I'm going, but I can tell you that pretty early on in the journey I identified that destination and have been following it ever since, and that is to find the deepest source of American music. And I believe that I've found it in gospel music, and specifically that is what is designated as African American traditions of gospel—not the white what's called '[contemporary] Christian.'"[15]

Shocked found the music she was looking for in the black Pentecostal church. This after she had run as far as she could from her Mormon fundamentalist upbringing and avoided—even savaged—religion in general. Shocked tells the story of her journey to conversion, as she must have been called on to do hundreds of times by now, with finesse and conviction: "Understand that I didn't start out looking for spiritual sustenance. I started out looking for evidence that there was a veracity to the idea that these vernacular roots were not just another version of whitewash, or more importantly, hogwash. And so I, like many cultural adventures before me, decided to take the mountain to Mohammed; I went straight to a black church. But it was also inspired not by my cultural curiosity but by my political convictions. Because it was a quote by the Reverend Martin Luther King [Jr.] saying that Sunday morning 11 a.m. is the most segregated hour in America. And how can the gospel of brotherly love justify perpetuating this type of segregation? How can it be that even with a black president in the White House that we still are able to make a choice of whether we go to a white church or a black church? So I felt like it wasn't much. It was just one woman's small effort at addressing [the problem]. But, you know, I thought, 'Well, they're sure not coming to my shows, so I'm going to go to theirs.'"

Shocked recounts the thought process she used to justify her repeated church attendance to herself: "It was easy to justify because you say, 'What's not to love about a gospel choir?'

You intuit that there's a spiritual sustenance, but you're, you know, pretty much very deeply enraptured with your own kind of secular humanism, your own, you know, intellectual hipsterism, your own rising above the . . . fundamentalist, narrow-minded, born-again hypocrites. That's not you. . . . The way I explain it is that I went, I went for the singing, but I stayed for the song. And I remember thinking, 'You know, this music would be so great if they would just get rid of all that Jesus crap.'. . . I mean what kind of marketing is that? . . . But there was a conviction and a power to it. . . . [T]he way it's said in the tradition is God had made an appointment with me. And basically he used whatever means were necessary to get me there."

How jarring it must have been for some of Shocked's long-time fans to hear the author of "God Is a Real Estate Developer" and "Campus Crusade" make an album with as obvious and as heartfelt gospel leanings as *Good News*. "And then to name it so blatantly . . ." she emphasizes. "You gotta know my ex-husband's like 'What are you thinking? You are destroying everything you have worked so hard to build. You are driving people away. It's almost like you're sending out invitations to say, "Please don't come." ' "

The worries were justifiable, but Shocked was undeterred. The same performer who had chafed under the authority of both the Church of Jesus Christ of Latter-day Saints and Mercury Records willingly placed herself under the authority of West Angeles Church of God in Christ, pastored by Bishop Blake—the same Bishop Blake who appears in her liner notes. Needless to say, it was a gargantuan step. She joined the church even though some of her political convictions did not necessarily jibe with COGIC doctrine, particularly those related to equality of gender and sexual orientation. As in many Christian denominations that view the Bible as infallible, women fill roles that are not accorded as much formal authority as some of those that men fill. "Evangelists in the Church of God in Christ can be either male or female. [But] . . . the COGIC is adamant about women not being called preachers."[16] The denomination as a whole does not ordain women or let them serve as pastors. Nor is it affirming of lesbian, gay, bisexual, and transgender people.

That is not to say Shocked necessarily changed her mind about those issues; rather, in becoming a member of West Angeles COGIC, she knowingly entered into a complex relationship; she had a clear priority, and it was to take part in that community. "I guess the primary principle is an old one," she offers, "that you don't throw the baby out with the bathwater." She clarifies, "I encountered a lot of things being preached from the pulpit that just struck me as downright narrow-minded bigotry. But . . . I mean, if you insist on remaining on the outside of the thing, it's forever going to appear to you exactly as your logic reveals. You have to take a leap of faith."

For Shocked, the good of being at West Angeles far outweighs the bad; the good is being where she encountered vital music, and God; the good is not just critiquing the racial segregation of music and church, but *doing* what she can about it. And she really has stayed for the song. By the time she played her gospel set at Telluride, she had already been at West Angeles for a number of years. Soon after, she even joined the church's mass choir, quite a change from being strictly a solo act and yet another sign of the seriousness of her commitment.

Perhaps most telling is the way Bishop Blake introduced her in front of the church the first time she sang a solo with the choir. What he had to say is captured in a video accessible on YouTube: "Now, Michelle is one of the most renowned folksingers and musicians in our nation. I've had the privilege of going to the Universal Amphitheatre and seeing Michelle Shocked in concert, thousands and thousands of people. And, you know, she has sat quietly in West Angeles for—I don't know—ten, fifteen years just as a faithful, generous, supporting member; gave her houseboat to West Angeles, and we sold it to have the money.

Just gift after gift she has given to us and just without any special respect or admiration or adulation. She's just been a faithful member of West Angeles Church, and others in this group and in the audience. She's just so faithful and such a blessing to West Angeles Church, and we love you with all of our hearts."[17]

Why, if Shocked has found such spiritual and creative sustenance in gospel music, if she is so deeply energized by singing in the choir, if the music expresses so much of what she wants to express, does she not make gospel her primary songwriting focus from here on out?

"It's a good question," she concurs, "because on the one hand I've argued that this musical path has been a journey back to the deepest roots. And so, if I believe that gospel is the deepest roots, why would I not reach that destination and then stop there? But I think another force that is in place is that I've always known that I would never be a gospel singer. I just, I don't have the qualifications. . . . I think what I really had a sense of was that I was going to become my version of a gospel singer, and that meant that I had to keep traveling."

Authority—who has what sort and how it should rightfully be deployed—is something she cares a great deal about. She weighs those considerations as she chooses her words: "Maybe you can say I'm not a gospel singer, but I am rapidly aspiring to be a gospel songwriter."

Whether Shocked is singing gospel or writing it, or something like it, none of the above are specialties anybody was prepared to hear from Shocked the twentysomething, roots-minded, irreligious radical. And yet, by audaciously following her conscience in defiance of expectations of any and every sort, Shocked, the late-forties radical, still roots-minded, and now genuinely devout, determined those are among the forms of music making she ought to pursue.

"I actually give God the credit for the vision in the first place," she says. "I don't think I would have come up with it. Generally

it's just understood to be style for the sake of style or just dilet-
tantism or just outright perversity, you know. Yeah, I admit that
it's a complex vision; I admit that you can't really see the whole
picture yet in terms of all the pieces that are coming together.
But I've been on this journey for over fifteen years now, and I'm
starting to catch on."

5

Mary Gauthier
Outsider Art

A folk-country singer-songwriter respected for the quality and heft of her work, Mary Gauthier unflinchingly—and not at all unfeelingly—speaks of and to people on the social margins, identifying with them particularly through her own experience of being orphaned.

In a way, Mary Gauthier seems very alone onstage as she shushes the people conversing over by the bar. Though there is a fiddler with her, contributing sparse, shadowy bow strokes, she stands with her acoustic guitar at the microphone as a soul confronting feelings of profound alienation and reaching into the void, grasping for eyes and ears that will reflect back to her a shared sense of humanity. With a mixture of sternness and humor, she corrals the attention of everyone in the room: "If the people talking are bothering anybody in the audience, you have my permission to tell them to shut up." It matters not that she is in a rock club, decidedly *not* the quietest of venues.

Gauthier has just played a steely, haunting number titled "Snakebit" that plunges her, with jarring, first-person narration, into the dark inner dialogue of a person who has careened over the edge. She opens with the song—the first track on her *Between Daylight and Dark* album and one she cowrote with Texas country singer-songwriter Hayes Carll—because its misanthropy, its chilling burst of violence toward targets both human and spiritual owes much to one of southern author Flannery O'Connor's best-known short stories and most notorious characters: the Misfit in "A Good Man Is Hard to Find."[1] The occasion of the performance is a tribute to O'Connor and a benefit for the decaying Georgia farm, Andalusia, where O'Connor did the lion's share of her writing. Though they are hardly contemporaries—Gauthier, a Louisiana native, was born in 1962 and O'Connor died just two years later—there are sympathetic impulses in their work. Both go places that are too isolated and dark for delicate tastes. And more importantly, they go there with a sense of deeper purpose.

During one of our phone interviews, Gauthier laughs as she reads aloud O'Connor's wry response to a reader's unmet expectations in an excerpt from the essay "Some Aspects of the Grotesque in Southern Fiction." O'Connor writes, and Gauthier quotes, "I once received a letter from an old lady in California who informed me that when the tired reader comes home at night, he wishes to read something that will lift up his heart. And it seems her heart had not been lifted up by anything of mine she had read."[2]

Gauthier weighs in, "That sums it up, you know. At the end of the essay she says, 'I hate to think of the day when the southern writer will satisfy the tired reader.'[3] That's not the job. . . . The job is to crack the illusions, and to break the delusions and denials, and to show the truth."

Gauthier is amused especially because she knows a thing or two about this matter of being asked to do things that fall outside of her job description, as she conceives of it. And she has written her own bitingly witty retort to the askers with in-demand

Nashville cowriter Liz Rose, in the form of a New Orleans–style, trombone-laced stroll titled "Sideshow," and included it on her sixth album, *The Foundling.* "'Sideshow's' a little bit of a jab," she admits. "Because people, I go to these radio stations and I sit down, and they smile at me and I smile at them, and right before they turn on the mic to go live on the air, they say, 'Play something happy.' I just want to whack 'em with my guitar." Happy-on-demand is not a quality Gauthier has cultivated in her repertoire.

"You can either get mad," she concludes about such misunderstandings, "or you can find the humor in it." Having a healthy sense of humor, she chose to do the latter. Beyond being wickedly funny to those in on the joke, "Sideshow" and the dozen other unfunny songs on *The Foundling* are a watershed. Because they represent a pivotal step in her spiritual journey. Because, through them, she has worked out a way to close the distance between her radically alienating experience of being orphaned, of confronting life without roots to bear her up, and other people who live just as alienated lives on the social margins.

(No Home) Is Where the Heart Is

Gauthier came to songwriting fairly late compared to the usual timing of these things. But once she did take it up in her mid-thirties—after running away from her adoptive family in her teens and getting in a bit of trouble with the law, studying philosophy in college for a time, being beaten by, then beating, drug and alcohol addictions, and establishing a successful southern restaurant in Boston—she took it very seriously indeed as an outlet for expression and meaning making and as a craft. You would be hard-pressed to find a flip song in her entire catalog, save perhaps a too-cute honky-tonk caricature called "You're All I Want to Do" on her 1997 debut, *Dixie Kitchen*, which was named for the restaurant.

That album was a rough, self-released effort, but the songwriting was potent, if still a little raw; Gauthier recorded it before she had ever even performed in public. By 1999 she had sold the restaurant—her share of it, anyway—to make her next album, *Drag Queens in Limousines*. *Filth & Fire* came out on the independent, Massachusetts-based contemporary folk label Signature Sounds in 2002. And, for the span of two albums, 2005's *Mercy Now* and 2007's *Between Daylight and Dark*, she was on the roster of one of Nashville's more roots-minded major label imprints, Lost Highway. During all that time, Gauthier honed the acute poetry of her lyric writing, the visceral effect of her singing, and the heavy shading of her folk-country sound.

Those first five albums are rife with first-person testaments to spiritual and emotional restlessness and empathetic portraits of marginalized characters rendered in hard detail, with, here and there, a fleeting moment of greater communion. On 2010's *The Foundling*, released on the independent Razor & Tie, she drives home how blood-and-spirit real and all-consuming the experience of alienation is—for her, for anyone—with the story she knows most intimately: that of her own orphanhood. Gauthier was surrendered by her mother at birth and spent the first year of her life in St. Vincent's Women and Infants Asylum in New Orleans before being adopted.

Restlessness is no new theme for American roots music. Historian Bill Malone documents the longstanding fascination with the "rambler" in country music. But the enticingly unfettered figure he talks about is, quite explicitly, a man, be he a train-hopping hobo, an outlaw, a cowboy, or a boastful bluesman. "Country musicians," Malone writes, "have exhibited a fascination for the rambling man since the beginnings of their music's commercial history, and a few of them have self-consciously absorbed and projected lifestyles that seem to mirror the rambler and his flight from responsibility."[4] The consciously cultivated image is one of glamorized, romanticized freedom.

Now, Gauthier has lived some of those things. To run away at age sixteen, she stole her adoptive mother's car. She broke into somebody else's car. She did a little jail time. And so on and so forth. But she does not write songs to boast about the colorful sins of her past or to establish a dangerous reputation for her-self. The song that deals the most directly with her exploits, "Drag Queens in Limousines," is as much about the ragtag group she ran with, the sorts of people she gravitated toward—which, besides drag queens, included pot dealers, AWOL marines, and philosophizing drunks—as it is her feeling the urge to, and suc-ceeding at, breaking free of convention.

By and large, restlessness is not something Gauthier paints in a particularly romantic light. In her songs, it comes across more as a spiritual malady that she has to live with, that dooms relation-ships and makes real peace elusive. There is precious little hope for closeness and stability in songs like "Different Kind of Gone" and "Slip of the Tongue," both on *Drag Queens in Limousines*, "Just Say She's a Rhymer," on *Mercy Now*, and "Same Road" on *Between Daylight and Dark*. In "Different Kind of Gone," Gauthier pleads with her lover to understand and accept that needing to leave is part of her constitution. In "Slip of the Tongue," she backped-als after getting caught up in the moment and promising more than her heart is ready to give. The weary country waltz "Just Say She's a Rhymer"—written by the late country songwriting leg-end Harlan Howard, whose Nashville song-publishing company signed Gauthier—blames artistic temperament for the death of a relationship. The understated desperation of the ballad "Same Road" is similar in spirit to "Different Kind of Gone," an attempt to comfort her lover with the reassurance that her urge to leave is not meant as a personal blow. If there is any mystique attached to the restlessness in these songs, there is also a formidable emo-tional burden.

Rather than the rambler's traditional self-mythologizing, Gauthier is given to self-reflection. There is a song called "Good-bye," first included on *Filth & Fire* as a Caribbean-tinged country number, and revisited on *The Foundling* as a fiddle-sweetened two-beat, that addresses what lies at the root of her inability to feel at home anywhere for too long. She likens her power-ful inward propulsion to the unrelenting, elemental forces of thunderstorms and hurricanes and claims that living her life as one long string of good-byes is her inheritance from a mother who told her good-bye for good when she was born.

A couple of years before Gauthier wrote and recorded that album, she mused about the source of salient recurring themes in her songwriting: "I think that restlessness and homelessness is something that . . . I guess I'm becoming more and more aware that it has a lot to do with being adopted and never looking into somebody's face and seeing my own face reflected back to me ever—not once. And maybe it also is some sort of American restlessness. It doesn't seem to be something Europeans go through. Being from the South may have something to do with it, too. But I think the three, when you stack all three of them, you've got one restless son of a gun, no doubt about it."

After Gauthier confronted her past with a visit to the orphanage that sheltered her as an infant and followed the visit with a good bit of reflection and writing—songs that ended up on *The Foundling* and the beginnings of another project—it was clearer than ever to her that those decisive early events of her life had left her with a gaping hole where connective roots should have been; she realized, on some level, she is never *not* feeling or writing about being without them. "What's crazy is that I didn't know the drive behind a lot of the songs I had written up until this record," she shares. "I didn't know underneath all that need to leave was this terror of abandonment, that came from being abandoned. I didn't know that; I didn't know I left because I was afraid not to leave."

A Little Less Alone

Herein lies the paradox: Gauthier has lived her life feeling severed from people and place, and yet she cares very much about writing songs that can serve as profound points of connection between people. That posture of communal awareness, not to mention her ability to complete a song period, is hard-won. Both took work—Alcoholics Anonymous twelve-step, life-realigning, recovery-type work—after she had spent the better part of her young adulthood in the '80s addicted. "[T]he nature of the way that I was using drugs and alcohol made it impossible for me to connect with the muse," she admits. "I could not tell my story and write the way that I write and be an active alcoholic and addict at the same time. So I had to get sober first." And that she did, late in her twenties.

The way Gauthier portrays an alcoholic's attitude in "I Drink," it is no wonder addiction and songwriting could not coexist for her. The bluesy, sung-spoken country song—written with Crit Harmon, the Massachusetts songwriter-producer who worked on her first two albums—first showed up on *Drag Queens in Limousines* and reappeared on *Mercy Now*. Between the two, mainstream country singer Blake Shelton covered it in slightly more produced fashion. In the song's verses, Gauthier lays out the oppressive details of the alcoholic's routine; every night holds a TV dinner, beer, whiskey, and isolation. The chorus lyrics have the symmetrical simplicity of a children's book that teaches young readers to match people and animals with their natural inclinations; the alcoholic's is to drink. This is presented as though it is a fact of life, wrapped in stubborn denial and feigned indifference, as though the alcoholic really does not care about anything or need anyone. But of course, we know better than that.

Alcoholics Anonymous makes it difficult for participants to stick to the belief that they can go it alone—if they are going to make any progress in recovery. And it was in AA that Gauthier came to recognize that others shared her experiences of addiction and alienation. She muses, "I think the big deal is the first word of the first step [in the twelve steps] is 'we': 'We admitted we were powerless over alcohol.' I mean, being who I am and going through what I've gone through, there was a whole lot of 'I.' And getting to a 'we' has been a really big deal for me. With the disconnectedness I felt from my blood family and my adoptive family, it's just been 'I' for so long."

Gauthier elaborates, "It's an aloneness that transcends anything I can explain. So learning about 'we,' being in a fellowship and learning about 'we' . . . ha[s] given me the courage to write this stuff and get onstage and sing it. Because I know it's not just about me, and I know there's people sitting out there who know. And I connect with them and it means something to me. It means a lot to me. And I know that . . . I'm not alone, and ultimately being connected to the human race in a significant way, it wasn't gonna happen for me if I didn't get into a fellowship and get sober and learn how to have connection. That's the big deal of recovery for me: connectedness."

That Gauthier gained the focus and inspiration for her songwriting only after her redemption from alcohol and drugs is, no doubt, one reason why she approaches music making as such a serious calling. "Well, it is a spiritual role," she begins, trying to articulate her sense of what she does. "The words that I would choose would all sound so . . . New Age or . . . something gross. . . . There's not a lot of words to choose from that haven't been tainted."

Finding the words she is looking for, she tries again: "Look, it's a sacred trust. That's what it is. And my audience trusts me to tell the truth. That doesn't mean the facts. It means the emotional truth . . . the deeper truth. And so my job is to figure out what the hell that is, turn it into a song and then convey that. It's out of respect for the work and for the audience that I work so hard, because I don't want to let them down, and I don't want to let the muse down. I want to keep the channel open so I can keep working."

Comforting the Disturbed

Gauthier has been writing songs about people who are outsiders for as long as she has been writing songs—not for titillation, nor for sentimental appeal, but because they are people she believes ought to be given serious attention. Hers is a folksinger consciousness, in the tradition of the most influential American folksinger of the twentieth century, Woody Guthrie. "What is that thing Woody Guthrie used to say?" Gauthier wonders aloud, before answering her own question: "The artist's job is to write songs that disturb the comfortable and comfort the disturbed." Of particular importance to her own songwriting range, Guthrie was one of the earliest singing and writing figures to thoroughly blend autobiography and social commentary.[5]

Gauthier and Victoria Williams share in common their regard for scorned fringe dwellers as worthy protagonists. But while Williams lifts such people out of their oppressive realities and finds transcendence in their stories as an act of imagination and faith, Gauthier writes about them right where they are— stuck in inhuman circumstances with no end in sight—often with an undertone of socially conscious indignation (though usually with less bite than a political song by Michelle Shocked). There is an element of admiration to Gauthier's choice of song subjects, admiration especially for their seldom heard points of view. "I don't see them as marginal figures—I see them as marginalized," she emphasizes. "I think they're major figures.... I cherish the characters, the people who dare to step out on a limb and be different, who are willing to just be exactly who they are, whether or not people will applaud or boo. And just because they've been marginalized by the majority, to me they're not marginal. They're just frowned upon, which, you know, leaders usually are. I mean, prophets always are."

Given Gauthier's own range of experience, the choice to write songs about people with those kinds of experiences is also a matter of strong personal identification. "Yeah, I've always been drawn to characters that were marginal[ized], because I see myself as one," she laughs heartily. "I mean, good lord, I'm a freakin' poster child for marginal[ized] characters."

Dixie Kitchen features a pair of narrative songs that zero in on people on the social borders during the 1980s AIDS epidemic in a jarringly specific and hard-to-shrug-off way. The spare, finger-picked folk song "Goddamn HIV" is one, and the other is a brawny, Appalachian rock number called "Skeleton Town." Gauthier sings "Goddamn HIV" in the voice of "Michael Joe Alexandry," who is gay, estranged from his family, and powerfully shaken up by the loss of his close friends to HIV/AIDS. He wrestles with the condemnatory message that the virus is a curse on gay people but ultimately rejects it by turning the curse back on the disease itself. And the reversal of the curse is precisely where the song's strongly worded title comes in. In "Skeleton Town," Gauthier describes "Joey's" painful final days. She never names the mystery disease that is killing him, though it is quite apparently HIV/AIDS. Doctors and nurses in the hospital treat Joey—or, more to the point, do *not* treat him at all—as an untouchable. Even when his parents take him home to care for him, their neighbors rally to run them out of town. The story is grotesque, but for the time period it deals with, one characterized by heightened fear and prejudice, it is also disturbingly believable.

Gauthier's telling of these stories is distinctive for its explicitness. "I guess perhaps the work that I've done with my own journey, you know, therapy and recovery, has just given me a doorway into being able to tell the stories in a matter-of-fact way without having them be tainted by shame or homophobia," she offers, alluding to the fact that she herself has long been out as a lesbian woman. "The way that I see it is that we're all of equal value. I think anybody would tell you that, but we don't really believe it. We start to rank people right after that."

There are many other sorts of people who also stir Gauthier to empathy—not hierarchical ranking. She devoted a song on *Drag Queens in Limousines*, titled simply "Karla Faye," to Karla Faye Tucker, a woman infamously executed in Texas in 1998 for a drug-fueled double murder who had a life-changing conversion experience on death row. She focuses on two moments: a troubled young Tucker falling into the grips of addiction and the spiritual transformation of a by-then clean and penitent Tucker in her prison cell. And Gauthier condemns the lack of mercy Tucker found in the justice system. Being a recovered addict herself, Gauthier's righteous indignation was roused by Tucker's fate. "Well, I guess it's just that I understand her story," she offers.

"Camelot Motel" is a gritty group character sketch on *Filth & Fire* that captures people who have snuck off to a seedy motel to do things they would prefer no one see them do—say, hook up with a stranger of the same sex from a chat room or cheat on their spouse. Gauthier sing-speaks the verses over austere folk accompaniment, zooming in on their morning-after shame. But the chorus takes a dramatic turn toward full-band country rock. She reaches for more emphatic notes to convey the characters' desperation. What these people are really doing, she suggests, is trying to relieve their deep spiritual wounds.

"Wheel Inside the Wheel" is another of Gauthier's textured portraits, a second-line talking blues propelled by hypnotic, circling banjo on *Mercy Now* (which beach bum singer-songwriter Jimmy Buffett covered on one of his albums). The song shares its namesake image with the didactic folk spiritual "Ezekiel Saw the Wheel": the prophetic vision of the four supernatural living creatures unfurled in Ezekiel 1:16. But Gauthier heads in a different direction from the spiritual, depicting a party raging on beyond this world, a sort of earthy heaven. In attendance are people who represent New Orleans' culture, flamboyance, and hedonism—people like jazz trumpeter Louis Armstrong, voodoo queen Marie Laveau, Mardi Gras Indians strutting in their brilliantly colored feathered getups, drag queens belting out musical theatre numbers, jazz bands, and absinthe-sipping ladies of the night. Like Carnival in full swing, only, in the spirit realm.

During "Thanksgiving," the final track of *Between Daylight and Dark*, Gauthier turns her attention to people who are often socially and officially invisible: a grandmother and child whose loved one is in prison. Gauthier describes the prison guards' cold, gruff handling of the visitors on Thanksgiving Day and seizes on a small, revelatory moment; after they frisk the grandmother, she brushes their touch off of her dress, regains herself, and walks on. Gauthier highlights dignity in the grandmother's refusal to be dehumanized by her circumstances.

Gauthier also works in the space between first-person songs—ones she may not have actually lived, but *could* very well have—and songs that narrate detailed stories of fringe dwellers who are clearly not her. On each of the last two albums she recorded before *The Foundling*, there is a song that incarnates her radical shift from an isolated "I" to a collective "we."

The first of those, the title track of *Mercy Now*, is one of Gauthier's most indelible compositions. It is both a modern folk song and a prayer, and she sings it as though she is carefully handling an open wound. Verse by verse, the focus of the lyrics grows bigger and broader. Her gaze lands first on her father, whose life's work is decaying before his eyes. He could use some mercy. Next she thinks of her brother, who, from the sound of things, is physically and emotionally in prison. He could use some mercy, too. She moves on to her church and country, both of which have their share of problems, and proclaims their need for mercy. Then she considers all living things, at the mercy of people who abuse their power, and in need of mercy. Finally, she requests mercy for every spiritually broken one of us. In one generous, enveloping motion, she makes space for everyone.

Between Daylight and Dark has its own wide-angle song called "Can't Find the Way." Gauthier sounds deflated when she sings it, as though she can barely support the weight of the notes and has to catch her breath in the long breaks between phrases, before trying to take up the story again. Beneath her voice are fragile bits of finger-picked guitar, pump organ, and piano set to a muffled marching cadence. She speaks from the point of view of an impoverished Hurricane Katrina survivor; haunted by the memory of retreating to the rooftop and weeping as the levees gave way; alienated from strange, new, makeshift surroundings; and numb to everything except feelings of absolute homelessness and helplessness. In the bone-bare chorus, Gauthier distills the experience of displacement to two realities: time slips by without meaning, and the only thing desired is the one thing that cannot be had—home. The first couple of times through the chorus, Gauthier sings "I." Then she switches to "we." By the final, nearly whispered repetition, the song speaks for all people who are in any way cut off from their senses of home. "The camera lens moves out, kind of like what I did with 'Mercy Now,'" she explains. "It starts 'This is my personal hell.' Then, 'Wait a minute—no, look around me. This is not my personal hell—we're all going through this. Look at all these people. We're going through this together.'"

Mysticism over Matter

Gauthier would say that she arrived at that enlarged awareness and shored up her spiritual foundation by working through the twelve steps of Alcoholics Anonymous, which are not explicitly religious so much as aimed at spiritual transformation. "The Twelve Steps move the alcoholic toward an understanding of the world as sacred, or in AA's terms, as spiritual. In the world of AA, nothing is arbitrary, and nothing can be taken for granted. A Higher Power has a personal interest in every alcoholic, and the actions of the divine are evident everywhere."[6]

Still, Gauthier is not unfamiliar with organized religion. She was adopted into a Catholic family and sent to Catholic school. But the way she talks about her experiences with religion suggests that, at least in adolescence, she found it authoritarian and empty. "I was just going through the motions for most of my life with everything I did, including going to Catholic school and going to church—it was something that I was forced to do and so I did it," she says. "But I didn't do it because I chose to do it. . . . Nothing about the Catholic experience really spoke to me."

Every so often, though, traces of Catholic imagery surface in her songs. "Well, certainly the imagery is from my childhood, from a Catholic upbringing," she allows. "But I think . . . actually there's more twelve-step thinking in there than Catholicism. There's more surrender[ing] the will to God than there is dogma. . . . I think it's more twelve-step thinking than Catholic traditional gospel thinking. But I do mix them both in there, don't I?"

Gauthier, the adult songwriter, decades removed from being marched off to mass against her will, does take some liberties with Catholic imagery, refashioning it into a profoundly egalitarian spiritual vision. In "Our Lady of the Shooting Stars," on *Drag Queens in Limousines*, she gets creative with Mariology. "The thing is, there isn't one," she points out amusedly, referring to recognized revered images of the Virgin Mary. "I made it up. It's taking a Catholic word, but there isn't one. And you could look through the theology forever and never find her: my private Lady of the Shooting Stars."

Her "private Lady of the Shooting Stars" is right. The track is one of the most intimate musical moments Gauthier has captured on recording. She murmurs over a soft bed of keyboard, guitar, and percussion. She draws close to this ethereal yet earthy figure; she opens herself to receive; she prays for wisdom and guidance; she seeks an embrace—not only spiritual, but sensual, too. And she strays from orthodox Catholic theology; she can experience *her* vision of Her Lady in an unofficial and unmediated way.

The same goes for Gauthier and prayer; she can do it *her* way. On *Mercy Now* there is a driving Cajun country shuffle, laced with organ and plunging, purpled fiddle strokes called "Prayer Without Words." The lyrics are prickly and alliterative, and she attacks them like she is going up against a formidable foe. Here she revels in imagining prayer as boundless, gritty, incarnated, and unscripted, accessible to somebody who is coming down from a high, roaming restlessly, confronting injustice, or facing death. In this song, there is no requirement that a person have special knowledge of a special prayer for a special occasion.

"I know that coming from a Catholic family, with a mother who just repeats the same prayers ad nauseam and doesn't really think about what they mean, I think maybe part of it was a reaction to that," Gauthier muses wryly. "Like, 'Hey, I've got an idea—why don't you write a prayer?' She'd be appalled." To Gauthier, the idea of being able to make use of her own words and experiences is precisely the point: "I don't like prayers that are repeated endlessly. I feel as though we should write our own prayers and be original about it."

In the transcendent country rock song "Evangeline" on *Drag Queens in Limousines*, Gauthier delights in upending notions of unholy people and places. Evangeline, angelic as her name may sound, is an exotic dancer in a nightclub. And yet, when she is up on that stage, she disregards human eyes, forgets all about the other dancers, and not only takes pleasure in dancing but encounters a higher power right there in the middle of it. "It may be a place of perversion," says Gauthier, "but even inside perversion the longing is real."

By putting her own spin on mysticism and conceiving of it as a welcoming and egalitarian spiritual space that she can claim as her own, Gauthier is in good company. Medieval Christian women who were barred from formal authority in the church sometimes claimed authority by way of direct mystical access to the divine. "[Their] devotion was the devotion of . . . those who are lay *rather than* clergy, those whose closeness to God and whose authorization to serve others come through intimacy and direct inspiration *rather than* through office or worldly power."[7] Simply put, "Because of her visions, [the woman mystic] could claim power."[8]

The Weight of the Words

There is another important thing to note about Gauthier's most explicitly spiritual songwriting. "Prayer Without Words" is not at all what it claims to be; it is *packed* with words, and tangibly descriptive ones at that. Words are her vehicle for approaching spiritual experience *and* the social fringes. Her repertoire, probably to a greater degree than that of any of the other seven songwriters in this book, is defined first and foremost by its lyrics. Well before Gauthier started writing songs, she found word-focused compositions appealing. "I think," she says, searching her memory bank, "the first record I ever bought was 'American Pie,' a 45 [rpm record] with Don McLean's thumb painted on the cover." (For the record, "American Pie" may just have been the longest, most lyrically dense singer-songwriter hit of 1971.) Ask her what particular songwriters have made lasting impressions on her and she names some of the twentieth century's premier folk and country voices: Hank Williams, Woody Guthrie, Bob Dylan, John Prine, and Leonard Cohen. "You know, the word people," she sums up.

Whether on Gauthier's albums the songs are given austere, acoustic musical settings or accompaniment that musters sinewy intensity—but never *dance*ability—the point is that she can render them on her own, just her and her guitar, without them losing their power. The most important companion to her frank, thoughtfully crafted lyrics is her singing. "I've had to learn how to sing," she confesses. "Singing doesn't come natural. Writing comes naturally to me.... It's been a process of knowing what I'm capable of and what I'm not and making the most of what I've got." The progression of her singing from her earliest albums until now bears this out; if at first it seemed forced, it commands attention with quiet intensity now.

"There's lot of reasons that people . . . come to shows to see people play songs," says Gauthier. "One of the reasons is because they look good; one of the reasons is because they sing good; one of the reasons is because they have something to say and have stories to tell. I don't fall into the look good or sing good categories. . . . I think if I had to choose, I would choose that anyway, because that puts people there for the right reasons. I'm not a chick singer, you know. I'm a writer; I'm a serious writer."

Singing-wise, what Gauthier has learned to do is to deliver the words in a way that acknowledges their weight. Her recalcitrant drawl hangs low, confides, never blazes through too quickly. The rawness and presence of her singing vouches for the lyrics; that they can be trusted. She jokes about what would constitute an inappropriate audience response to her performance: "If you're clapping away, you're not listening to the lyrics, which is really all I'm offering. I'm not offering toe-tapping . . . I mean, it's not what I do."

The body is not Gauthier's primary musical target. She aims elsewhere: "Yeah—the heart and the soul and the mind." To do so is, to her, an equalizing move, and it allows alienated people to hear themselves in her songs. "And boy is that a good place to go: leave your body and transcend, really, the prison of self to connect to the . . . the unified we, to the us," she emphasizes. "That is what great art can do. You know, heroin can do it too, but it's not real. It ain't real. Great art does it in ways that transcend . . . the barriers that separate us, and I'm drawn to it and I'm passionate about it. It helps me, you know. It helps me to get past myself and plug into my community of souls that are here, now, with me."

For much the same reason—the removal of barriers for her listeners—outside of her most detailed narratives, Gauthier generally writes without revealing the gender of the characters; she includes no names or gendered pronouns, especially in songs about the inner workings of relationships. "That's the trick: don't use he/she—ever," she relates matter-of-factly of her informal rule. "I think it makes it a bigger song and I also think it makes it apparent that we're all going through exactly the same stuff." For a songwriter of folk and country music—neither of which are particularly known for abstract lyrics—writing about loving, leaving, and hurting yet rarely painting a tangible picture of exactly who is doing the loving, leaving, and hurting and what kinds of bodies they occupy goes against the grain. "It's confusing when my publisher goes to pitch [my songs]," Gauthier allows rather unconcernedly, "because it's like 'Is this a man's song or a woman's song? '. . . Well, you know, how about both? You know what? Spiritually I don't think we have a gender. [T]hat's how I see the world and that's how I write. I think it's a gift that I've been given that I wasn't even aware of until I started really getting deeper into the [music] business and seeing that not everybody writes like that."

Facing the Story

The Foundling is Gauthier's most potent expression of marginalization to date; potent not only because of the force of its storytelling and emotion and the heft of its subject matter but also because it is at once an intensely personal account *and* a voice raised passionately and empathetically for an entire group of people: those whose lives have been shaped by the severing of biological ties or the improvising of new ones. It is her most "us" album to date. Considering that recovery through Alcoholics Anonymous is an ongoing, intensely self-reflective, and deeply spiritual process, it makes sense that it would take her five albums and several years to get to the point that she would be ready to revisit that painful early chapter of her life, to want to know the truth, and to find the gumption to write about it. Once more, as she has changed, so has her songwriting.

"I'll be twenty years sober in July," Gauthier observes. "I had to have a long period of looking at myself, and I had to have some real distance from this. But yet I had to go find my birth mother and I had to do this work around adoption and abandonment in order to be able to tell it. So I couldn't tell it until now. I had to make myself ready to tell it spiritually."

She thinks better of this idea: "Although, I don't know if I made myself ready. I think I just became ready through the work that I have done in my recovery from drug and alcohol addiction and my work in therapy. . . . There's so many different levels of clearing out the brush that had to be done before I could see, you know, the freaking house standing behind the overgrown bushes."

And, having seen the house—or, to put it slightly less poetically, having come to the realization that nothing in Gauthier's life or songwriting is untouched by her experience of being orphaned—she did not beat around the overgrown bushes. Through *The Foundling*'s thirteen tracks, she unfurls a striking story. And like a good storyteller, she establishes the central character right at the start in the title track, a minor-key Eastern European waltz replete with mournful strains of accordion and violin vibrato. This character, the Foundling, merits the tragic musical setting, for she or he—we are not told which[9]— is anonymous, unwanted, abandoned, and set up for a life of suffering. During "Mama Here, Mama Gone," we hear the Foundling's instinctual, childlike loneliness channeled through Gauthier's hushed, slackened singing.

The story reaches its dramatic climax at the album's midpoint. Rarely has Gauthier rocked as hard as she does during "Blood Is Blood." A churning rock groove hauls the track along at full steam. She howls at those who would minimize the bizarre and lonely torment of being both blood-bound to and cut off from one's identity, while the fiddler's serrated, scraping attack amplifies her rage.

The very next track, "March 11, 1962," also cowritten with Liz Rose, is a window into what may very well be the most vulnerable moment of her life: her one and only phone conversation with her birth mother. She recites her side of the exchange during the verses, heaping so much on her words that her delivery drags low over the slow-burning country rock. She tracked her mother down; she made the phone call. Having gotten her mother on the line, she identifies herself by the date of her birth, a date her mother cannot help but remember. She waits to see if the woman to whom she has reached out will make any effort to reach back. Her grave trepidation turns to agitation as her mother deflects, suspects, asks her why she is calling. Gauthier can respond only that she does not know.

"Hell, I know why," she adds bluntly, after the fact. "But I don't want to say I know why. I'm trying to find a connection to this person who gave me life. But I can't say that to her, because she's not allowing me the opportunity to be that vulnerable. Like 'Who are you and what do you want?' is what I got from her. . . . That's not exactly inviting. . . . What am I supposed to say? 'I want you to love me? I want you to embrace me? I want you to know me? I want to know you?' You can't say that to someone who's so defensive and so out of touch with their own emotions. So the character says, 'I don't know why.'"

Gauthier sings her mother's side of the exchange with anxious, straining notes. Her mother evidently has regrets, but she feels she cannot change anything, cannot bring herself to unhide the daughter so long hidden, cannot handle even talking to her from a safe distance. Remarkably, Gauthier ends the conversation with generous empathy, acknowledging that she is not the only one in pain—her mother is, too—and offers a reason for why she called: to thank her mother. It is an emotionally wrenching six minutes, something like hearing her Gauthier be abandoned all over again.

How striking, then, when during a country waltz called "The Orphan King" near the end of the album, she playfully recasts the Foundling as a sort of ragged antihero, whose great power is willfully open-hearted illogic. She runs down a list of the circumstances stacked against the Orphan King, reaffirming her or his abiding belief in love after each one. The song is not exactly upbeat, but it is not defeated either. If anything, it is defiantly hopeful.

Between the first and last notes of *The Foundling*—both chanted by Gauthier, a capella and alone—she tells the story from multiple vantage points. She steps back into the position of third-person narrator; she plunges herself into the middle of things in first person. She gives sweeping descriptions; she gives specifics. She wants to make clear that as much as it is about her, it is not about *only* her. It is personal *and* representative of a

great, overlooked number of people who have never known normal—not *really*. In the liner notes she dedicates the album "to all
adoptees, birth mothers, birth fathers and adoptive parents who
still suffer."[10] There is that paradox again: her loneliest collection
of songs is also her most communal.

"I guess it's inevitable," Gauthier says, "that people are going
to see [*The Foundling*] as about just me. But my experience is not
unique. My experience is a universal experience that almost
every adoptee I've talked to feels and has. It's the break of the
bond between mother and child. We've lived in an environment
where that's been—how do I put it?—where everybody pretends
like it's no big deal. And it *is* a big deal. It's a really big deal. So
while it was traumatic for me, and I didn't realize it till I was
almost fifty years old, it's not just me."

As a sonic backdrop for the theme of lacking a true home,
Gauthier and producer Michael Timmins, of the Canadian alternative rock band Cowboy Junkies, gave much of the album a flavor evocative of gypsy music, particularly the title track and the
recurring instrumental interludes that echo it. Whether or not
the dark, lyrical melodies carried by accordion and fiddle—two
instruments often identified with gypsy music—are anything
close to the authentic musical styles of the Roma, or Gypsy people, the sounds are popularly associated with them and conjure
images of wandering and rootlessness.

When you get right down to it, what Gauthier makes is rootless roots music. "This is the story that Mary Gauthier was born
to tell," she says emphatically. "You know, for adoptees, going
back to your roots means going back to your unrootedness. It's
not a place you want to go. It's not a place that anybody wants to
go. And to go there requires a tremendous amount of . . . Well,
you know, I guess, courage. You have to, I had to look at things I
really didn't want to look at and see things I spent my whole life
trying not to see."

It should be said that everybody and their (birth or adoptive) grandmother has written songs about orphans, and even

more have sung them, from songs of the Victorian era, like Will
S. Hays' nineteenth-century sentimental number "Nobody's
Darling on Earth" up to contemporary songs borrowing on traditional idioms, like Gillian Welch's late-twentieth-century,
old-time-reviving "Orphan Girl." But people have not necessarily assumed that the singer of such songs is drawing on her or
his own autobiography in any literal way. A century ago, when
orphan songs were especially numerous, they might be aimed
at stirring sentiment, whether pity for orphans or self-pity of a
nostalgic, homesick soul.

Where Gauthier is coming from, sentimentalism does not
hold water. She is well aware of how different her songs about
looking back are from many of the wistful "back home" songs
out there. She reaches behind her and finds nothing solid bearing her up—no roots to get back to. "Usually when you think of
going back to your roots and returning to where you came from,
you get this feeling of connectedness," she says. "But adoptees
get a feeling of profound isolation and disconnectedness. We
don't go there. We like to pretend like being adopted's the same
as being in a natural family. We like to pretend like our adoptive
parents, those are our real parents. And, yeah, they are. But, no,
they're not."

Gauthier does not let alienating realities or misconceptions
squelch her spirit. She has staked out her own place, on the margins, and it is from there that she writes songs. She never for a
moment forgets she is there. She never for a moment forgets she
is not the only one. And she never stops wrestling with how to
do justice to her outsider experience, and others'. It is, perhaps,
her ultimate paradox: "You have to have some faith in connection to be able to communicate that, don't you?"

Of course, she already knows the answer to that.

6

Ruthie Foster
Don't Be Shy about What You've Got

A Texas singer-songwriter partial to blues, spirituals, folk, and soul and possessed of a warm, spirited voice, Ruthie Foster teaches boldness by example, in the spirit of her mother and the celebratory church services of her youth.

Professional singers will often tell the stories of their musical origins a particular way: they have, they aver, always wanted to sing, dreamed of singing, and believed to their souls that they could make their dreams a reality. Their assuredness is meant to convince us that they in themselves had what it took—not just ability, but confidence and drive—and that they are, without the shadow of a doubt, in the right career. Ruthie Foster's story starts off a little differently than that; it involves more than one central player, and, to begin with, less self-assurance on Foster's part. But when, in that story, she reaches her moment of singerly conviction, her footing is sure.

As a young teenager in tiny, unincorporated Gause, Texas— a good eighty miles northeast of Austin—she was teaching herself to play guitar. But singing, particularly singing in public, was where she drew the musical line, since the fervent, forceful singing of a number of her cousins, aunts, and uncles in their rural African American church, New Hope Missionary Baptist, seemed to her a hard act to follow. "They didn't sing—they *s-a-n-g* sang," she emphasizes. She, on the other hand, found it "just too intimidating and too up front and letting everybody see who you are. That was not what I was about at all."

Yet *somebody* was not content to see Foster just hole up and strum away in the privacy of her bedroom—which was pretty much what she had been doing—and this somebody did not hesitate to say so. "Yeah, my mama," Foster clarifies. "[M]y mother came in one day after school. I was sitting and playing [guitar] after I'd done my homework. . . . She burst my door wide open and she just stood there with a dishrag in one hand and her hand on her hip in the other and said, 'Girl, just open your mouth and sing.' I didn't even know she could hear me, was even paying attention or listening to me."[1]

That was a pivotal moment for Foster, and she has retold the story many times, in many ways. Witness this inscription in the liner notes of her self-produced 1997 debut, *Full Circle*: "Special dedication to my mother, Shirley 'Puddin' Jones 1943–1996. . . . 'Open your mouth and sing, girl!'"[2] Foster's commemoration of her mother's challenge is set off from the affectionate thanks that she directs toward some twenty other friends, boosters, and colleagues, as if to affirm that nothing has mattered more to her music making than that relationship and those words.

If a mother prodding her daughter to do something seems like an unremarkable occurrence, there was more at stake in Foster's case than a simple battle of adult and adolescent wills. Ruthie's mother had apparently sensed in her teenaged daughter a pent-up spirit, a potent voice that had yet to find an outlet. And she did not want to see her daughter remain barricaded in silence by insecurity. "I think it was definitely that she was trying to just unleash that, unlock that person on the inside that really can sing, wants to sing and come out of that bashful shell," Foster muses. "I was really, really shy as a kid. In fact, when I would talk, a lot of it was stutter. So singing was a way to overcome that."

And her mother's mother, Ruthie Deborah Johnson—"Big Mama" to the younger Ruthie—also had a hand in getting her granddaughter to speak up. The day a fourteen-year-old Foster sang her first solo in church—the Fanny Crosby hymn "Pass Me Not, O Gentle Savior"—she was making the leap from soft, solitary bedroom singing to projecting her voice over her cousins and the rest of the choir—a choir that may not have been huge but was still plenty spirited and plenty loud. Big Mama's powerfully affirming reaction transformed the moment and had no little affect on Foster: "I let loose and my Big Mama, her neck swung around and she looked over and she was smiling so big. And I knew I was all right then. I could hear her 'Yeah, baby, sing it.'"

On top of that positive reinforcement, Foster was the recipient of informal, one-on-one public speaking lessons of a sort. "Big Mama would work with me on Saturday evenings with just a little paragraph or little poem or something to say in church," she remembers. "I had a lot of cousins, but none of them wanted to stand in front of the church and do the welcome. And Big Mama thought that would be a great job for me, the shy one. . . . I got, actually, pretty good at it."

To become the hearty, uninhibited performer she is today, Foster had to get pretty good indeed at talking and singing in front of people. Her mother and grandmother egged her on and uplifted her spirit; their presences were vivifying where the absence of such family figures were just as powerful a shaping force for Gauthier. Foster, in turn, has learned to lift her own spirit and others', imbuing her joyful, frequently participatory live performances with bold sensibilities passed from one woman and one generation to another. Embedded in her work, onstage or recorded, is a conviction that all people have valuable voices—though those voices too often get buried or muted by the harsh realities of their lives—and a sense of possibility that they can be reclaimed. And she has absolutely no qualms about nudging her listeners to get on with the reclamation process; she is, in a sense, still at it herself.

Style Collecting

Besides interpreting songs that Foster did not write—a practice that remains important to her repertoire—she has, at least as often as not, lent her voice to her own original compositions. A good many songs from her pen grace each of her six albums: 1997's *Full Circle*, 1999's *Crossroads* (both self-released), and 2002's *Runaway Soul*, the 2004 live set *Stages*, 2007's *The Phenomenal Ruthie Foster*, and 2009's *The Truth According to Ruthie Foster* (all four were put out on the small, Austin-based roots label Blue Corn, and the latter helped earn her a Blues Music Award for Contemporary Blues Female Artist of the Year). Her decade and a half's worth of recordings display a progression of musical style and growing artistic assurance. But she had already traveled quite a distance to arrive at that first album at the age of thirty-three, and both her early roots and the experiences collected along the way have a lot to do with the music that fills those recordings. "Once you've been introduced to a style of music, it doesn't leave you," Foster reasons. "You can pull out a little reggae in the middle of a country song, if you please. There's a way to connect any and everything, because it is all connected. I think it's all connected through the spirit, how it makes you feel."

Foster's first instrument was piano, though she picked up guitar in early adolescence, supplementing her efforts to teach herself with the know-how of an electric guitar–playing Holiness preacher who lived next door to her growing up. She explains, "He'd come in from work and he'd play in his kitchen, and his kitchen faced my mother's window. And I would sit in my mother's window and just listen to him play all the time. I noticed he'd do blues, but I'd hear him go into the Gospelaires and, you know, Sister Rosetta [Tharpe]; I'd hear that kind of stuff coming from him too. I thought, 'That's cool. Now that's what I want to play.' I got my courage up to go over and ask if I could just sit and watch him play in his kitchen, and that's where I spent a lot of my time after school, just listening to him play. . . . He just had an old amplifier and a Fender guitar, and he'd just sit and pick out rhythms. . . . He gave me really simple things to start with, with just being able to use as little as possible, almost like the Pops Staples sound. And how much sound and how much rhythm, how much music you can get out of just using a few strings."

The first semiprofessional solo performing Foster did—after the "Pass Me Not" experience—was in local churches. "Playing in church was something that was a huge part of my musical growth," she affirms. "So I took the guitar and taught myself a few more chords. And then I got into those Dorothy Norwood songs and little simple songs that I could sing and play on guitar, and I would do those in my church. And I would be the visiting musician for other churches. And I did that all through my teenage years: 'Sister Ruthie's going to play a couple of selections—the visiting musician from New Hope Missionary Baptist Church.' I played my little guitar and did my two songs, 'Jesus Is the Answer' and something by maybe Shirley Caesar, or something like that. And they'd take a collection and that's how I got paid." The guitar she was playing was almost always her acoustic (like the preacher next door, she had an electric, too); as she sensibly points out, "It's not easy to find a place to plug in in some of these old churches."

Besides gospel and blues, Foster took in an abundance of soul and R&B, thanks to her mother, who had not only a sizable record collection but a formidable voice of her own, and enjoyed singing around the house. "My mother, she was a beautiful singer," she remembers. "You know, when I was pretty young she would put on these records, and I just figured that was her [singing on them] for the longest time. That was nothing for me to hear Aretha [Franklin] and then think, 'Oh, well, that's just mama.'"

McLennan Community College in Waco, Texas, provided Foster with formal vocal training—as formal, even, as operatic arias in French and Italian. Foster can condense her formative downhome-to-classical years into one brief, bemused description: "I grew up picking tomatoes on the Brazos River. And then I went to school and studied music and learned a lot about the elements of music and what supposedly works together and what won't."

The navy, of all places, was the next stop on Foster's musical journey—not that she enlisted for musical reasons; at first she served in a helicopter squadron in San Diego. Then she auditioned and became the lead singer for a navy touring band called Pride. "We had a pretty funky band," she recalls with evident pleasure. "We did Top 40 and funk with a horn section and synthesizers, because that was the sound at the time: Keith Sweat and Bobby Brown.... We were a recruiting band, if you will. We would show up in our little ice cream suits and just rock the place. They called me the secret weapon."

It was during that time that Foster began dabbling in songwriting—and, as in the guitar playing years before, she did it in the privacy of her own home. When she left the military, after four years with Pride, she started performing a few of her songs—interspersed with familiar folk tunes and not-so-typical selections, like acoustic covers of '60s pop-soul—at a strip club–turned–folk club in Charleston. "Well, the strip club part I'm not sure what it was called," she says. "But after [the owner] turned it into a folk club, it was called the Soft Rock Café.... And I'd be doing my Sam Cooke, along with a few songs that I had managed to write on my own.... And we had the same clientele that would show up every now and then, very confused." As surreal as the setting may have been, it was another important season of discovery for Foster. She recalls, "That's when I started really studying folk music and picked up the Woody Guthrie, the book on his life and all that; that's how I found out more about [singer of spirituals and folk songs] Odetta and all these just beautiful singer-songwriters."

Not So Black and White

"Singer-songwriter" is a term that, since entering pop music parlance forty years ago, has most often been associated with a particular image—a white man with an acoustic guitar, none more recognizable than Bob Dylan. And if not a white man with a guitar, a white women with a guitar—say, a Joni Mitchell (who, admittedly, also plays piano some of the time). Of some importance to the development of the singer-songwriter concept were '60s folk revivalists who wrote original songs that were taken seriously as the writers' original, lyrically substantial expression, like Dylan after his first album. Even then, forty-plus years ago, seeds were already planted for the image of the white singer-songwriter. Notes Craig Werner, "Despite the presence of Odetta, Josh White and a few other black folksingers, the folk revival was mostly a white thing."[3] Rock music would have its own heavyweight singer-songwriters—like Bruce Springsteen—but, then, since the days of Bo Diddley and Chuck Berry, rock has been a genre overwhelmingly populated by white performers. As black performers have continued to pioneer urban, plugged-in, rhythmically dynamic, dance-friendly styles of music—from soul to hip-hop and contemporary R&B (little of it explicitly placing lyrics ahead of music in importance or centered on a solo singing acoustic guitarist)—acts like Stevie Wonder, who *do* compose their own material, have not been thought of first and foremost as singer-songwriters.

But Ruthie Foster is, indisputably, a singer-songwriter. And she is black.

Those shortsighted racial-musical categories particularly touched Foster when she departed Charleston for a development deal with Atlantic Records in New York City—the very same

Atlantic that had released Aretha Franklin's late '60s hits. At the time, Tracy Chapman epitomized the African American female singer-songwriter "type"—she being the only successful one people knew of. People walking in off the street to the small blues venues Foster was playing in New York mistook her for Chapman more than once. She alludes to those cases of mistaken identity in a ruminative song called "Lost in the City" on her first album. "Yeah, there were people who would walk in and see me with a guitar," she says generously. "I don't think I had dreadlocks then, but they definitely related me to Tracy Chapman, you know, being the black girl up front who's sitting and singing, playing guitar. You know, I can see that."

Foster even chuckles at her then–record label's futile attempts to shape her using an existing musical mold; perhaps she could be like Chapman, or like jazz-tinged R&B singer Anita Baker or some other act. "I think maybe Atlantic was kind of looking at me as maybe an Anita Baker–type of a singer, because they didn't really have their own," she muses without the slightest hint of acridity. "All the record labels had their version of someone. I can say that because I had a photo session where I took these pictures with a very prominent photographer . . . I sent a postcard to my dad with a picture on the front, and then he called a couple of days later and he said, 'You know, I got this picture in my mail, and the first thing I wanted to know was who is this white woman with my baby's nose?'"

No image-tweaking that anybody tried, and not much that Foster wrote, really felt right to her until she turned her attention toward her roots and started mining her own rural background in her songwriting; it gave her the sense of direction she had lacked. "I got to where I realized, 'I just need to write about what I know.' Because I got into writing with other people about other things, and it's funny—none of those songs come to mind, because they're easy to forget, because they weren't about my life at all. But these are the songs that came out of that time that I connected to, because it was about what I knew."

She continues, "That's when I started to realize it was not so much about, you know, being in New York and writing, but what I have to say. And that's when the songs started coming that had a lot to do with Texas. I started writing about Texas like I was just homesick. And I think I was. I was just really starting to find my own voice during that time, that last year I was [in New York]."

Some of the songs that Foster wrote then and recorded a few years later for her debut—fittingly titled *Full Circle*—sounded like the musings of a young artist newly appreciative of her roots. One of them, "Lost in the City," captures the feeling of being swallowed up in a sprawling, impersonal place; another, "Home," waxes nostalgic for the simpler way of life Foster knew in childhood.

Foster moved back to small-town Texas to care for her ailing (and now deceased) mother in 1993, and it was there, after spending a few years away from music, that she began a more self-determined, satisfying, and decidedly grassroots season of her music career. "What the Atlantic [Records] people couldn't figure out, they didn't know how to categorize me, because if you're from Texas and if you grow up around the music of Texas, there is no category," Foster reasons. "Everybody listened to and played everything where I came from. So coming back home gave me a chance to just be who I am musically and not have to worry about being categorized." Just as important as coming back home was the fact that she had left and learned, with the perspective that distance affords, what she valued most about her roots.

Her Mother's Daughter

Homecoming, for Foster, was not strictly a geographical proposition. Home meant her community, too, and her family in particular—none more important than her mother and grandmothers. They helped her find her voice, and use it proudly; and she still finds spiritual and creative sustenance in their memories.

The storyline of "Mama Said," a country soul song on Foster's fifth album, *The Phenomenal Ruthie Foster*, ought to have a familiar ring to it: a daughter recounts her mother's stern yet affirming life instruction. Against a swinging, sure-footed backbeat, she recalls her mother's admonition (that she had better tend to her spiritual life), testimony (that her mother had tried to set an example of perseverance), and prayers (for her to live right and be loved). Foster's supple, thrumming vocal delivery is engrossed in the memories, until, at particularly emphatic moments, she seems suddenly to channel her mother, fiercely bearing down on the lyrics. This is no tossed-off performance on Foster's part. "Full Circle," the title track of her first album, also mentions her mother urging her to boldly express herself. What we hear in songs like these is not a woman idealizing or sanctifying her mother or trying to regain youthful innocence by sloughing off adult responsibility. Quite the opposite; we hear a confident woman taking responsibility for herself.

Twice during her song "Mama Said" Foster sings, in her mother's chiding voice, of needing to save her own soul; the onus has been placed squarely on her shoulders. The sort of soul-saving Foster has in mind has little to do with traditional Christian concepts of sin and salvation—though, given her upbringing, she is undoubtedly familiar with the weight that that language carries in church.

While Foster's intentions may be nontraditional, they are anything but flippant; she is as attentive these days as she has even been to what she is communicating in a song. "I think that I prepare for singing in a different way," she says. "I actually pay attention to whether I have something to say, more than anything else. . . . I guess because I feel I have something to say, it's gonna come from another place. And that's been really recent. That's something that is starting to come about even today. You know, I was just in St. Thomas the other week . . . and that's when I heard the news about Odetta passing away. And just something about that, that and it was real close to my mother's birthday, and I'm just doing a lot of reading about songwriters right now, and black women in songwriting in particular.[4] It's really got me . . . knowing that I've got to pay attention to what I say now, you know. I've got to pay attention to what I want to say and the story I want to tell, even if it's my own. It's like mama used to tell me: I have a soul to save and it's mine. And if I have to sing that, then that's what I'll do. I have a story to tell and a soul to save."

Foster uses those two phrases, "story to tell" and "soul to save," habitually and interchangeably; in neither is she talking about the state of her eternal soul, but a way of living that is very much planted in the here and now. Or, as she puts it, "Saving . . . that sense of who you really are and what you came here for. Finding that again." Behind the seemingly plain phrases there is an urging toward self-discovery, self-expression, and listening to one's gut.

A number of Foster's songs emphasize inner strength. On *The Truth According to Ruthie Foster*, "Stone Love" fixates on the resilience it takes to maintain an internal wellspring of emotion; "Truth!" is emphatic that there is truth worth heeding inside people; and both aim advice directly at the listener. These sorts of songs—first-person, testimony-style declarations—are well represented in her repertoire. Most of the time, though, Foster gets her convictions across with considerable warmth and seems as likely to be trying to get a message through to herself as anyone else, which makes the lessons in her music easier to take. "With the songs that I've written . . . sometimes it is therapy and I can look at a song and learn from it," she observes. "Sometimes the songs come as an answer to the questions I've been looking for. And 'Truth!' was definitely one of those."

Foster also has a third pet phrase that is akin to the other two: "sing your song." It shows up in some form in her songs "Crossover," "Another Rain Song," and "Dues Paid in Full." Ordinary as they sound together, it is the history behind those three words that gives them weight. "That's something Big Mama used to always say—'Baby, you sing [your song],'" Foster explains. "That's something they would say in churches, even today—'You sing your song. Sing it. Sing your song.' It's about singin' yo' story."

Even when Foster does not invoke her female elders in a song in any explicit way, their presence can often be strongly felt. "I'm actually starting to use more of their wording in my writing, too, which is kind of cool," she points out. "I don't know. I guess maybe as a songwriter in a lot of ways I'm growing, but I'm also regressing." Or, drawing more on her roots.

Whether or not Foster actually plucks them from her memory, the lyrics she writes tend to be simple and sturdy, earthy and spiritual; not terribly groundbreaking in and of themselves. To say what she wants to say, she does not feel as though she needs much in the way of words, either in number or in complexity. In a way, that, too, is her creative application of what she learned from the speech of her elders. "You know," she begins, "my grandmothers [came] from a simple time when you didn't use a lot of words, so the words you used meant something. And I think, as a songwriter, to be able to grasp that, to be able to get that and put it into, you know, this melody and this rhythm— when somebody's grooving but . . . they're learning something from that—I think that's a gift to be able to do that."

Nowhere is Foster's desire to empower her audience more evident than in the musical adaptation of Maya Angelou's poem "Phenomenal Woman," the centerpiece and namesake of her fifth album, *The Phenomenal Ruthie Foster*. Foster learned the song—a poetic reappraisal of physical and spiritual traits that are oft-overlooked sources of beauty and power for women— from Canadian pop singer-songwriter Amy Sky, and fashioned it into supple, slow-burning soul. She takes obvious pleasure in singing it and sounds thoroughly dignified as she arcs her sustained vibrato over the choruses.

"I'm really particular about when I choose to do the song and where I'm doing it," Foster shares, "because it just says so much. It says everything that I was taught, and then want to say to someone else: 'It's okay to step into who you know you are.' I grew up, as I said, a bashful kid. But I knew that there was something special about me, and I think every kid does, every young person realizes that at some point. . . . There's always something that makes you feel like you're not worthy of that."

"And I think that's something that that particular song, 'Phenomenal Woman,' touches on, you know, when it starts off just talking about your physical qualities, and how they may not be perfect, according to someone else's standards, but they're just right. It's just what you need to put yourself out in front of people and let them know who you are and that you're special and you are a beautiful person. I love doing that song."

Older, Bolder Soul

Foster's desire to open her mouth and sing, to make use of her voice, is still with her, affecting not only the words she sings but how she sings them and the styles of music toward which she gravitates. Over time, she has drawn more of that varied, rootsy-to-formal musical background of hers into her album making, and sounded a surer singer and songwriter because of it. "I guess," she muses, "I've just . . . in the last four or five years come to a point of figuring out how all of those things are connected. . . . Because it's all there." But in another sense, she had been trying, in smaller ways, to connect the dots all along. The feel she developed for kinetic, gospel-style piano playing when she was young later made her something other than a typical acoustic guitar–playing singer-songwriter. "And, you know, I liked the idea of doing something different than everybody else. Another version of Grateful Dead, another version of Peter, Paul and Mary, that's all great . . . I love folk music. But just having something a little more rhythmic in the mix kept me interested in wanting to keep playing, just to be able to . . . do something different with the guitar."

Foster's first couple of albums, *Full Circle* and *Crossover*, show a flexible folksinger-songwriter who works in occasional tinges of soul, country, blues, or reggae. "Stories" and "Changes (Annie's Song)," both on *Crossover*, pair introspective lyrics with finger-picked acoustic guitar. Her guitar playing yields different results elsewhere: fluid soul during "Another Rain Song," from *Crossover*, and sprightly R&B during "Rain from My Shoulders," from *Full Circle*.

Congenial as those initial albums are, they are also quite evidently the work of an unseasoned recording artist. Since she made them, Foster has become a nervier singer and songwriter by reviving and reworking styles from her younger days. She fortified her third album, *Runaway Soul*, with country blues and spirituals alongside her usual singer-songwriter fare. On it is a cover of Texas singer-songwriter Terri Hendrix's "Hole in My Pocket"—which inaugurated Foster's present tradition of covering songs by other female Americana singer-songwriters on her albums—and an understated rereading of her song "Home" from *Full Circle*. "I think the record *Full Circle* was really about just doing the songs, getting them out [there]," she reflects. "One of the reasons I'm pretty sure I decided to redo a few of them is because I could [really] use my own voice on the songs. And songs grow." (Grow, that is, in their meaning and impact.) "When you're doing them as much as I have, they just, they grow."

On *Runaway Soul*, Foster also attacks rousing, downhome originals like the title track and "Joy on the Other Side" and spirituals like "Woke up This Mornin'" and "Death Came a Knockin' (Travelin' Shoes)" with newfound, blazing authority. "I incorporated a lot of those songs, spirituals, songs that made me feel good to sing on top of the . . . storytelling," she says. It could not have hurt the robustness of the results that she had also elevated her studio game, enlisting an outside producer for the first time: Texas steel guitarist Lloyd Maines, perhaps best known for his work with his daughter Natalie's band, the Dixie Chicks.

Foster leavened her next studio album, *The Phenomenal Ruthie Foster*—this one produced by Austin bluesman Malcolm "Papa Mali" Welbourne—with electric southern soul. The differences are evident from the opening strains of the lead track, "'Cuz I'm Here," written by Austin funk band Greyhounds. The groove is all unhurried, molten syncopation; above it Foster sounds energized and in command. She was, she says, "just really, really getting my ears back into what I really grew up listening to, and what really, really came natural for me."

The album's more full-bodied sound matches the empowered sentiments of tracks like "Mama Said" and "Phenomenal Woman." Alongside those songs are a couple of confessional numbers, Foster's sensual, sumptuous reading of Lucinda Williams' "Fruits of My Labor," and gospel and blues selections, including a pensive, minor-key interpretation of Sister Rosetta Tharpe's "Up above My Head" and a defiant, foot-stomping a capella rendition of Son House's "People Grinnin' in Your Face." Foster proved how comfortable she had become in her skin by revisiting a song from her first album: "Heal Yourself." She had started writing it way back when she was playing the Soft Rock Café, giving herself her own motherly "open your mouth and sing"–type push: "I wasn't really big into playing out in front of people, you know, playing guitar and singing. I looked at myself as a singer, more than anything, but not really . . . someone who could sit up there or stand up there and play and sing. . . . I'd done it in church, but this [was] different."

The second time around, the song has a new, politically charged verse, and Foster plays it on Wurlitzer electric piano instead of acoustic guitar—not that that had been her plan, so much as an intuition on the part of her producer. But doing it that way did seem to help her get the lyrics' emotional urgency across. "Actually," she explains, "we had just recorded 'Heal Yourself' . . . on guitar. And [Papa Mali] . . . said, 'Hey, that was really nice, Ruthie. I was wondering if you could, ah, swing over to that Wurlitzer over there and see what kind of sound you can get from that, too.' I didn't know, but he was actually rolling tape when that happened. And the [players] in the next room just picked up on what I was doing." She adds, "Yeah, the Wurlitzer was part of my early, early music training. You know, piano classes that's what you played—Wurlitzer—when I went to school for music. So all of that just started coming back to me."

A couple of years later, Foster followed those performances with an even more electrified Memphis soul sound on *The Truth According to Ruthie Foster*, recorded, in point of fact, at Memphis' Ardent Studios with local players—including Hammond B3 organ player Charles Hodges, who had backed Al Green, and the late keyboardist Jim Dickinson, who had played on (and sometimes produced) records great and small, including the Rolling Stones' *Sticky Fingers*. On this album, Foster's voice is more up-front than ever, and her musical support more muscular: smoldering electric guitar, percolating organ, and bright, blasting horns. She tears through ferocious funk-rock originals, "Dues Paid in Full" and "Truth!"; slow-burning blues "Tears of Pain"; and tortured soul covers "(You Keep Me) Hangin' On" and "Nickel and a Nail" (the latter two learned from early '70s recordings by Memphis soul singers Ann Peebles and O. V. Wright, respectively); she maintains the singer-songwriter and gospel streams of her work with a rendition of Patty Griffin's "When It Don't Come Easy" and a countrified rereading of her own "Joy on the Other Side." "I do have, I think, a pretty good mix of positive songs in there," she affirms. "But, there again, *The Truth* is really about [how] you can find your truth and truth in anything, in all of these songs, in despair and getting your praise on at the same time."

Playful as they no doubt are, *The Phenomenal Ruthie Foster* and *The Truth According to Ruthie Foster* are not the kinds of titles an artist chooses if she feels unsure about the finished product. And there would be no reason for Foster to feel that way; both albums have greater breadth, spirit, and rootedness in her past than anything she had previously done. They assemble the array of musical styles and modes of expression that feel familiar and relevant to her life. She favors songs that emphasize the message of the lyrics; *and* she favors songs that lift up the spirit by way of the body.

"I think for me," she offers, "it was just about being moved . . . whether it's by the lyric or something melodic or even just the timbre of somebody's voice, you know. Because I can remember early on as a kid in church, not really getting what this particular gospel song's saying that my uncle, my great uncle, is singing. But I could feel . . . what was going on in his voice that let me know that . . . 'My uncle's feeling it today. He's feeling it.' You pick up on that energy. And I think with gospel and soul, that's what a lot of people are connecting to, whether they know what's being spoken or not—whether you even speak the same language; there's something about the feel of Aretha Franklin's voice and the feel of Sam Cooke and the feel of Shirley Caesar. You know that they're feeling what they're talking about."

And on the subject of feeling it, on these last two albums Foster has rekindled her interest in song interpretation; like Franklin, she is up to the challenge of making other people's compositions her own with conviction and poise. This is one point where the more formal and rustic elements of Foster's background meet; she knows how to get the most out of her voice, and she knows whether or not a performance rings true. Foster is not a blues or gospel shouter, but she can muster power, elegance, and much joy with her supple, peppery instrument. "I just love big and beautiful voices," she says, "and . . . when you've got a singer who's using training on top of being able to use what they [have] naturally."

When it comes to song sources, Foster has significantly broad tastes; tastes that willfully ramble all over the so-called musical color line; tastes governed by no standard other than what feels right and familiar to *her*: transgressive performers of gospel and blues like Son House and Sister Rosetta Tharpe; soul singers like Sam Cooke, Aretha Franklin, and Ann Peebles; folk revivalists like Pete Seeger and Odetta; and Americana singer-songwriters like Terri Hendrix, Lucinda Williams, and Patty Griffin.

Something for Everyone

Given that breadth, it should not come as a surprise that Foster's live shows feel like several shows in one. "I like mixing my blues with my gospel," she declared with relish during a Saturday night set in a Nashville club a few years back. Her gospel is what Jon Michael Spencer, who has written at length on the subjects of black music and religion, would call African American spirituals—folk in origin, bare bones in structure, and lyrically simple "reflections of a long-standing practice of liberation"[5]—as opposed to urban, evangelical gospel, inspired by Protestant hymns.

Foster started working spirituals, traditional and original, into her repertoire because she finds them tremendously joyful and communally uplifting to sing. "That's why I pull songs like that into my set, usually toward the end of the set . . . and sometimes in the middle of the set because, you know, I know that's what's going to make me smile and keep me happy," she explains. "All of those tunes, [like] 'Woke up This Morning,' which different people have different memories of that song, from church to the civil rights movement. For me . . . it has both. . . . Plus, it's this connection that I have had with Odetta, because I had a chance to open for her a couple of times and she actually came up and sang with me on that one. . . . And it's just really about . . . something Pete Seeger would say to me, and that was, 'The human voice is just magical.' There's just something about singing that opens you up, frees the spirit. Those songs allow you to do that."

What Seeger, beacon of the folk revival, was most likely getting at was the power of singing *together*. Usually, when Foster takes the stage, she is not alone. And there is a certain symbolic power, on top of creative compatibility, to the musical partners she chooses; throughout her solo career, she has often worked with women. Earlier on, she performed as an acoustic duo with white percussionist and singer Cyd Cassone. These days, she has a versatile power trio with bassist Tanya Richardson and drummer Samantha Banks; together, they make a skilled, all-female, all–African American band. Even now, with more women working as professional musicians than did so in earlier eras, that is no small thing. Male and female audience members alike respond to the sight and sound of three women with chops and an intuitive feel for the music.

"We try to keep our little happy family together," says Foster of her band. "Because we know that . . . just us walking in the door and being on stage together . . . I think that alone, before we even sing a note or play anything, says something. People walk in and they see three, you know, black women on stage . . . getting ready to play. First of all, you walk in and you see that and you know something's about to happen; something good is about to happen."

Foster, Banks, and Richardson have been playing together long enough that they no longer give much thought to their uncommon lineup. But surrounded by primarily male blues musicians on the Legendary Rhythm and Blues Cruise a few years ago, they felt their uniqueness rather acutely. For one thing, notes Foster, their musical approach—centered on uplift and groove—was different from many of their male counterparts' fixation on busy instrumental soloing: "We were the women trio, and we rocked that boat. We rocked it. We put a little gospel into the blues, 'cause that was kind of missing. . . . If you're a player, you've got all this manpower and all this testosterone and all these guys standing there yanking on those guitars, and everybody tries to play as many notes as they possibly can in twelve bars. . . . We can do that, now. I can handle that. But we also brought in an element that was missing, and that was truth and a little bit of inspiration and a shot of joy, you know. Bring the feminine aspect back into it, and it just rounded it, really rounded it for us."

On any given night, during any given performance, Foster creates a profoundly welcoming space by invoking her roots in a way that makes everybody in the room feel like familiars. She wants them to really *get* where she is coming from and to not only enjoy but participate in and respond to her jubilant conjuring of memories. Songs give way to animated storytelling. Onstage that night in Nashville, she prefaced her rousing rendition of Brownie McGhee's gospel-blues "Walk On" with an insistent churchly shuffle and a flashback. "This is a groove my uncle would play on the piano every Sunday to let the pastor know to wrap things up," she explained, before doing a few impressions of the wild, colorful ways members of her family expressed their spiritual ecstasy. Her back-home theatre drew laughs and cheers; if the most vocal of the audience members had not experienced for themselves exactly what Foster was talking about, they were at least mightily entertained by her scene-setting. She even got a few people—including gospel singer Odessa Settles—dancing unself-consciously next to the stage before "Walk On" was over with.

Foster's live album, *Stages*, captures a similar moment on a track that is simply and appropriately titled "Church." For a full seven minutes she memorializes the zeal the women of her family displayed during church services; her Aunt Cora's unabashedly shrill singing in the choir; another aunt who had a habit of getting so spiritually overcome that she would physically lose her wig; Big Mama stirring up fervor in "the amen corner"—a place where, as gospel music chronicler Anthony Heilbut puts it, "a group of old-timers sits . . . and 'moans' the spirit into presence."[6] During the portion of the show captured on the recording, Foster discovers that somebody in the audience has a church fan—used by congregants to survive the heat in church sanctuaries since pre–air conditioned times—and invites the person to demonstrate how it can come in handy when a service is in full, sweaty swing.

"That's the spirit I like to bring to my shows," she says. "You can call them a show, but it's really just an experience. I am in every word and every note, and I want everybody else to be, too—to feel the joy that I get from just singing. It's that same ele-ment that I grew up with in the church, without religion and the right or the wrong behind it, but just the spirit—that energy." So, even though Foster stopped attending church long ago, she still stakes her claim to the spirit of the Missionary Baptist ser-vices of her youth; not only that, but she puts her own spin on it, infusing her shows with fervency and communal uplift.

Not every song in Foster's repertoire contains a directly appli-cable message or a motivational challenge, but, as if to acknowl-edge the sort of impact her mother and grandmother had on her, a number of them do; the messages themselves, though, are of her own authoring. There is "Heal Yourself," with its call to cor-rect one's own way of thinking, being, and doing—whether that means summoning the courage to perform original music or fac-ing unpleasant social and political realities with eyes wide open; "Phenomenal Woman," a model of sensual self-assurance; and "Truth!" a blues-rock proclamation that the truth we ought to be searching for is that which lies within people—not in politics, in the media, or even in religion. But didactic as some of the songs may be, Foster would never compare what she communicates at the microphone with what a minister has to say from the pul-pit. "I guess I do see myself more as a messenger, not necessarily preaching," she says. "But I try to teach as I go, too—teach what I've learned, anyway." And if her singing and songwriting ever gets close to preaching, she, as much as anybody, is the intended audience: "I'm preachin' to myself."

Behind the empowerment that Foster proclaims with warm-hearted conviction is the authority of experience. Speaking about singing and songwriting, she insists, "Well, I know what it's done for me. You know, music has helped me; it's helped me get over, process what's going on if there's something that just doesn't seem right or feels like I'm in the wrong place."

Some three decades ago, Foster's mom spurred her on toward her first big musical breakthrough. And Foster, the pos-sessor and user of a bold voice, has taken it from there.

Elizabeth Cook
Staying Downhome, Getting Somewhere

A regular on the Grand Ole Opry and the daughter of an aspiring country singer, Elizabeth Cook is also a keen, often irreverent songwriter, as affectionate toward her humble roots as she is determined to do her own thing.

A good twenty miles south of Nashville sits a boxy community center with a scuffed wood floor. Inside, a contemporary pop-country song blares from a lone speaker and a middle-aged woman stands at the back wall, facing a dozen or so children and adults, calling dance steps in a sweetly prodding southern accent via a wireless microphone. The dancers follow her instructions in unison, shuffling their toes, kicking and bending their legs, sliding forward and backward on the balls of their feet, and rocking back on their heels, the tambourine-like jingle taps on the bottoms of their lace-up shoes producing a syncopated metallic clicking on the wooden floor boards.

What they are doing is clogging, an American folk step dance that, despite its modernization over the past few decades—some youthful groups now even incorporate hip-hop moves or amped-up electronic music—still conjures images of the rural Appalachian Mountains for a lot of people. Elizabeth Cook is one of those dozen dancers. She is enjoying herself, just like the rest of them; carrying on a pastime that she, like several of them, first took up in childhood at her parents' encouragement; and, decidedly *unlike* anybody else in the room, polishing dance steps that she will break out during the next show she plays in a small rock club somewhere in the United States, or perhaps abroad. Not that her fellow cloggers are necessarily aware of that last part, because she would rather not dwell on the differences between her performing career and their work, blue-collar and otherwise.

"When they asked me if I . . . could come to [a clogging performance] and I was going to Europe [on tour], I would just be like, 'I'm going to be out of town,'" Cook explains, a little apologetically, in her petite, sparkling twang. That, of course, raised more questions than it answered: "'What do you do?' And I told them I worked for a radio station, and I left it at that. One day there was one lady [in clogging class] that was insistent that I had clogged on the Grand Ole Opry. I was like, 'No, I have never clogged on the Grand Ole Opry.' Which is true."

Now, *singing* on the Grand Ole Opry, Nashville's storied country music stage show, is another matter entirely. That is something Cook has been doing for the past decade. Just shy of forty, she is still one of the Opry's younger voices, since plenty of the regular performers are now in their sixties and beyond. But when it comes to singing stone-cold traditional country material, she can hold her own with just about anyone. It is also true that she works for a radio station; two of them, in fact. Opry performances are broadcast live on WSM, as they have been since 1925, and Cook is also the captivatingly quirky host of a weekday show on SIRIUS Satellite Radio's Outlaw Country channel called Apron Strings. Plenty of people have come to know her entertaining abilities through both avenues.

But the songs of her own that she writes and sings are really her greatest offering. To date, she has filled five albums with them: 2000's *The Blue Album*, an independent collection of song-publishing demos that was not widely distributed; 2002's *Hey Y'all*, a one-off major label country album that garnered some critical praise but failed to make commercial waves; 2004's *This Side of the Moon*, an independent album she made after her record deal came to an end; and two albums on an indie label, 2007's *Balls* and 2010's *Welder*, that both showcase her singular personality, songwriting, and singing, and the wild-eyed electric guitar playing of her husband, Tim Carroll. While Carroll has his own singer-songwriter career, he also leads her band with his punkish take on country music.

Growing Up Country

Cook's humble background lends color, texture, and roots to her songwriting. She treats it as an important part of her identity, without letting it circumscribe who she is, how she sees things, or how people see her. She makes something—her own novel something—out of her roots, deciding for herself which direction she will go, her moves informed, but not limited, by where she has been. The newer and older elements Cook holds in play come together in ways that may surprise but never seem forced. Hers is a body of work in which a song as knowing, hip, and offbeat as "El Camino"—best described as a garage rock bossa nova talking blues about being seduced by a sketchy retro character—can exist alongside "Mama's Funeral," a pedal steel–sweetened country ballad and tender family portrait edged in grief, on the very same album, *Welder*, and it not be a stretch, or ironic.

In his book *Meeting Jimmie Rodgers: How America's Original Roots Music Hero Changed the Pop Sounds of a Century*, critic and historian Barry Mazor masterfully illustrates a performer's journey from humble roots to grounded popularity. He asks an all-important question of Jimmie Rodgers, the Mississippi-born father of country music and plenty more besides: "How did he happen . . . to originate the path for 'up from down home' American roots stardom?"[1] The route Mazor lays out for Rodgers is one that has applied to many a performer since, including Cook, in her own way.

There can appear to be quite a distance between Cook's anachronistically rustic upbringing and her thoroughly modern outlook. That may be one reason her profilers have sometimes gotten hung up on particular details of her past, winding up with a partial portrait at best or, at worst, caricature or outright misinterpretation. "There is a tendency," wrote Grant Alden in *No Depression*, "to render the story as if she were a supporting character in one of those tawdry Erskine Caldwell novels."[2] Chief among the colorful cited bits is the fact that her Georgia-born father, Tom, did time for running moonshine and learned the stand-up bass in the prison band—a talent he would subsequently use to play hole-in-the-wall honky-tonks with her country-singing mother, Joyce, once they got together. By that time, they were both in their forties, with five older children apiece from their previous marriages. And then Elizabeth came along in 1972.

Geographically speaking, where Cook comes from is backwoods Florida. This point calls for clarification, since Florida generally connotes jet setters baking themselves on Miami beaches, families vacationing at the Disney World compound in Orlando, and snowbirds seeking condos and wintertime shorts weather. *That* is not the Florida in which Cook grew up. She laughs recalling how often she has had to explain the difference between what people think they know about the state and what she lived: "I have come to just about blows at times at shows where people ask me where I'm from. And I say 'Florida.' And they say, 'Well, where did you get your accent?' And sometimes some people are more elegant in asking me that than others. It can sound a little accusatory."

"And so I found myself saying things to fans that have paid to get into the show like 'Well, where do you go when you go to Florida? Do you go to the beach? Do you go to Disney World? It's a *big* state. It's like the fourth largest state in the union. So you've never been down [rural highway] 301. You don't know nothing about it.' And they don't. You know, they don't know what a hodgepodge Florida is, that there's a strong southern contingency there."

Bobby Braddock, a native of Cook's home state and the writer of iconic country songs like George Jones' "He Stopped Loving Her Today" and Tammy Wynette's "D-I-V-O-R-C-E," echoes her point with a bit of historical context in his autobiography *Down in Orburndale: A Songwriter's Youth in Old Florida*: "At the time of the Civil War, when most of its population was in the northern part of the state, Florida was among the deepest of the Deep South, and was the third state—after South Carolina and Mississippi—to secede from the union."[3]

Even though Cook was born in the '70s—hardly the olden days—hers was a genuinely backwoods, southern, blue-collar upbringing in the small, crossroads town of Wildwood, Florida. Sandy soil, scrub palmettos, and alligators were regular features of the landscape. Besides her parents' music making, her dad worked as a mobile welder, saving the day, and the crops, when irrigation pipes would break out in the fields. Sometimes, in his line of work, he would run across turtles, and he liked to have his wife fry up their meat. Cook is amused by this particular memory of home life: "Mama wouldn't eat it and I wouldn't eat it and he'd get mad; 'Y'all don't know how to live off the land.'"

Cook's family was not particularly religious. Her mother would, however, send her to Sunset Park Church of God on Sunday mornings, a nearby Holiness-Pentecostal church that the neighbors attended, and the experience made quite an impression on her. "They would watch me make the corner and then she'd stay home and fry chicken," she remembers. "Later it occurred to me, 'Does she know what she's sending me to down there? This is a crazy scene.'"

Cook's parents got her not only clogging and going to church but also singing country music, first onstage with them beginning at age four, then as her own act. "Once daddy quit drinking, [their days of playing in bars] sort of became a thing of the past," she says. "Then it was more I was the kid singer. That's when I got my own band. They were going with me. I was playing arts and craft fairs or opening of a feed store, county fairs."

At the age of nine, Cook recorded a little 45 rpm record—impossible to find anywhere now, aside from the handful of copies squirreled away in her basement—featuring two songs her mother had written for her to sing. On side A was "Homework Blues," a country novelty number about what a drag it is to have to do homework instead of playing, and side B held "Does My Daddy Love the Bottle?" a country weeper lamenting that her father's hard-drinking ways had stolen him away from her. Her daddy indeed loved the bottle, but he laid it down for good when he heard his youngest daughter singing that song. The voice captured on the vinyl recording is itty bitty and lacks the vocal control that Cook would have later, but her spirit and spunk can already be felt.

She hung all of it up at twelve years old—the hard country songs, cowgirl stage costumes, and county fair performances—and began exerting her independence from the music she had learned to love through her parents, getting into other more contemporary stuff. "At that age, your parents are so not cool; whatever is opposite of them is going to be cool," she reasons. "My first concert was Conway Twitty and Loretta Lynn. I was like four or five years old. My second concert was Madonna, on the Like a Virgin tour."

Cook's dad was the one who drove her friends and her to the concert, waited in the car while they worshipped at the altar of Madonna, and bought cross earrings for his daughter from the pop superstar's merchandise table. "That's how sweet and open and forgiving that they were," she says, of her parents' support throughout her changing interests. "Because they spent a lot of money on cowgirl outfits and a PA and tapes to learn songs and music equipment and stuff. And I was completely unplugging from that."

The only place Cook was singing at that point was a place her parents did not often go—the Church of God. "[A]round twelve, thirteen, fourteen years old . . . I got really involved in the music there," she says. "Some of them remembered me as a little local child singer. . . . The next thing I knew I was in the ladies' ensemble and the ladies' trio and just doing all kinds of singing in a number of different groups . . . within the church, which was extremely active and extremely impressive southern gospel live-band rock 'n' roll. It was fantastic."

Cook's ultimate act of unplugging—eclipsing even her retirement from the kid country singer gig—was deciding that she would find a way to go to college. Her family did not have much money and nobody had been through college, though an older sibling or two also started taking classes around the same time she did. She graduated from Georgia Southern University with dual degrees in accounting and computer information systems, landed a position at the Nashville branch of the accounting firm Price Waterhouse, and stayed there for all of eighteen months before turning her attention back to her childhood dream—on her own terms—and taking a gargantuan leap into music with only the flimsiest of safety nets: a little publishing deal with Bro 'N Sis Music.

"Definitely when I was at Price Waterhouse it did not feel true," she reflects. "I went there and I was somebody else. Just like a lot of people feel about their jobs." And no wonder it did not feel true. Cook is about trying to make something of herself; about taking responsibility for her happiness; about pouring herself into and putting her spin on whatever she does. And Price Waterhouse was not the place for her to do all that: "There was no way that I could challenge myself everyday or try and shine or try and do anything, really. . . . It was just very defined and rigid."

Family Ties

Cook's roots lend her songs grounding and heart, and the way she confounds all manner of stereotypes gives her writing nerve. She had her Florida stomping grounds in mind when she cowrote "Ocala," a country ballad that closes *Hey Y'all*, with Hardie McGehee, a songwriter signed to the same publisher as her at the time. In it, she describes distinguishing characteristics of the decidedly un-Disneyfied inland spot she called home—sunning alligators and Silver Springs' glass-bottom boats, for instance—and makes clear that it still has a hold on her heart.

But physical place is less prominent in Cook's oeuvre than the people who have her affection. Early on, she wrote "Mama You Wanted to Be a Singer Too," a straight country song addressed to her mother and featured on both *The Blue Album* and *Hey Y'all*. It was a hefty song to write at the start of her adult career, one that acknowledged that the dream of being a country singer was her mother's before it was ever hers, and that the hard facts of her mother's life—having five children with a first husband who repeatedly abandoned the family without money or food in a remote West Virginia holler—had made pursuing it unimaginable. Cook, in a sense, carries her mother's musical aspirations along with her own.

"I remember specifically when I started writing the song, daddy would make [mama] sit down at the table with him while he got the bills out and told her how much to write the check out for," says Cook, recalling the song's down-to-earth inspiration. "And there was a little documentary on about Tammy Wynette and they were interviewing her and they were showing her house. . . . And mama kept getting distracted by that. . . . I wrote it and sat it out on the kitchen counter late that night. . . . She got up the next morning and she came into my room crying." Cook ventures a guess as to why: "I think she thought it was a good piece of writing. And I think she was probably also touched that it was her story."

Several years later, after Cook's recording and publishing deals dissolved and her career was in a sort of limbo, she invoked her mother as a source of unfailing comfort and steadying strength in "Mama's Prayers," a heartfelt two-beat on *Balls*. Knowing that she was *someone* to her mom, regardless of the circumstances, overshadowed the chafing reminders of all that she had yet to accomplish in music. Because her mother passed away between *Balls* and *Welder*, the song has become even more poignant. "She was just insistent on it—insistent that her family be close; insistent that she was gonna hold it together, no matter what," says Cook. "I don't think we all realized what a rock and a touchstone this sort of tiny little country woman was for all of us."

Though Cook's mother is no longer here in the flesh, she can be felt on *Welder*. In the aching country song "Mama's Funeral," Cook describes her mother's impact in terms of lives touched; a good many people came together on the rural plot of Tennessee farmland to which Cook's parents had retired and helped shoulder the grief of losing her with a thoroughly informal funeral. The song says much about the resilience of her family; there was laughter, and beer drinking, right along with the mourning, all part of one big home-style package.

In a different era, before Cook ever picked up pen, paper, and guitar to express herself in an original way, her mother was the one writing the songs, first as an outlet for her own thoughts and emotions, and later for her daughter to sing. On *Welder*, Cook plucked a song from the former category for her own use. That song is "I'm Beginning to Forget," a heart-dragging country weeper—the plea of a soul trying to get over somebody who keeps coming back around, stirring up old wounds and feelings all over again. It was not just a plausible scenario that her mother dreamed up. "I imagine now," shares Cook, "that that was about her first husband that continued to come home and keep her pregnant and leave and kind of had her trapped. You know, when she finally just had to let go, that the father of her children was not going to be present, that was hard. He was real good at building the fantasy up. Repeatedly."

Besides being in the songs, Cook's mother, and father, got to be close to the action. For one thing, they saw her grace the Grand Ole Opry stage more times than she can count. The Opry's historical and cultural significance may outweigh its commercial clout in contemporary country music, but her mother could surely remember the star-making institution it had once been. Cook calls singing on the Opry "the single most important thing that I ever did for her in my career, performance-wise."

Sometimes when she played elsewhere in middle Tennessee, her mom and dad would do more than watch; they would dust off their old honky-tonk repertoire and open her show with a short set of their own—that or sit in with her for a song or two. Cook's dad still hauls his electric bass onstage at some of her local shows to cut up for the crowd with his country songs and hillbilly humor, and to brag on his daughter. *The Blue Album* features recordings of her parents reminiscing, and playfully disagreeing about, how they got together in the first place, and what role music played in that story. In the liner notes of *Welder*, she honors them both, noting that the album title was partially inspired by her dad's work as "sole proprietor of Cook's Welding in Wildwood, FL," and dedicating the project to her mother's memory.[4] "I mean, my parents especially, being musicians and loving country music and just loving people and being around country shows and stuff, always have stuck really close," says Cook. Involving and invoking them in her music has been a way of staying connected to her roots, even as she lives, and writes about, a life that has taken a different direction.

By no means have Cook's parents liked *everything* she has done musically—nor has suspecting they would not like something stopped her from doing it. "I knew that I'd have to make it my own and do my own thing," she says. "[My mom] certainly doesn't understand—or did not understand—everything I was doing. She did hear 'El Camino' before she passed away." "El

Camino," recall, is Cook's funny, out-there account of unlikely seduction. In titillating detail and cool jive talk, she describes the shady qualities of the seducer's truck-car, as well as his psychedelic shirts, mullet hairstyle, and choice of air freshener scent: Piña Colada. And did her mother get it? "No, she didn't get it," laughs Cook. "She did not understand it at all. She would say, any time I did anything that she didn't like or wrote anything she didn't like, she would just go, 'Elizabeth, *reaaally.*'"

Cook's mom did not get the chance to hear the way she merged gritty realism with familial feeling in "Heroin Addict Sister" on *Welder.* The song is a pained close-up portrait, with Cook's brittle, bruised singing laid over finger-picked guitar. She tells it absolutely and unadulteratedly like it is, yet she is also fiercely affectionate toward the song's subject: her real-life heroin-addicted sister. The verses are packed with vivid description of her sister's personality traits—some destructive, others lovable—her pleas for help, her past crises, and their emotional aftermath. Cook sounds deeply concerned for her sister, as she contemplates the ravages of the drugs and the dangers and indignities of the streets, but also, in fleeting moments, genuinely tickled by her sister's more harmless exploits.

It is a revealing song—about the sister's troubles *and* about Cook's commitment to directness. She has a hard time talking about that relationship, and, from the sound of things, found it no easier to write about. Still, she did. It has been a great relief, she emphasizes, when people have picked up on the empathy in the song: "Oh, good. I don't sound like I'm pissed off or mad because I'm just sort of spewing my observations about it." And Cook does not take those interpretations of "Heroin Addict Sister" lightly. "My mother, if she instilled anything in me, that you don't . . . ," she trails off. "She was crazy about all of her children, and no matter what any of them do, you better not ever be harmful to each other in any way. And so out of respect for her, that maintains."

Addressing matters that hit *that* close to home, especially for the people Cook cares about, and doing it in such an unvarnished way—or, as she lightly puts it, "spewing"—is not an easy undertaking. The fact is, she often needs a certain amount of space from her family to write songs without censoring her point of view: "Because it's hard to do art around your family—it is for me."

Cook describes the nerves she felt the first time she attempted "Heroin Addict Sister" live. "I was in Washington State at a casino opening for [veteran country singer] Mel Tillis," she recalls. "There was absolutely no one there to see me. . . . I remember doing it and kind of feeling as I was going through it that it was definitely tense. . . . But then when I was through I sensed that it was good. And then I had people come up and talk to me about it, a brother and a sister in particular." Knowing that someone is relating to what she is singing, she says, makes her discomfort worthwhile.

Exiting the Mainstream

Cook's newer songs, like "Heroin Addict Sister" and "El Camino," show more candor, specificity, and willingness to go out on a limb than her earlier writing. It is hard to imagine these songs getting played on commercial country radio or being welcomed on the Opry; it is also hard to imagine that she had either of those aims in mind when she wrote and recorded the songs. There was a time, though, when she *had* to care about such things. Even she is a little stunned by how radically her career and priorities have changed since then. "There's P.B. and A.B.," is how she puts it. "Pre-*Balls* and after-*Balls* is how you define my life."

Being a country singer and songwriter of an alternative stripe was not an option that was anywhere on Cook's radar to start with. She emphasizes, "I thought I would be a mainstream country star. No question. That's what I grew up knowing, understanding. . . . I was in Nashville, Tennessee; I got a major label record deal. Pretty quick, though, I looked around and just felt really, really alienated. At awards shows, at label functions. There were a few artists that I got close to and a few even of the executives and stuff that I worked with that I was able to have a rapport with. But I was pretty alienated from what was going on; musically, socially, culturally, just didn't fit at all."

The true-blue country songs she was writing then, many of which recalled harder-edged strains of country music of the '60s and '70s, and the fact that she was writing, or cowriting, almost all of her songs, did not fit the popular model for women in country music at the time. Cook prods rhetorically, "Who's the girl singer-songwriter, you know, in mainstream country music in the late '90s? Who would that be? I mean, that's just not what it was. It was girls with diva outfits and big voices singing, like, power ballads and they're all trying to compete with Celine Dion. And it was just not what I was interested in doing. Not what I was good at." Indeed, the second major performer of the '90s that Mary A. Bufwack and Robert K. Oermann profile in their definitive history of women in country music is Faith Hill, who fits Cook's description of a non-songwriting, glamorous pop crossover singer to a T.[5]

As for Cook, her relationship with a mainstream country major label was short-lived. She had initially been signed by Atlantic Records in Nashville; the label was quickly absorbed into Warner Brothers, which put out *Hey Y'all* but gave it little promotional support. It would be her first and last major label album. She soon asked to be released from her contract, inaugurating a rather unmoored period in her music career, which found her supplementing her tour earnings first by waiting tables, then keeping the books for a local boutique's shoe department. And during that time, her songwriting changed. Partway into the transition, Cook put together an independent album called *This Side of the Moon*. The songs were written with several different cowriters and recorded in several different studios. Some, like "Here's to You," used soured romance as a metaphor for how her major label relationship had turned out. But when her publishing deal ended, so did her days full of cowriting appointments. She moved toward expression that was more robustly *her*.

"It's really, really demoralizing for me to go sit in a room all day and try and be creative and a lot of times give up ideas or lines that I really find entertaining or quirky that [make] the other person think I'm a complete freak," reflects Cook. She takes care to qualify, "And I've written with some *great* writers, and still have relationships with some great writers and probably will write with some other people more going forward. But I think overall that was the only [big change] that I made." That is, taking full advantage of her freedom as an independent recording artist by writing solo and hanging onto each and every off-beat line, if she so desires.

In Cook's newer compositions, she speaks to contemporary experiences in a way that is tangible and down-to-earth but also allows her irreverence to come through. "So I'm getting more and more to that point to where I'm able to communicate what I see maybe a little more clearly or . . . clear's not the word," she tries. "But in a more poignant way, where you can say . . . this really specific thing, and everybody knows what you mean when you say that—or people that are gonna listen to your kind of music know what you mean."

A perfect example is "Rock N Roll Man," a strutting rock 'n' roll number on *Welder*, featuring the searing guitar work of one Tim Carroll. With her tough delivery and punchy blues phrasing, she brings to life what it is like dating the small-time, gigging rock musician, who is almost broke, not particularly responsible, and sliding toward middle age while still harboring big dreams. She nails his musical taste (Elvis Presley's early rockabilly recordings on Sun Records, but not his later material, and *definitely* not the Grateful Dead); his habits (investing what little money he has in guitars); his way of showing affection (a tattoo of his girl-friend's name); and his decorating style, or lack thereof (sheets on the windows). The funny, fresh, humanizing picture she paints of this character could hardly be any truer to life. She *gets* him, and his girlfriend, too. To be portrayed so truthfully is to have one's dignity and experience affirmed. Relates Cook, "I thought that I was speaking for a lot of girls, you know, that maybe they're in their town and they date the guy that has the blues band, and what their experiences of that might be."

Out-Countrying Country

Cook was never an abstract songwriter. "Mama You Wanted to Be a Singer Too" was an early example of her concrete writing. But in pursuing hard, intelligently observed detail that has not been recycled in a hundred other songs, that is informed both by her backwoods, blue-collar roots *and* the urban environs of her funky, racially, economically, and educationally diverse East Nashville neighborhood—without denigrating or whitewashing either sensibility—she has headed the opposite direction from most contemporary mainstream country music.

"When I listen to Top 40 country radio today, I hear almost nothing . . . that suggests the working-class society that originally nurtured this music," laments Bill Malone.[6] He hears something else instead: "[E]ven when the young country entertainers sing their occasional songs about blue-collar life, they sound like what they are—suburban men and women interpreting those experiences through middle-class lenses and sensibilities."[7] As much as it might pain him to say so, Malone also allows that this contemporary version of country may simply be an outgrowth of lives that look a lot different from those of generations past.[8]

But there is also this reality: the songs that get played on country radio took a sharp turn toward "increasingly bland, increasingly 'happy,' and increasingly less interested in the realities of everyday life" when the Telecommunications Act of 1996 deregulated radio and a few corporations were able to buy up the stations and, eventually, systematize and homogenize the playlists.[9]

It is no wonder, Cook being the type of sharp-eyed, in-touch songwriter she is, that she has a hard time connecting with contemporary country radio—forget getting played on it. "I guess, I mean, whenever I do hear something—and not to complain about mainstream country music—but I can't believe how *reverent* it is, to this very singular-minded message," she marvels. "And it really underestimates the country music fan. That's sad." It seems part of what bothers her is the thought of songs failing to speak to people's lives on a deep level, and instead casting them in the role of consumers who express their identities primarily through what they wear and drive and drink.[10] "It's a simple badge they can grab and slap on their shirt or on their ball cap, that helps them be able to walk into Walmart or the grocery store and let everybody in there know what kind of person they are," she observes. "And it's oversimplified."

Cook takes personally the feeling of being underestimated as a country listener. "Maybe I'm . . . naive about that," she admits. "But I *am* one of those people; I come from that. You know, my daddy drank, went to jail. My mama was uneducated, couldn't drive a car. Because of that, I feel like, 'Well, I was there.'" Between there and here, Cook has accomplished a remarkable thing with her music: proven that the true picture of her life is far more complex than the stock images offered in some mainstream country songs. She celebrates the influence of her downhome roots in her writing, her singing, and her self-presentation, *and* she puts her intelligence and varied experience to good use.

Richard A. Peterson separated country performers into two types—"hard-core" and "soft-shell"—yet Cook confounds that dialectical schema as thoroughly as anybody out there. Her southern accent and sayings, the twang in her singing, the concreteness of her songwriting, her readiness to let the audience in on mundane details of her life and her humble origins are all "hard-core." But she also has qualities "hard-core" country singers are not expected to have: education, professional accomplishment in an unrelated field, and a broad, expertly descriptive vocabulary that she puts to good use in her lyric writing.[11]

Not Just a Pretty Face

That is not the full extent of Cook's unconventional identity; she is, after all, a petite, attractive, blonde, southern female singer *and* an extremely smart, serious songwriter. "It's so easy to be dismissed, if you're blonde and under a hundred and twenty pounds, as far as having anything to say or to offer," she testifies. "And how to overcome that and still be feminine and attractive and relevant to the discussion is highly challenging."

"Having a southern accent's a whole other thing," says Cook. "I sat down with a music business lawyer once to discuss a contract. . . . And she said to me, in the middle of the conversation, 'Your vocabulary is surprising.'" She repeats this part for emphasis, taking a thoroughly condescending tone to do justice to the story. "She said, '*Your vocabulary is surprising.*' I was polite in the moment. But I remember that and now it really, really rubs me. . . . I was like, 'Here you are with all your education, from Los Angeles, California, and you don't know no better than to say that to me.' I mean, unbelievable."

Cook has a pretty effective strategy for being taken seriously: "I am interested in being a really good songwriter." She has also written songs that cleverly dismantle some of the biases. *Hey Y'all* features one of them, a Bakersfield-style shuffle called "Dolly." Rhythmically reciting the verses, she sounds exasperated and knowing. Then she sings the chorus in a sweet-and-salty twang, describing scenarios in the music industry in which a man wanted one thing and one thing only from her—sex, that is. She portrays those men as unprofessional and highlights how unfair it is when a woman's looks are rewarded and her intelligence is not. But considering that she wrote the song several years back—a lifetime ago, in terms of her career—she did not give the lyrics or her vocal performance quite as much bite as she might if she were writing and recording it now. "Yeah, I think at the time that I wrote that I thought it was pretty cutting," she reflects. "And now it would cut much harder, probably even lyrically."

The Dolly to whom Cook appeals for sympathy and advice in the song is, of course, Dolly Parton, who has had her share of experience with superficial characteristics—such as her own sex appeal and backwoods sensibilities—getting more attention than her smarts and talent. Cook's "Dolly" has drawn comparisons to a sassy song that Parton recorded in the late '60s called "Dumb Blonde"—written, in point of fact, by male country songwriter Curly Putman. In it, Parton plays the part of a woman taking up for herself and her intelligence when a lover treats her like a fool.

Cook also invokes Parton, and another famously feisty country-singing woman, Loretta Lynn, during her defiant honky-tonk number "Sometimes It Takes Balls to Be a Woman," the centerpiece of *Balls*. Before Cook names them as examples of female courage, she depicts women being sorely underestimated: a woman seeing right through a huckster car mechanic's attempt to sell her work she does not need; a hard-working woman defending her right to get a few things that she wants. Cook wrote the song with Australian country singer Melinda Schneider in a moment of solidarity, frankness, and levity. "She really was going through a major transition, with her husband, who happened to be the president of her record company," explains Cook. "She was going to have to be decisive and sort of make some of her situation happen. And it was not gonna be easy. . . . So I said that to her in the conversation; I said, 'Sometimes it takes balls to be a woman.'"

It is not at all insignificant that the song has proven to connect with all sorts of women—and men. She has sung it at a political fund-raiser, on a bill with progressive-minded, veteran singer-songwriter Nanci Griffith, *and* at a NASCAR rally. "So there was a serious songwriter, more cerebral group, you know, folk-whatever," says Cook, describing the gig with Griffith. "And then there was this other [group of] just everyday women that don't have time to have a record collection and work at the bank or whatever. It translates completely across the board. And even men—even men who have a strong woman in their life or recognize, whether it's their mother, their sister, their boss, a coworker; I have men come up and buy the album for somebody."

In this song and elsewhere, Cook's sharp wit is hard to dismiss. She is aware of assumptions made about her, but they do not keep her from writing, singing, and saying what she means—if anything, they make her want to go further. "I think I'm a smart-ass," she confides, with pleasure. "And because I sorta have this little voice and, you know, long blond hair, I get away with it, a little more than some other people might. And I have no problem using that in order to get away with it. It's not a choice; it's just biologically what I have for a larynx makes me sound like a sweet little girl. And it's not true." She cannot help but laugh at the thought of how far off such a benign, simplistic image is from the savvy, complex person she is and the layers she reveals in her writing.

Welder's "Yes to Booty" is a more recent addition to Cook's string of songs that speak to frustrations of hard-working women. It is a song Loretta Lynn could be proud of: a hipper, rawer hard country cousin to Lynn's 1966 hit "Don't Come Home a Drinkin' (with Lovin' on Your Mind)." Where Lynn's song is all obstinacy—tough-talking words of a woman fending off late-night sexual advances from a drunken husband who shows no regard for what she is feeling—Cook makes her point with a mood swing of sorts. "Yes to Booty" starts off as a country waltz in 6/8 time, and she sets the scene with her coy, feminine delivery: both partners in this working couple are ready to relax at the week's end. Much to the woman's dismay, the man wastes no time reaching for a twelve-pack. And *then* he wants sex. The chorus kicks in, the tempo picks up, and Cook shifts into good-natured, straight-talking mode. The woman prods her man to put "booty" before beer and do the drinking later. That way they can both enjoy themselves and each other. It is a message that scores laughs, even as it hits home.

Cook writes with just as much awareness about the present realities of her career. *Balls* opens with "Times Are Tough in Rock 'n' Roll," which, despite its title, has old-time string band flavor: the rustic, spring-loaded droning of juice harp and a raw-boned fiddle and banjo lick. She sings about being on the road with her band; traveling to gigs, performing, then repeating the cycle—but not making any money at it. She does not try to make the lifestyle seem glamorous, or even appealing in a bohemian sort of way, but wryly lays out the facts: which are, according to her straightforward summary of the song and the truth behind it, "that I am in a van with some guys and we hope to all make fifty dollars today."

Just Doing It

Cook's way of dealing with challenging situations in songs and life is, simply put, to do something about them, and then, as much as possible, to cultivate happiness with being wherever she is in the journey. This may sound terribly obvious, until you consider that there are other options—such as not doing anything and waiting for better days and better things to come to you. The sole country gospel entry in her catalog, "God's Got a Plan," one she cowrote with Carroll, has a title that might suggest it was written in praise of God's sovereignty. And at first blush, it indeed seems like an affirmation of the theological concept that God alone is in absolute control of events, and that God being in control is what gives her the confidence to assert, during the first verse, that if she lost her job she would get a new one in no time flat.

Further along, though, it becomes clear that that is not what she is getting at. The track opens with a recording of a Mississippi Southern Baptist preacher proclaiming, in a stirring Deep-South drawl, his determination to meet the challenges of this time, while a churchly piano and organ intro swell and settle into the chords. Then the piano pickup walks the band right into a hearty country gospel two-beat, and participatory church house touches energize the chorus even more: hand claps on the backbeats and bright harmonies from the veteran father-and-daughters bluegrass gospel trio the Whites.

In sound and power of conviction, the song clearly draws on the southern gospel sensibilities Cook encountered in church, but the chorus makes clear that she is doing her own thing with them. She sings the confident statement captured in the song title, then she follows with an assertion of *her* active participation; *she* knows when to move on, and does so; *she* takes steps forward. In other words, she is not singing about waiting helplessly for God to act on her behalf. The song depicts divine–human partnership. She clarifies, "I'm not saying that if I lost my job today, God would give me another one. *I'd* find another one. . . . I think I've probably seen the resiliency in my father and how he just absolutely *refuses* to not have a full, happy life." Later, upon further reflection, she adds, "I think that I sort of put that responsibility of finding faith on myself. I think that it's sort of my responsibility to find hope and light and justice and grace and all those things. That it's sort of my job to seek that out and find that."

This is not a sentiment one would find in the typical southern gospel song. In the revival hymns of that musical tradition, music-knowledgeable Baptist theologian David Fillingim identifies precious little that depicts people playing an active role to improve life in the here and now. Instead, he notes, the songs "encourage believers to trust Jesus to soothe their affections while waiting for their heavenly reward."[12] Sandra Sizer, in her analysis of nineteenth-century revival hymns, writes that gospel hymn rhetoric "portray[s] the human condition as that of a passive victim," and the proposed solution "is equally passive: to rest in a safe place."[13]

Cook, though, is not one for passivity. In "Gonna Be," a catchy, upbeat number on *Balls* that she cowrote with Carroll, she rejects the "has-been" connotations that can follow a performer who leaves a major label for somewhat smaller pastures and gives notice, with a touch of bite, that she is headed some-where worthwhile, and getting there under her own power. "There was a little bit of judgment on me there for sure after leaving the mainstream world, music world, and then getting into the more indie thing," Cook affirms. The song "[let] people know that may have thought that I had fallen off the map that I was still out there; I was still out there doggie paddling. Probably some of them would wish that I would go away. . . . I think it was a little bit of a retort to the doubters."

Cook's reluctance to sit back also surfaces in "Girlfriend Tonight," a powerfully affecting country ballad on *Welder* that captures a time when the marital fires have fizzled. Rather than complaining, she sings about doing something to rekindle the chemistry: getting dolled up like she used to in high school—tight jeans, big hair, and all—and indulging in the kind of frivolous passion that tends to disappear as the shared respon-sibilities and baggage multiply. The urge to act is also there in "Yes to Booty," a song that she cranked out on the spot in the recording studio; she acknowledges that a mansion and a plati-num American Express card are out of reach but is gung ho about going after something that is not so cost prohibitive: a mutually satisfying sex life.

Lyrically, "Yes to Booty" is the work of a woman who feels free to say what she wants to. The ragged, raucous track is no straight-laced musical exercise either. "Rock N Roll Man" is even less so. Cook sees a link between her days at the Sunset Park Church of God and her lack of inhibition now. "I mean, I really think it was a musical revelation," she says of her church experience. "It was probably my venturing into that kind of spirited music, where, you know, the country music was so much more conservative and low-key and mournful. And this was rock 'n' roll to me. It was music played loudly with reckless abandon."

There is another essential ingredient in the feral attack of "Rock N Roll Man" that Cook found a long way away from her roots: her punk rock guitarist-husband Tim Carroll. He is the one propelling that track with meaty, distorted chording and slicing the air wide open with wailing, note-bending licks. Hearing her describe what they each find appealing about the other—from her perspective, anyway—says much about her salient rootsy identity *and* readiness to push boundaries. "I think that I was really wowed by this reckless, thrashing guitar player," she says of Carroll. "That he plays guitar like *that*. He shoots from the hip. It's very wild. Never has played the same solo twice in his life. Couldn't if his life depended on it, because he's so in the moment and so really just swinging for it like every pitch is a fastball. . . . Very dangerous. Very, you know, naughty."

"And I think for him—and I don't know, I'm guessing—that he had come to discover when he was in a punk band, a lot of those people really like early George Jones records and Loretta Lynn," ventures Cook. "And he found this girl that exists that is from this really kind of pure country place and sings like that and was kind of like a real country girl, in the city, you know, in Nashville. . . . He probably likes about me what I totally take for granted, and I like about him what he takes for granted."

Carroll is the one who launches into a train song called "The T.G.V." in the middle of Cook's show so that she can share another talent that hearkens back to her roots: clogging. As out of place as those clogging breaks might seem for a twenty-first-century rock club performance, you can be sure that there is nothing put-on or ironic about them on her end. She does her throwback dancing because she has the skills, because it reminds her, and the audience, where she came from and because it is flat-out entertaining. "I enjoy it because it breaks things up," she says. "You know, I'm a singer-songwriter and I'm doing all my songs and sometimes it's kind of heavy or sometimes it's silly and it just sort of changes the vibe of the show at that point, and allows you to go somewhere else."

To go somewhere else, but stay in touch.

8

Abigail Washburn
The Joy of Joining In

A bilingual, clawhammer banjo-playing, old-timey singer-songwriter with a distinctly modern mindset, Abigail Washburn embraces Chinese folk music alongside traditional American fare and aims—through musical blending, collaboration and mutual exchange—to foster a sense of global interconnectedness.

For a singing, songwriting, solo independent recording artist who enjoys all the creative freedom in the world, Abigail Washburn has a surprising take on her approach to music. Over lunch in an East Nashville cafe, she agrees wholeheartedly with the suggestion that collaboration and mutuality are at the heart of her work. Then she muses aloud, "I do kind of wonder: When am I going to have my diva, like, 'I know exactly what I want and how I want it and I can tell you all how to do it'? Is that going to happen? Am I going to have that?"

The question is, does she want it? "Not right now. I only want it if I have such a strong vision that I know . . . ." She trails off midphrase, regroups, and follows with a statement she is absolutely sure of: "I love people changing each other. And I, whenever I get into a collaboration situation, I feel so strongly that that be the center of how we collaborate. . . . So, yeah, I do lose my center a lot, but it's calculated; it's on purpose."

Officially, Washburn—who is just into her thirties—has released two proper solo albums, 2005's *Song of the Traveling Daughter* and 2011's *City of Refuge*; two recordings with her name out front of a group, 2006's *The Sparrow Quartet* EP and 2008's *Abigail Washburn and the Sparrow Quartet*; one cobilled benefit effort with the Chinese American electronic outfit Shanghai Restoration Project, 2009's *Afterquake* EP; and two albums as a member of the all-female stringband Uncle Earl, 2005's *She Waits for Night* and 2007's *Waterloo, Tennessee*. Each one of them, even those strictly under her name, bears the influence of the musicians she was partnering with at the time. But in losing her center—if that is, in fact, what really happens in those instances—*she* does not ever get lost.

A Big Change of Plans

Washburn may well be the only person on earth doing exactly what she does in the way she does it. Lots of performers blend or borrow cultural flavors, Latin or African maybe, to arrive at more exotic musical hybrids. But her pairing of American old-time revivalism and Chinese traditional music—down to bilingual singing in English and Chinese—and her intentional courtship of both American and Chinese audiences—sometimes even in an ambassadorial role at the request of the U.S. government—stand out in a big way. On top of that, she does not play either of the singer-songwriter's standby instruments, guitar and piano; she plays banjo, and in the older clawhammer style at that. (Clawhammer banjo's bristly down-picking style was overshadowed half a century ago by the popularity of bluegrass banjo and its more fluid three-finger rolls.)

That Washburn embraces unconventionality is obvious. But being unique is not what she identifies as her primary motivation. "My whole reason for making music is to communicate," she explains, "to say something and be heard. And in order to be heard by someone, you have to have empathy for their position and what makes them hear you. So I try to think about that. I try to think about the people who would be listening and what will make them hear what I'm saying."

To Washburn, encounters with other musicians or audiences are opportunities not only to influence them but also to be influenced *by* them. In the way she looks at individual people, and at the entire rapidly changing, globalizing world, she welcomes the possibility of bona fide two-way exchange. And her readiness to plunge herself into situations that may utterly transform the way she sees the world, or the way she makes music, is by far the most modern—or postmodern—outlook among the eight songwriters in this book. "I think human beings themselves, each individual is an experiment in the crossing of cultures," she philosophizes. "It's an experiment in how much can the human soul, mind, and spirit be flexible and expandable, to the point that it can allow differences in, and that discernment actually becomes a process of expanding."

Washburn puts a lot of thought and theory into her musical efforts; more, probably, than most people would expect of a musician—at least a nonclassical one. "It's so interesting, people's perspective of musicians," she remarks. "I ride on airplanes all the time along with my banjo. . . . And I sit down and get into a conversation with somebody and nine times out of ten, they just figure I couldn't be that educated or that I'm some kind of creative spirit; I couldn't be tied down. . . . It's hard for people to contemplate that there's another kind, there's other kinds of people who choose to live a creative [life]."

Washburn is one of those "other kinds" of people. Not a decade ago, she was pursuing a career path that would have struck any chatty stranger on a plane as seriously ambitious. Music was not it. She emerged from Colorado College, a small liberal arts school, with a degree in Chinese studies and philosophy; eco-philosophy, psychoanalytic theory, and French feminism, she says, were particular areas of interest. She had also spent time in China and was fluent in Mandarin Chinese. An internship with a Beijing consulting firm led to good job offers. And she worked for a couple years as a lobbyist in the Vermont State House. Her next move was to be law school in Beijing—the launch of a career she hoped would serve as a bridge between the United States and China.

Then came a plot twist to rival any dramatic novel: Before Washburn could leave the country, she was offered a record deal—an unsolicited one at that, which, for the record, is not exactly a common occurrence. "It was like a pivot point," she marvels. "It was like '*Bam*. Ooh, I guess I'll go that way.' Yeah, that was right when I was getting ready to go off to Beijing to go to law school there and got offered this record deal with [the independent roots label] Sugar Hill, just because they heard me singing some Appalachian songs in a hallway at the IBMA [International Bluegrass Music Association] convention."

Less because of the label interest than the public cultural platform it portended—a platform Michelle Shocked had recognized twenty years earlier—Washburn decided to ditch law school, settle in Nashville, and give music a chance. However rash the move might sound, it was not a light-minded decision. "There's two things that propelled me in this direction," she begins. "One is the cultural tie, the understanding . . . that culture could be that bridge that I stood on to have the dialogue through music and artistic events, to talk about—or not actually even talk about—but just to experience language . . . not even so much lyrically, but through sound and vibration and pitch and shared ideas, or not-shared ideas, of what that means and where the roots is in music or where it isn't, just by experience, by making music, not by talking about it even. So culturally is one aspect."

"And then the other," she continues, "really is psychologically, what it means to feel like the 'other.' And how does the concept of self change when you start to understand the other better? That's probably the piece I'm even the most passionate about is that, because my experience, and the reason I'm [making] music in general, is because being in the face of things Chinese and living in China I was forced to try to explain where I came from, and I realized I wasn't very well equipped to do that. And it led me back to things American, the banjo being one of them."

The Good Old-Timey Days

China's centuries-deep cultural roots made Washburn conscious of how shallow her own were by comparison. Clearly, though, there is more to the story of how the one thing led to the other. How, for instance, did a person born in 1979 in Evanston, Illinois, raised first in the Washington, D.C., suburb of Gaithersburg, Maryland, and then in Minnesota, by parents who favored the soft, smooth sounds of "John Denver and Air Supply" get acquainted with old-time music in the first place?

Since the connection between Washburn's roots and her roots music—unlike Elizabeth Cook and her direct line—is less than obvious, she offered the brief explanation in the liner notes of her debut, *Song of the Traveling Daughter*. And she did not intend it only for the people who were hearing of her for the first time: "I guess I was probably thinking about not my immediate family necessarily, but my relatives; like, how would I explain this to them? What would they think about this? You know, like the cop on the south side of Chicago, the aunt that works at Claire's and sells jewelry, my cousin who's teaching science in a public school in northwest Chicago, my grandma that runs a roller rink. How does this relate to all them? How does it relate to where I'm coming from?"

There was not room on that squat, CD-sized page for Washburn to go into great depth, so she related that she had taken up American old-time music on a quest to strengthen her attachment to where she comes from. She had also been looking for something she felt was lacking in her personal roots, and feeling a sort of nostalgia for things not of her lifetime. Her childhood musical taste is a good place to take up the story. "Specifically," says Washburn, "I always loved black gospel music since I was a little kid. It had nothing to do with my parents. . . . I don't know where it came from, but the first time I heard Whitney Houston singing a gospel song I was like 'Oh my god.' . . . I just thought it was the most compelling music in the world. . . . And I just was always so sad that I couldn't sing black gospel music."

"I could," she clarifies, acknowledging the difference between opportunity and ability. "I sang in my black gospel choir—it was called the Black Gospel Music Choir—at my college, [and it] was half white. And then when I moved to Vermont, I sang in the community black gospel choir—again three-quarters white or whatever. But I just, I could never really actually do it. I couldn't sing like my heroes. And when I heard old-time music, I realized I *could* sing like my heroes. I mean, I wasn't singing exactly like them, but it was accessible to me."

Why did music from well before her grandparents' time feel more accessible? "It's not about technique; it's not about execution or anything. Which a lot of the black gospel music requires. There was a lot of heart—*oh my gosh*—singing heart and soul. But [also] a lot of 'Are you good enough for this melisma . . . hitting that high note?'. . . And I wasn't the person that was great at that, at least not naturally, or easily. But when I picked up the banjo and sang an old-time song, it felt like I was doing it; I was in it. Immediately. *Immediately.* I learned [the traditional folk song] 'Shady Grove' off of a Doc Watson record and I played the banjo and I sang. And it was great."

Washburn never lost interest in gospel music, though. She simply tapped into earlier strains of it; strains that preceded electric amplification; strains that date back to, in the words of Anthony Heilbut, slaves "combin[ing] the revival hymns of eighteenth-century England with an African song style and creat[ing] our greatest national music."[1] "I'd always loved the black gospel tradition," she says, "and then as I started to get more and more comfortable with traditional [music], started to open up more and more into early black gospel and early blues, without the sort of modernisms that made it a little less accessible, for me, vocally."

Avoiding the more contemporary stuff, Washburn has found plenty of gospel music that she can throw herself into singing wholeheartedly and compellingly, from both black and white tributaries. "Strange Things," an apocalyptic song inspired by a 1952 sacred blues performance by black singer-guitarist Henry Green, is one of the most electric—though literally unplugged—tracks on *Abigail Washburn and the Sparrow Quartet*. Washburn and the rest of the players attack the song as though they aim to rub nerves raw with her breathless delivery and their churning, impatient rhythms, until they all become unhinged. Cello, fiddle, and banjo burst into frenzied runs, but her murmuring, shrieking, belting voice is by far the most dynamic instrument.

Uncle Earl recorded her a capella original "Divine," a welcoming vision of heaven, on *She Waits for Night*. And *City of Refuge* draws to a close with a pair of gospel songs: "Divine Bell," an old-timey call-and-response warning of God's judgment that she wrote with Ketch Secor of Old Crow Medicine Show, and the yearning traditional Appalachian hymn "Bright Morning Stars." And that is a much abbreviated list; gospel songs are important to her for powerfully therapeutic, if not traditionally religious, reasons. "I, basically, just as a human being, am sort of built to see people suffering really easily," she says. "And so these songs let it run through me rather than get stuck inside of me. And it's just something I need, I really need, in my life."

Washburn's path to old-time music was a well-trod one. During the first half of the '60s, a good many college students and twentysomethings latched onto recordings of folk music made thirty years earlier by people living very different lives than theirs, and learned to play the songs for themselves in their search for broader, deeper, purer tributaries of meaning and expression than they had yet found in their more urban experiences. Robert Cantwell describes what was going on as "a kind of nonviolent cultural disobedience dedicated to picking up the threads of a forgotten legacy to reweave them into history."[2] In learning old-time songs from Doc Watson and Carter Family recordings; in gravitating toward her fellow young devotees of the music, especially the picking and singing women of Uncle Earl; in internalizing the music as a way to graft herself onto greater musical and cultural roots, Washburn was, in a sense, acting in the spirit of the '60s urban folk revival—though, unlike many of the revivalists, she is no traditionalist when it comes to the way she performs that traditional material. Often she has drawn songs, or songwriting inspiration, from some of the same sources that they did—Harry Smith's odd yet influential *Anthology of American Folk Music* and John and Alan Lomax's field recordings—always taking care to specify her sources, something else that many of them did.

"That's really important to me," she says. "Definitely a part of traditional folk music, modern traditional folk music in America, especially for the people like me who are probably part of something more akin to a folk revival than actually being from a tradition of folk music. . . . I grew up in the suburbs. They didn't [play] that [music] there. There's an awareness that preservation is an important piece of it, because it's not something that I actually had readily available to me. So when I finally got it, I covet it, and I feel like it's an important thing to have around for a long time, and to be remembered."

"I just find comfort in being a part of it, that's the other thing," she continues. "That's part of the reason I like to point out where it came from, is because, 'Hey, this is my community and this is a line of music that I get to be a part of.' I like to point that out, too: 'Hey, I'm not alone.'" Since she values community, and folksongs are, ostensibly, communal property, it is no wonder she has claimed them as her own.

Halfway between East and West

The intellectually and spiritually open attitude of Washburn's music making, like her music itself, has both Eastern and Western influences, one of the latter being Unitarian Universalism. As American liberal religious traditions go, Unitarian Universalism is one of the most theologically flexible; the denomination welcomes people from such diverse viewpoints that there are groups within it for people who identify with Christianity, humanism, Buddhism, and so on.[3] "I was raised a Unitarian Universalist," she says, "and they're just all about social movement of equality and harmony and interconnectedness and all of that."

That Washburn encountered ideals of spiritual harmony does not mean that all was tranquil all the time in the ruminative recesses of her interior life. There were stormy periods of change. "Oh, it must have been so annoying for my parents," she jokes, "because I had this total existential despair because I was a philosophy major in college. And I was like 'Woe is me, woe is me; there is no point. Keep peeling back the layers to nothing. *Nothing.*'"

"Yeah, I went through a real period of just true depression, feeling like I'd be a fool to believe anything," she shares. "It took me a long time, and I had to sort of reason it out. . . . My professor, John Riker, came up with the idea of eco-philosophy, which everybody's talking about now. . . . But just the idea of how relational our existence is, that meaning comes from our relationality—not the individual.[4] That was a beautiful, beautiful course that I took where I was like, 'Oh, man. I see.'"

Washburn also took an interest in Buddhism and the Dalai Lama. "Discovering the Dalai Lama was totally amazing," she says. "And after I came home in my monk's robe, my parents, my poor parents, they just didn't even know what to do." Plenty about Buddhism, and Chinese culture as a whole, present challenges to Western individualism and dualism, and she took those perspectives to heart. "It's about being a part of something much, much larger than you even have the right to try to identify; but [having] the duty to obey," she summarizes. "Yeah, there's something very profoundly different there . . . good and evil has no place in it. There's just no place for it. It's just a matter of balance; it's a matter of the elements in relation to one another." This idea comes through in a song like "Halo," a peaceful meditation on approaching without fear death, dark, and the unknown on *Song of the Traveling Daughter*.

Girls Pulling the Strings

Balance seems to be a principle Washburn applies to music making; she creates, readjusts and creates again, responsive to her collaborators and audience—or, rather, audiences. Very little is set in stone if it might create a barrier. "I love the act of uniting with kindred spirits to create a sound that's about more than just one person's idea of what it should be like, but sort of a symphony of that connectedness," she says. "Yeah, I just think that's a really beautiful thing and it helps me grow so much to be around other musicians."

Washburn's first real band was Uncle Earl: an exceedingly joyous, all-female, old-time stringband, then rounded out by singing, songwriting pickers Kristin Andreassen and K. C. Groves and singing, songwriting fiddler Rayna Gellert. "They just were in love with traditional music, and Appalachian music in particular," says Washburn. "And I thought, 'Well, how cool. I'll learn from these people about [old-time music].' Because I was just new to it and a few months into really digging into it. So it became a channel for me to learn, to learn from each of them what they know about the tradition, and then to create music, have fun with a bunch of rowdy women. I mean, they're so much fun."

The two Uncle Earl albums that feature Washburn, *She Waits for Night* and *Waterloo, Tennessee,* are group efforts in the truest sense of the word; everybody spiritedly engaged in the writing of songs, the adopting and arranging of material—some traditional, some merely old—the lead singing, harmonizing, and playing. Every voice is felt, as is the camaraderie between them and the excitement of getting caught up in the music together. Observes Washburn, "Felt like with Uncle Earl . . . there was a continual sense of balance that everyone had in their mind; how we all could share in the limelight; how to all be at the center at one point or another; how to have communal songs, you know."

A lot of the music they played was music meant for dancing. The traditional fiddle romp, "Streak o' Lean, Streak o' Fat"—over which Washburn comically hollers out original lyrics in Chinese—got its own deliriously campy music video, a sort of mashup of a kung fu movie with bad voice-overs and a team clogging competition—surely the only example of any stringband doing any such thing. There is a scene in which Washburn, Gellert, Andreassen, and Groves take the floor and clog together in matching silver shoes: a fun and fitting visual representation of their solidarity.

History does not document very many well-known female stringbands; the Coon Creek Girls—led by clawhammer banjo player Lily Mae Ledford—was one of the first, a group that projected a thoroughly downhome image on Kentucky's Renfro Valley Barn Dance radio and stage show beginning in the late 1930s. Washburn would eventually make Ledford's signature song, "Banjo Pickin' Girl," her own on *Abigail Washburn and the Sparrow Quartet.* In writing it, Ledford did a rare thing for her time: she made the free wheeling, globe-trotting, banjo-playing protagonist a woman. If her man thinks he can persuade her to give it up and stick close to home, he might as well save his breath.

Washburn is the contemporary embodiment of an independent woman using her music to travel far from home. "Of course,

I have to do that song," she enthuses. "I just couldn't believe it when I realized that Lily Mae Ledford in 1928 wrote those lyrics sitting in her east Kentucky home." Also with Uncle Earl, Washburn recorded "Walkin' in My Sleep," a song learned from Hazel Dickens and Alice Gerrard, a duo who made significant inroads into a '70s folk and bluegrass scene dominated by men.

Birds of a Feather

The year of Washburn's first Uncle Earl album, 2005, she also recorded *Song of the Traveling Daughter* with a different, virtuosically inclined group of musicians. She headed for China with three important ones in tow: singer-songwriter and cellist Ben Sollee, fiddler Casey Driessen, and Béla Fleck, the world's premier boundary-pushing, three-finger-style banjo player, who is also now her husband.

"We didn't think, 'Oh, this is the perfect band—banjo, banjo, fiddle, and cello," she says, alluding to the fact that that is anything but a traditional lineup by bluegrass *or* old-time standards. "They were all connected to me and knew each other. So I thought, 'These are people I'd really love to go to China with.' So I asked them and they said 'Yes.' . . . We got invited back in 2006 to be the first American cultural mission in Tibet. That kind of solidified a sense between us that we have been called on to serve a special purpose, certainly in that situation we were. And it just felt like if we continued to work together that kind of stuff would keep happening."

And it did. The Sparrow Quartet, as they came to be called, also received an invitation from the U.S. ambassador to China to play at the American embassy during the Beijing Olympics. "But then President Bush had some other ideas in mind," Washburn says dryly. "He wanted to bring over the Gatlin Brothers to sing inspirational Christian music."

The Sparrow Quartet had not officially formed when Washburn made *Song of the Traveling Daughter*, but Fleck, Driessen, and Sollee were right there in the middle of things, helping flesh out her ideas with polished variegation. Fleck was one of her coproducers on the album, a role he would reprise on two subsequent projects. You can hear the three of them sweep in around her on "Red and Blazing," a song that displays her ability to emotionally embrace traditional material, her way of making folk music personal. At first she is alone, picking chords on the banjo, clear and constant as a ringing bell, and bending her voice to the laden, lilting melody. Then she is borne aloft by billowing strings, and transported into a new, expansive landscape. "That song was totally inspired by [a 1928 recording of singing banjo player] Buell Kazee," she explains. "That melody of that song almost directly comes from [Kazee's] 'The Dying Soldier.' . . . He feels badly in his voice about the loss. That's what inspired me to write about the loss of my cousin in my life, and instead of talking about the dying soldier I was talking about my life."

By the following year, there was officially a Sparrow Quartet, and they had made their first recording as such, *The Sparrow Quartet* EP. It was a laidback affair, consisting of five traditional songs—vaudeville blues, gospel, and old-timey dance tunes—arranged by the four of them together and given a jazzy, improvisatory feel. There were some highly innovative moments, like the bait-and-switch from a regal, reverential performance to a hot, playful one during Washburn's favorite gospel song, "His Eye Is on the Sparrow." Their version lays her energetic embellishments of the vocal melody alongside a jaunty exchange of solos between Driessen and Fleck and the springy, driving feel Sollee creates by playing his cello as one would a stand-up bass. A genuinely collaborative dynamic was emerging, and Washburn welcomed it.

Just after the full-length, and fully realized, album *Abigail Washburn and the Sparrow Quartet* came out, she said emphatically, "I never thought of this band as a group of sidemen. Never; no way. Each person is so unique in their individual musical approach and artistry that that's what I wanted to take advantage of. I have no interest in working with people to tell them exactly what to do. I want to work with people who have musical genius, and I want their musical genius to shine when I work with them. So that's why I work with these people, because I think they're incredible. I have no interest in anybody quelling their greatness to conform to a sound for me. I think that's going to be my artistic approach for the rest of my life, too."

The words to the songs were mostly Washburn's—sometimes with input from Sollee—but the music was everybody's. And breathtakingly intricate it was, composed and arranged as if to stay a good three steps ahead of the listener's expectations. She says of writing with the quartet, "If I spell everything out in advance, it takes away the freedom and the space for there to be more creative possibilities. So a lot of times I would just bring the songs to the group and say, 'Here we go. What should we do now?' I was very minimal about what I brought, partly because I knew that something that everybody had to contribute was extremely ingenious compositional ideas."

Fleck, having spent three decades pushing into far-flung musical territory with instrumental dexterity and a hungry mind—that territory including bluegrass of all stripes, jazz fusion, classical music, and collaborations with African musicians—influenced Washburn's sensibilities in a particularly lasting way: "I would say the biggest thing with Béla is that—and it's such a gift and it's become a part of my primary way of functioning—is that he always tries to think of 'How can we do this differently? What's an unconventional approach that will open our eyes to new possibilities?' That's always how he approaches everything."

Often, Washburn's culture-bridging vision served as a jumping-off point for the group's compositional ideas. In her way of looking at things, globalization is not a sinister, oppressive, homogenizing force, though that is how it is sometimes seen. "That's at the heart of what I'm doing here, in this lifetime," she says. "It's looking at globalization, and seeing the common perspective of globalization, which is mostly understood to be terminology in discussing corporate interests and consumers around the planet. . . . To me, I just come from such a different place. I come from such a perspective of honoring and valuing culture—native culture, culture that's being, you know, manifested daily by all of us—that I just believe . . . some portion of that term should be ours. . . . It should be about the people and who they're becoming, not just on the psychological level, but on the community level and on the cultural level."

"My whole thing," she adds, "is we're not just passive subjects, we're not just passive beings in this process of globalization. If we want it to be less about corporate interests, we can make it less about corporate interests. So why don't we? Let's start now, you know." There is, as Washburn seems to sense, a lot less reason to fear or to fight change when a person can claim the agency to help shape it.

Washburn sang in Chinese and blended Chinese and American sounds on *Song of the Traveling Daughter* and with Uncle Earl. But she explored the connections between East and West far more thoroughly, and vividly, on *Abigail Washburn and the Sparrow Quartet*. In "Great Big Wall in China," she and the quartet map out an alternative geography. The song begins gingerly, with her soft yodeling and plucked arpeggios on the banjo. Her apparently American speaker imagines a flower growing on the other side of the moon, much too far away to see. Then things shift; the banjo slips into rolling 3/4 time, no more emphatic than the intro, but signaling motion at least. Washburn's speaker has found a vehicle to carry her to this faraway bloom: a spaceship.

In outer space, there is another shift; all four members of the group tumble into a frolicsome, Stephen Foster–style waltz, conjuring the optimistic frontier spirit of nineteenth-century America. Gazing on the earth from this high orbit, she makes out the Great Wall of China. Then Washburn switches to a speaker who is apparently Chinese, her presence announced by a precise Asian melody. From the other side of the globe, she has seen the very same celestial sights, the same lunar bloom. Soon, the quartet members are waltzing again, and the first speaker is reorienting herself. She has all but forgotten the flower, drawn instead to the real marvel—the land of this Great Wall; it stands beneath the same sky that she does. She wants to go to this kindred land. Before repeating her wish a final time, fiddle and banjo vamp on a ruddy, optimistic, quintessentially American melody that sounds a great deal like Foster's "Oh, Susanna."

Ask Washburn about her songwriting inspiration, and you are as good as guaranteed a thoughtful answer. In the case of "Great Big Wall in China," she offers an impressive annotation: "What we did was we went and listened to [Puccini's opera] *Turandot* and decided to write our own melodic lines based on his interpretation of the [traditional Chinese folk song] 'The Jasmine Flower,' even though we know 'The Jasmine Flower.' . . . I thought it would be pretty fascinating, since the song, to me, is very much about how our own perception of ourselves and the world changes based on being in another culture or empathically understanding another culture."

There is plenty more musical blending to be found; "Overture," the meandering opening track, is the sort of thing that only roots musicians with classical chops—which Sollee, Driessen, and Fleck all have—can pull off. Brushing against nearly every musical theme on the album in the course of a single composition, they drive home just how broad a territory they are covering. "Kangding Qingge / Old Time Dance Party" is a Chinese folk song set to a Fleck instrumental with a buoyant groove and pronounced backbeat—not at all the feel the former usually has. Late in the song, after much trading of solos, the other players pull back to reveal Washburn performing it straightforwardly, a glimpse of tradition set within considerably funkier innovation.

Moments like that highlight a uniquely modern tension in Washburn's priorities: how to hold on to roots while embracing and adapting to global change that is inevitably coming. "It's a good question," she acknowledges, "especially for someone like me who's purporting this idea that globalization, cultural globalization is a good thing. I think . . . it's just as important to recognize the treasures of local tradition. Just as important. I think it's a hugely important thing to remember that, and I think once a person starts to think about themselves as a global human being, they start to see the potential for conformity that will wipe out the traditions. And I hope that becomes a very real awareness as a part of this whole dialogue . . . that people are holding onto what's beautiful about where they're from."

Washburn has sought out and cultivated a strong attachment to not one but two "folk" cultures: Chinese and American. If anybody has the imagination, intelligence, and limberness of spirit to live with that tension, it is her. The regal ballad that closes *Abigail Washburn and the Sparrow Quartet*, "Journey Home" (cowritten with her Chinese-teaching friend Jingli Jurca), is all about dwelling between; about living in motion. It is as though the two words that meet in the title mean one and the same thing. "Basically," she summarizes, "home is in the looking for it."

Knowing When to Bend

Washburn has plenty to balance in her relationship with her audiences. Her music itself is many-layered; the Sparrow Quartet album, especially, is anything but straight-ahead. "And that," she says, "was one of the things I felt like I needed to be very careful of when I was working with such virtuosic collaborators, was that I knew the potential for ability to take us to really obtuse places, and that being an awesome thing, but also being the thing that could make it inaccessible or less meaningful material as well. . . . Luckily they were very respectful of my opinions about that. And that was probably the time I would speak up the most, was when I was concerned that it was going somewhere too out-there."

Reaching one audience is a challenge in and of itself, but Washburn is dedicated to reaching two—and they do not like or respond to all of the same things. But she is quick to reshape her repertoire and performances when she feels anything may be getting lost in translation. She has, from the start of her recording career, written songs in Chinese; she began doing it less once she learned that Chinese cultural values do not jibe with the American premium on self-expression. "It's different with the Chinese," she explains. "Individualism isn't as appreciated, so songwriting isn't as appreciated in China. . . . I will tell you what is absolutely appreciated across the board is when I sing their folk songs that they know. That is seen as reaching out, an intention to show my respect for their culture. Me taking their language and doing stuff with it as a foreigner? Eh, I don't know." Her response to this realization was to reverse the ratio of Chinese folk songs to originals in Chinese between *Song of the Traveling Daughter* and *Abigail Washburn and the Sparrow Quartet*; on the former, it is one to three, and on the latter, three to one.

Washburn has also changed the way she transitions from one song to the next live. Now the name of the game is less exposition, more letting the songs and performances speak for themselves, engaging, more than educating an audience. "Honestly, it was the Sparrow Quartet that helped me understand that," she relates. "Two things: Sparrow Quartet sort of saying to me after shows . . . 'You know, there's a lot of talking. We probably could have done two or three more songs if you hadn't talked so much.' And me getting kind of defensive, you know, like, 'I'm saying things I think are really important.' So that was one thing that made me really aware. But then I listened back to the show at Beijing University where they had said that about it, and I totally agreed with them. I was like, 'Oh my god! I'm talking so much! Lord.' So that's what shifted things for me."

Letting yourself be corrected when the subject matter is that near and dear to your heart is no small thing; even more dramatic was Washburn's willingness to bend, in practically every way, with *Afterquake*, a benefit album for the region of China devastated by the 2008 Sichuan earthquake. Though the project bears her name, it features none of her songs, none of the musical sensibilities for which she is known, and none of her singing. She and Chinese American DJ and electronic producer Dave Liang—who makes music under the moniker Shanghai Restoration Project—traveled the remote Chinese countryside, recording schoolchildren from some of the ethnic groups hit hardest by the disaster singing their own folk songs and the construction noise of some of their parents rebuilding their homes. Liang spliced and sampled what they captured in the field and, in her words, "put [it] to hip-hop beats and Chinese dance music beats and stuff, so that it can become a part of pop consciousness, you know, try to get it out there." In other words, Washburn purposely tailored the project to Chinese popular tastes.

Even before that collaboration, she had had Liang do dance-pop remixes of a couple of tracks from *Abigail Washburn and the Sparrow Quartet*; "It Ain't Easy" emerged stretched over a mellow hip-hop groove, and "Old-Timey Dance Party" took a decidedly new-timey, synth-heavy club turn. "The guys in the band did not like it all, because it's sort of pop," she recalls amusedly. "But I'm like, 'This is awesome. The Chinese people might finally like my music.'"

With *City of Refuge* Washburn wanted to broaden her appeal, especially with her American audience. As she put it well before the recording process commenced, "I'd like to entertain." For her, that is a different way of thinking about her musical intentions: "[With other records] I've been more, maybe, conceptual and heady about how it will impact the world than [I have been with] this record. And yet I think this record . . . has a bigger potential to reach more people and have an impact." Her approach consisted of "just making up music [and] not worrying about having a point so much."

There are no songs in Chinese on the album, and none anywhere near as sinuous as "Great Big Wall in China"; nor is it a strictly, or even mostly, acoustic affair. But to a greater degree than ever before, the choruses announce themselves as moments to get caught up in—as *hooks*—and there are steady grooves that feel direct and keep things moving straight ahead, that are easy to latch onto. "Burn Through" is a perfect example; the chorus has both a crisply delivered, catchy, cascading melody and a lighthearted eighth-note pattern on the tom-toms.

Washburn has a way of finding collaborators who will get deeply invested in the spirit beneath her music, and in the give-and-take of creating it. Those she enlisted for *City of Refuge*—with the exception of Jeremy Kittel of the chamber group Turtle Island String Quartet, who arranged and played the string parts—are about as unlikely partners for her as a dance music DJ. They do not hail from any remotely traditional music, but the world of indie pop and indie rock. Into the producer's chair she welcomed Tucker Martine, best known for his work with the Decemberists, a band inspired by literature, sea shanties, and British folk-rock psychedelia. He laced the album with all sorts of modern, atmospheric flourishes, notably, glimmering electric guitar, and glassy washes of pedal steel. She also sought out under-the-radar singer, songwriter, and multi-instrumentalist Kai Welch, after hearing him playing with a Nashville indie band called Tommy and the Whale. He helped her complete a number of songs, sang sympathetic harmonies, and played keyboards, trumpet, guitar, and more besides.

"Kai's had a huge impact on how I think about music and how I communicate," she observes. "Part of what I think I really wanted to do with this record, subconsciously if not—I don't know if it was subconscious; maybe it was conscious; I don't know—was just make something that more people would want to listen to than listened to my records in the past, something that felt more like present popular culture than the traditional music. . . . And, you know, I'm not worried about losing my traditional music passion or center, because that's where I come from when I do anything."

If anyone can harmonize these things—old-timey roots and modern pop flourishes, tradition-honoring values, and change-embracing ones—it is her: "I don't feel, like, off-center; I just feel like I have a new stronger center that can reach in more directions."

Washburn simply wanted to mix in some more contemporary—and conventional—elements, the sorts of touches that can help a song stick in pop-calibrated ears. "Kai's approach of trying to find a strong hook was a new notion for me," she says. "Even though a lot of old-timey music, for example, will have something that repeats a lot, that you come back to and it feels like a touchstone, I would never think of it as a hook. Now I kind of do think of things as like a hook in a song that really brings people back to your message again and again." She points to a transcendent surge in the melody that starts the chorus of "Bring Me My Queen" as an example of Welch's influence.

Washburn's commitment to openness, to letting herself and her music be affected by others, has its risks, as does any relationship genuinely grounded in mutuality; depending on one another is, at some point, necessarily part of it. In the case of *City of Refuge*, she shares, "It's a little scary because it means now that [Kai's] stamp is all over this material and he's the only one that can do it and one who really gets it. . . . There's a few places where things are almost totally his contribution, which was out of my comfort zone, to tell you the truth. Because I'm making my record and I'm doing a song that he wrote with Tommy [Hans] from Tommy and the Whale ['Chains']. That shocked the shit out of me. I never thought I'd do somebody else's song unless it was a cover from the old days or something."

Even so, there is no mistaking Washburn's sensibilities at the heart of things; she would no more want her voice to disappear from the music than she would want her music to shut everybody out. From the album-opening title track on, you can still hear her way of gracefully spreading a hard-edged, earthbound, old-timey melody like wing feathers on a soaring bird and her distinct, circling clawhammer banjo figures. She has changed some things, held onto plenty else, and not done either flippantly. "I believe so much in it being beneficial to everybody, you know, in a room wherever I go," she says. "There's a center-piece that I won't let go of, but most stuff is something I can bend on if it helps someone."

City of Refuge may not be as conceptually complex as some of her previous recordings, but it is no hastily or thoughtlessly assembled thing. There were big decisions to make; what to bend on, what to hold onto, and why. Concedes Washburn, "There's something theoretical about my approach on this one, too; that embracing the amount of joy that this music brings me and peo-ple around me and the audiences will have even bigger impact."

She feared there might be cause for worry when she could not, for the purpose of a press release, immediately supply her publicist with a concise explanation of what the album is about: "I went back and I talked to Béla, and I was like, 'Béla, I just feel like I stumbled through this thing. I don't have anything to say about it.' He was like, 'What are you talking about? You know, from the very beginning you were saying that you really wanted this to be a lot about the story of people and their sense of belonging.' I think that really is what the record's about, and I forgot. I sort of lost touch with that through the process of hav-ing to make the thing happen."

So there is something of a central concept after all. The dif-ference is, Washburn turned her attention to what it must feel like for all sorts of people to try and find their places in a shrink-ing, globalizing world—instead of, say, taking on the big idea of globalization itself. The emotion in the songs hits you first; only then do you begin to contemplate exactly who is speak-ing, and from where. In "Dreams of Nectar," an old-timey song cradled by a collective inhale–exhale of harp and horn, vapory guitar, and thrumming voices, an immigrant pines and prays to see delivered the promise of a good life—the promise for which he has given up so much; in "Last Train," a rather refined train song as train songs go, a ne'er-do-well flees, wondering if there will ever be an end to the flight, and a home at the end; in the heartland pop number "Burn Through," a soul struggles to see the light and follow it, hard as it is to make out; and in the pulsing, anthemic song "City of Refuge," a privileged white woman is unhappily trapped in her life and wants out. Offers Washburn about the latter, "The character that really, you would think she had everything just from hearing the description of her: '. . . I basically have everything I need. But I still don't feel right.' And for me, that's sort of the embodiment of . . . that illusion of freedom in America, and what does it really mean to be free here? So that's one piece of it, but it's also that question of belonging and where do I belong?"

These are the sorts of songs that can strike a chord either in the heart or in the head—or both. And Washburn would certainly love to reach both.

The fact is, there are other ways she could be trying to build bridges between people, cultures, nations, and continents; there are other options for her besides music. She could have gotten that law degree and could be working as a lawyer, lecturer, consultant, or diplomat. You get the sense she could do all that yet. But for now, she is on what she finds to be a more joyful path—blazing it, really—as a compelling new breed of roots singer and songwriter: one who sought out cultural rootedness not only for her own grounding, her own sense of belonging, but for the sake of mutual relationship. So that she would have something to offer when she encountered people halfway around the world—people who can tell her where they came from, and want to hear the same from her.

Washburn is still early in her music making; she wants to help shape the future—and not only the musical future. "I definitely think that what I'm doing is not just these individual albums," she says. "I have a profound belief—it's a spiritual one; it's a faith—that absolutely everything I do has an impact, and my intention will have a lot to do with what happens in the world, and how our world is created in the future has to do with what I do right now. It has to do with my spirit, if I'm happy, if I'm sad.

Intellectually, it has to do with what I think about things and how I try to change them or participate; everything. . . . I guess I believe in karma, or something of the sort, where everything is having a continual impact."

"And the more I build a tendency towards kindness now," she reasons, "the even more likely [chance] I would have to be kind to myself and others an hour from now or two days, or much less fifty years down the line. I think we're building ourselves piece by piece. And, yeah, in terms of the body of work that I'm creating . . . I want it to create the world that I want to live in."

Conclusion
The Art of Changing

It is 1990. Lucinda Williams is two years beyond the release of her self-titled third album—an album that strongly suggested she was, and would be, a songwriter to be reckoned with. Folkways, the historic folk label that had been acquired by the Smithsonian just a few years before, is reissuing her self-financed second album, 1980's *Happy Woman Blues*; it had been the first showcase of her original songs.

To veteran music journalist John Morthland, who has been given the job of writing the album's updated liner notes, Williams describes how *Happy Woman Blues* strikes her ears now that that she has spent ten additional years living, writing, and singing: "It definitely sounds like I was younger then, it's more innocent musically." She adds, ". . . [B]ut at the time I was real pleased, real excited, by it."[1]

Being young is not necessarily the same thing as being innocent. But, as is sometimes the case with performers who seem destined to remain active and creative music-makers for a good long while, Williams had not yet found her thing when she made that second album. Of course, she was younger then, too; twenty-seven as opposed to thirty-seven.

Michelle Shocked, at the age of twenty-six, proclaimed her playfully serious faith in what she would be and do later on in life with a song on her *Short Sharp Shocked* album called "When I Grow Up." Even Washburn—the youngest of this group and the last to embark on a music career—hears a different voice on her debut than the one she sings with now. "I was new," she reflects, "new to this; a new musician. That's how I felt."

As of 2011, two more decades have passed since *Happy Woman Blues* was reissued, and in that time, Williams' expression has changed even more than it did during those first ten years; it has gotten more cutting, more knowing. Along the way she has outgrown the song-critiquing mentorship of her poet father, Miller Williams, and chosen her battles—with the industry, the media, maybe even the fans—in order to continue her exploration and development as a writer.

Our contemplation not only of Lucinda Williams' body of work but those of these seven other distinctive singers and songwriters—Julie Miller, Victoria Williams, Michelle Shocked, Mary Gauthier, Ruthie Foster, Elizabeth Cook, and Abigail Washburn—has yielded this all-important insight into their journeys: they have done right by their roots by not staying *right by* their roots, rather maintaining a sense of their roots— a more powerful, active, and present force than mere memory. They have, at varying paces, shed their innocence, grown in their awareness, and put their gifts to more demanding uses. To say it another way, it has taken a little time, and distance, for them to discover and develop their voices and to figure out what matters to them. But their progress means more, and can be seen most clearly, against the backdrops of their roots.

Perhaps part of the work of the long-haul singing, song-writing roots recording artist is trying to make sense of how, and how much, she has changed; marking the miles she has put between herself and the place she started, yet also fashioning what she has chosen to carry with her—or not chosen, but carried anyway—into something meaningful and something she can authentically claim where she is now. That process, as we have seen, is not always a pleasant one—for a performer or an audience. But it surely reflects the realities of life.

And because I have partnered with these eight in the telling of their stories, because I have determined which parts are most important to tell, and how they ought to be told, you have, admittedly, seen the realities of their lives and music as filtered through my eyes, my interests, my assumptions.

It was late in the writing of this book that I finally realized why I was writing it—not why the book was worth writing, but why it meant something to me to be the one writing it. The story of my connection to it is one that can be told best in reverse. I was, just a few years ago, a witness to the scene that opens the chapter on Elizabeth Cook; I was one of the cloggers. At that point, she and I had not met. Though I knew of her music, I also understood why she was there and why she would prefer the focus be on everybody's dancing than on the particulars of her performing career. I, too, was there to rekindle my enjoyment of a pastime of mine from a lifetime ago—from an era when the answers to questions of belonging had come effortlessly. While, busy touring musician that she is, Cook could not keep dancing with the clogging group for all that long, I stayed on, and over time my fellow cloggers became friends—friends who understood that the fact that I was writing a book sometimes prevented me, too, from making it to rehearsals.

I might never have seen a way back to a relic of my past like clogging if I had not encountered songs of a certain sort. As a punk-music-loving college student, I felt alienated from my extended family's small-town southern roots; roots I was so innocently and intensely proud of as a kid. In my early twenties, I realized that my relationship to the faith tradition I grew up in had become a good deal more fraught and complicated than it was when I professed my youthful commitment many years before.

But I found that there are songwriters who work within these tensions, and—most reassuringly—who do not pretend they have found neat, once-and-for-all resolutions. Listening to them sing fragments of their stories helped. It helped me imagine how I might gather up the pieces of my own background and make something of them. The result would not be a facsimile of my old relationship to my roots—nor should it be—but it could be true to now.

That is, I could get right with my roots.

The songwriters in this book are a few of those who have mattered to me. I am not the only one who has ever lived with these questions and sifted, rummaged, and dug for satisfying answers. And I suspect, and hope, I am not the only one who will find these songs and stories to be pointing where answers might be found.

Discography

Lucinda Williams

http://www.lucindawilliams.com/

Ramblin'. Smithsonian Folkways, SF 40042, CD. 1979. Reissued by Smithsonian Folkways 1991.

Happy Woman Blues. Smithsonian Folkways, SF 40003, CD. 1980. Reissued by Smithsonian Folkways 1990.

Lucinda Williams. Rough Trade, 47, CD. 1988. Reissued by Koch, KOC 8005, CD. 1998.

Sweet Old World. Chameleon, 61351-2, CD. 1992.

Car Wheels on a Gravel Road. Mercury, 558 338-2, CD. 1998.

Essence. Lost Highway, 088 170 197-2, CD. 2001.

World Without Tears. Lost Highway, 088 170 355-2, CD. 2003.

Live @ the Fillmore. Lost Highway, B002368-02, CD. 2005.

West. Lost Highway, B000693802, CD. 2007.

Little Honey. Lost Highway, B0011434-02, CD. 2008.

Blessed. Lost Highway, CD. 2011. (At the time of this writing, not all release details have been confirmed.)

Julie Miller

http://buddymiller.com/
Meet Julie Miller. Myrrh, 7016895386, CS. 1990.
He Walks Through Walls. Myrrh, 7016928381, CS. 1991.
"Emily's Eyes." On *Emily's Eyes/Cry of the Heart.* Broken, 84418-8806-2, CD. 1992.
Orphans and Angels. Myrrh, 7016957381, CS. 1993.
Invisible Girl. Street Level, 49002-2, CD. 1994.
Blue Pony. Hightone, HCD 8079, CD. 1997.
Broken Things. Hightone, HCD 8103, CD. 1999.

Buddy and Julie Miller

Buddy & Julie Miller. Hightone, HCD 8135, CD. 2001.
Written in Chalk. New West, NWA 3039, CD. 2009.

Buddy Miller (featuring Julie Miller)

Man on the Moon. Coyote Records, CR 5001, CD. 1995.
Your Love and Other Lies. Hightone, HCD 8063, CD. 1995.
Poison Love. Hightone, HCD 8084, CD. 1997.
Cruel Moon. Hightone, HCD 8111, CD. 1999.
Midnight and Lonesome. Hightone, HCD 8149, CD. 2002.
Universal United House of Prayer. New West, NW 6063, CD. 2004.

Victoria Williams

http://www.victoriawilliams.net/
Happy Come Home. Geffen, GEFD-24140, CD. 1987.
Swing the Statue! Rough Trade, Rough US 50, CD. 1990.
Sweet Relief: A Benefit for Victoria Williams. Thirsty Ear/Chaos/Columbia, OK 57134, CD. 1993.
Loose. Mammoth, 92430-2, CD. 1994.
This Moment in Toronto with the Loose Band. Mammoth/Atlantic, 92642-2, CD. 1995.
Musings of a Creek Dipper. Atlantic, 83072-2, CD. 1998.
Water to Drink. Atlantic, 83361-2, CD. 2000.
Sings Some Ol' Songs. Dualtone, 80302-01126-2, CD. 2002.

Mark Olson/The Creekdippers (featuring Victoria Williams)

The Original Harmony Ridge Creek Dippers. Koch, KOC-CD-8254, CD. 1997. Reissued 2001.

Pacific Coast Rambler. Original Harmony, 323, CD. 1998.

Zola & the Tulip Tree. Atlantic, 0480, CD. 1999.

My Own Jo Ellen. Hightone, HCD 8127, CD. 2000.

December's Child. Dualtone, 80302-01123-2, CD. 2002.

Creekdippin' for the First Time. Fargo, 20393, CD. 2003.

Mystic Theatre. Glitterhouse, 605, CD. 2004.

Political Manifest. Glitterhouse, 610, CD. 2004.

Michelle Shocked

Shocked maintains her entire catalog in print on her label Mighty
Sound. A more detailed discography is available at http://
www.michelleshocked.com/releases.html.

Texas Campfire Tapes. Mercury, 834 581-2, CD. 1987.

Short Sharp Shocked. Mercury, 834 924-1, LP. 1988.

Captain Swing. Mercury, 838 878-2, CD. 1989.

Arkansas Traveler. Mercury, 314 512 101, CD. 1992.

Arkansas Traveler (Bonus Tracks). Mighty Sound, MS 1006, CD.
Reissued 2004.

Artists Make Lousy Slaves (with Fiachna O'Braonain). Mood Swing,
CD. 1996.

Kind Hearted Woman (black cover). Private Music, 82145, CD. 1996.

Good News (with the Anointed Earls). Mood Swing, CD. 1998.

Deep Natural. Mighty Sound, MS 1001, 2CD. 2002.

Texas Campfire Takes. Mighty Sound, MS 1002, 2CD. 2003.

Don't Ask, Don't Tell. Mighty Sound, MS 1007, CD. 2005.

Got No Strings. Mighty Sound, MS 1008, CD. 2005.

Mexican Standoff. Mighty Sound, MS 1009, CD. 2005.

ToHeavenURide. Mighty Sound, MS10, CD. 2007.

Soul of My Soul. Mighty Sound, MS11, CD. 2009.

Mary Gauthier

http://www.marygauthier.com

Dixie Kitchen. In the Black/Groove House, 48003-2, CD. 1997.

Drag Queens in Limousines. In the Black/Groove House, 41962, CD.
1999.

Filth & Fire. Signature Sounds, SIG 1273, CD. 2002.

Mercy Now. Lost Highway, B0003570-02, CD. 2005.

Between Daylight and Dark. Lost Highway, B0008965-02, CD. 2007.
The Foundling. Razor & Tie, 79301 83099-2, CD. 2010.

Ruthie Foster

http://www.ruthiefoster.com/
Full Circle. M.O.D., 91022-0579-2, CD. 1997.
Crossover. M.O.D., RF 9912, CD. 1999.
Runaway Soul. Blue Corn, BCM 70202, CD. 2002.
Stages. Blue Corn, BCM 0403, CD. 2004.
The Phenomenal Ruthie Foster. Blue Corn, BCM 0602, CD. 2007.
The Truth According to Ruthie Foster. Blue Corn, BCM 70901, CD.
    2009.

Elizabeth Cook

http://www.elizabeth-cook.com/
The Blue Album. Bro 'n Sis Music, CD. 2000.
Hey Ya'll. Warner Bros., 9 48289-2, CD. 2002.
This Side of the Moon. Hog County, 462536, CD. 2004.
Balls. 31 Tigers, TOT3101, CD. 2007.
Welder. 31 Tigers, TOT3102, CD. 2010.

Abigail Washburn

http://www.abigailwashburn.com/
Song of the Traveling Daughter. Nettwerk, 06700 30423 2 1, CD.
    2005.
The Sparrow Quartet EP. Nettwerk, 06700 32170 2 6, CD. 2006.
Abigail Washburn and the Sparrow Quartet. Nettwerk, 06700 30792
    2 8, CD. 2008.
Afterquake (with the Shanghai Restoration Project). Afterquake
    Music, download. 2009.
City of Refuge. Rounder CD. 2011. (At the time of this writing, not
    all release details have been confirmed.)

Uncle Earl (featuring Abigail Washburn)

She Waits for Night. Rounder, 11661-0565-2, CD. 2005.
Waterloo, Tennessee. Rounder, 11661-0577-2, CD. 2007.

Notes

Introduction

1 Abigail Washburn, liner notes, *Song of the Traveling Daughter*.

2 Washburn, liner notes, *Song of the Traveling Daughter*.

3 Cantwell, *When We Were Good*, 318. Barker and Taylor, *Faking It*, trace the increased emphasis on "personal authenticity" from the 1960s through the 1970s—a decade characterized by highly auto-biographical songwriting—and into the 1990s and 2000s, during which time the practice of performers writing about their lives in "real" and "honest" ways ascended to a new level of importance. Before the '60s, this had not been the case.

4 Barker and Taylor, *Faking It*, 129–30.

5 Frank, "Pop Music in the Shadow of Irony," 44. As part of his discussion of the artificiality of genre trends, Frank highlights two options available to irony-employing young musicians in the '90s: either find kitschy cultural artifacts that remained undiscovered by their peers or go the whole hog and—with the ultrairony of seeming to be unironic—feign genuine appreciation for some "bad" earlier fad. Even those who chose to do the latter, he implies, wanted people to get that they were being ironic—that

they were too sophisticated to actually like whatever stuff they had chosen to emulate.

6 Peterson, *Creating Country Music*, 154–55. Peterson has shown that pop or "soft-shell" leanings have existed in country, and pre-country, music just as long as styles that are regarded as traditional—or, in his preferred description, "hard-core." They alternate in popularity, he says, according to "both aesthetic and commercial" forces.

7 Marcus, *Mystery Train*, 50.

8 Pecknold, "Selling Out or Buying In?" 40. Pecknold's chapter-length analysis of Americana as an industry, and an industry that in many ways parallels the beginnings of the mainstream country industry—only with more moderate sales expectations—is one of the savviest treatments of the subject available.

9 For instance, the first two aims Latina theologian Ada María Isasi-Díaz lays out for mujerista theology are "to provide a platform for the voices of Latina grassroots women" and "to develop a theological method that takes seriously the religious understandings and practices of Latinas as a source for theology" (*Mujerista Theology*, 1). Also, subjectivity and specificity are at the heart of the ways of thinking, doing, and being elaborated by womanist ethicist Floyd-Thomas: "[A] womanist is radical because she claims her agency and has a subjective view of the world in which she is not a victim of circumstance, but rather is a responsible, serious, and in-charge woman" (*Mining the Motherlode*, 8–9).

Chapter 1: Lucinda Williams

1 Marcus, *Mystery Train*, 35.

2 Werner, *Change Is Gonna Come*, 71.

3 Davis, *Blues Legacies and Black Feminism*, 24.

4 Williams, "Notes in a Minister's Hymnbook," 15–16.

5 O'Connor, "Wise Blood," 1–131.

6 Frey, "Lucinda Williams Is in Pain." The writer of the piece did not really entertain the possibility that Williams, in her perfectionistic drive to experiment with different players, producers, and sounds, might have been striving toward a vision, or that her exacting standards might, in the end, yield a masterpiece worth the trouble. The tone of such characterizations might have differed a little if she were a male recording artist. After all, Bob Dylan rerecorded half of his 1975 album *Blood on the Tracks* at the eleventh hour and more or less got away with it as an artistic move.

7 Facing critical and commercial risks if she altered her songwriting style, Williams drew courage from watching Bob Dylan make significant changes to his own approach: "[H]e had just come out with *Time Out of Mind*, and I loved the sparseness of it, the songs and the production and everything, you know. And I remember reading in the paper . . . the reviewer was criticizing it, saying the songs weren't developed enough and 'This isn't the Bob Dylan we've known and loved over the years.'. . . And I thought, 'Well, wait a minute. I don't agree with that. I like that record; I like those songs; I love the simplicity and the starkness.'"

8 Schlansky, "Lucinda Williams."

9 Ellison, "Keeping Faith," 130.

10 Here are three examples: "Lucinda Williams' Wedding—First Avenue—Minneapolis—September 18, 2009" (Video, 2009), http://www.youtube.com/watch?v=nVSoUos1Png (accessed July 26, 2010); "Lucinda Williams Wedding" (Video, 2009), http://www.youtube.com/watch?v=oKe8RHt_6kg (accessed July 26, 2010); "Lucinda Williams Tom Overby Wedding Vows!!" (Video, 2009), http://www.youtube.com/watch?v=-aCWO0Mw4Ek (accessed July 26, 2010).

11 Barker and Taylor, *Faking It*, 191.

Chapter 2: Julie Miller

1 To give a sense of Buddy Miller's stature in the roots-country world, he was, for one thing, named Artist of the Decade in the final print edition of *No Depression* (Alden, "Buddy Miller," 94–109). He was also selected as the Country Music Hall of Fame and Museum's Artist-in-Residence for 2010, following in the footsteps of previous not at all lightweight artists-in-residence like Kris Kristofferson and Vince Gill.

2 In the *Encyclopedia of Contemporary Christian Music*, Mark Alan Powell unpacks the genre descriptor rather insightfully. "Contemporary," of course, refers to the style of the music, a style leaning toward pop or rock as opposed to southern gospel or traditional (black) gospel. "Contemporary," he also points out, was a less threatening option than calling the music "rock." The Christian-ness of the music has largely been determined either by its explicitly devotional lyric content or the fact that it is written or performed by person who is a Christian. Powell offers a third alternative: that the music be defined according to the audience it draws. However, the fact remains that the content-based

definition is the one that holds sway in the contemporary Christian music industry and the one the Gospel Music Association employs (Powell, *Encyclopedia of Contemporary Christian Music*, 12–13).

3   McFague, *Models of God*, 17. Writing in the shadow of nuclear war in 1987, McFague argues, with more than a little urgency, that naming and identifying God primarily with an image of dominance—like Ruler, Lord, Monarch, all-powerful Father—leads to inadequate and counterproductive responses to global, looming threats (there are certainly other powers besides Russia that would fit that bill now). With that kind of concept of God, people might stand back and welcome a nuclear attack as God's will or wait passively for deliverance, and do either with "no sense of . . . shared responsibility." Here McFague is also drawing on Gordon Kaufman's *Theology for a Nuclear Age*.

4   McFague, *Models of God*, 103.

5   Patoski, *Willie Nelson*, 238.

6   Friskics-Warren, *I'll Take You There*, 83.

7   Hagstrom Miller, *Segregating Sound*, 102–4. In late nineteenth century literary and journalistic portrayals of Appalachian people, geographical and cultural isolation were played up beyond all reality. As a symbol, Karl Hagstrom Miller writes, Appalachia "connoted a racial commonality between subject and reader, yet inscribed a geographic, class, cultural, and temporal distance." And although music scholarship has shown that the mountain dwellers were exposed to outside influences—for instance, getting sheet music and instruments by mail order—and were not the musical products of just a single Anglo culture, vestiges of that image of Appalachia seem to linger as popular myth–truth and to affect how people hear and feel the music.

8   *Raising Sand* was another Burnett production, an album that brought together former Led Zeppelin front man Robert Plant, Alison Krauss, the bluegrass-pop star, and roots-blues material. Buddy Miller, as it happens, handled guitar duties when Plant and Krauss took to the road, and he produced Plant's subsequent album, *Band of Joy*.

9   Another noteworthy outcome of the Millers' meeting with T Bone Burnett was that Julie Miller discovered Victoria Williams' voice. To make a point about good songwriting, Burnett played them recordings of singer-songwriter Peter Case, with Case's then-wife Williams singing harmony in the background. Much to Burnett's

consternation, it was the latter who grabbed Miller's full attention. She remembers, "[He] was like 'I'm not trying to play Victoria Williams for you here. I'm trying to show you [Case's] '[Old] Blue Car.'. . . [H]e kind of like tossed off this little crazy story about this little crazy Victoria: 'She's way far up on the mic and then she gets right on the mic and breaks it.' As soon as I heard her voice I felt like 'Who's that girl? Because I have to find her. Now she's my best friend.'"

10 Goff, *Close Harmony*, 35–38.

Chapter 3: Victoria Williams

1 Barker and Taylor, *Faking It*, 189. Barker and Taylor describe the rift that grew between commercial pop and rock music beginning forty years ago; it has reached the point now that to call music merely entertaining is almost an insult. To be taken seriously, songs in an artist's repertoire need to contain soul-baring of a personal nature.

2 Williams has shared similar sentiments in other interviews, dating back at least a decade (Ochs, "Sweet Relief").

3 Williams seems here to be distantly referencing a theme from the book of Psalms—specifically, one found in Ps 66:1, 81:1, 95:1, 98:4, and 100:1.

4 L'Engle, *Walking on Water*, 74.

5 Welty, *One Writer's Beginnings*, 10.

6 Williams, *Happy Come Home*.

7 Casmier and Matthews, "Why Scatting Is Like Speaking in Tongues," 168.

8 Cox, *Fire from Heaven*, 82.

Chapter 4: Michelle Shocked

1 Pete Lawrence, liner notes, Michelle Shocked, *The Texas Campfire Tapes*, COOK 002, 1986, LP.

2 The section she speaks of can be accessed at http://www.michelleshocked.com/neckofthewoods.htm.

3 Werner, *Change Is Gonna Come*, 48.

4 Michelle Shocked, liner notes, *Arkansas Traveler*.

5 Mercury Records, liner notes, *Arkansas Traveler*.

6 Russell, *Blacks, Whites and Blues*.

7 Miller, *Segregating Sound*, 15. There is also a very good chapter tracing out the artificial and prejudicial manipulation of the musical categories "folk" and "blues" according to the race of the

performer, and offering as a case study Mississippi John Hurt—
who was something closer to a black folksinger, though he was
pegged as a bluesman—in Barker and Taylor, *Faking It*, 29–99.

8   Cohen, "Shocking."

9   Michelle Shocked, liner notes, *Kind Hearted Woman*.

10   Here Shocked is paraphrasing John 15:5.

11   That Shocked opened her Telluride side and *ToHeavenURide*
     album with Sister Rosetta Tharpe's "Strange Things Happening
     Every Day" and extemporized midsong about the "strangeness"
     of Tharpe playing in both churches and nightclubs was no empty
     gesture. Tharpe is an inspiration for Shocked. In her biography
     of Tharpe, Gayle Wald hits on the sorts of qualities that Shocked
     admires: "Rosetta . . . attempted to inhabit an in-between place
     where the worlds of religious and popular music intersected and
     overlapped. She performed church hymns on secular stages. . . .
     Even when limiting herself to a church repertoire, she stuck out as
     a loud woman: loud in her playing, loud in her personality" (Wald,
     Shout, Sister, Shout! x.)

12   Jones, *Wade in the Water*, 50.

13   Jones, *Wade in the Water*, 59.

14   Cone, *Spirituals and the Blues*, 95.

15   Shocked has good reason to refer to contemporary Christian
     music as "white." The highest-selling and highest-charting per-
     formers in that genre are, consistently, white, and the same is
     true for those who win the Gospel Music Association's Dove
     Awards. Even though contemporary Christian music is ostensi-
     bly a racially neutral category, the prominence of the genre led
     to the racial qualifier "black" being placed in front of "gospel" to
     distinguish traditional gospel—with its origin in African Ameri-
     can churches—from mainstream, and mainly white, Christian
     music. Lisa C. Jones addresses much of this (Jones, "Are Whites
     Taking Gospel Music?" 30–33). I also draw on an unpublished aca-
     demic paper of my own (Hight, "Monochromatic Christian Music
     Industry").

16   Church, "Accommodation and Liberation of Women in the Church
     of God in Christ," 85–88.

17   "Michelle Shocked—Yes God Is Real—michelleshocked.com"
     (Video, 2007), http://www.youtube.com/watch?v=xJq11taAJgY
     (accessed January 14, 2010).

Chapter 5: Mary Gauthier

1 O'Connor, "A Good Man Is Hard to Find," 137–53. Like the speaker in "Snakebit," the Misfit in O'Connor's short story feels cursed—doomed to be punished worse than he deserves, doomed to never have his questions answered, and incapable of faith or goodness. When he is reminded of all that by a desperately chattering grandmother, he lashes out in a primal attack, lodging three bullets in her chest at point-blank range.

2 O'Connor, *Mystery and Manners*, 47.

3 O'Connor, *Mystery and Manners*, 50.

4 Malone, *Don't Get Above Your Raisin'*, 119.

5 Barker and Taylor, *Faking It*, 129.

6 Swora, "Rhetoric of Transformation in the Healing of Alcoholism," 188–89.

7 Bynum, *Fragmentation and Redemption*, 137.

8 Petroff, "Medieval Women Visionaries," 35.

9 It is no accident that "The Foundling" does not reveal the gender of its subject. "'The Foundling' is intentionally genderless," Gauthier explains. "It's not a foundling *he* or a foundling *she*—it's just a foundling. . . . I wanted to try to connect with men as well as women."

10 Mary Gauthier, liner notes, *The Foundling*.

Chapter 6: Ruthie Foster

1 Foster retold the story in a similar way during one of our subsequent interviews: "Yeah, it was definitely my mother. I guess she got tired of me just playing guitar. I'd come in from school—this is early on, junior high or so—and I'd pick up the guitar and that's where I'd be, in my room playing guitar. And I think she just got tired of hearing that one day and came in and she burst through the door and she said, 'Girl, just open your mouth and sing. You're sitting there playing, but I don't hear no voice coming out of this room.'"

2 Ruthie Foster, liner notes, *Full Circle*.

3 Werner, *Change Is Gonna Come*, 48.

4 A book that Foster had been reading, and recommended to me, was Lashonda Katrice Barnett's collection of interviews *I Got Thunder*.

5 Spencer, *Protest and Praise*, 8.

6 Heilbut, *Gospel Sound*, xvi.

Chapter 7: Elizabeth Cook

1 Mazor, *Meeting Jimmie Rodgers*, 11. Mazor's writing about Jimmie Rodgers helped me wrap my head around the arc of Cook's journey and inspired this chapter's title.
2 Alden, "Everyday Sunshine," 50.
3 Braddock, *Down in Orburndale*, 13–14.
4 Elizabeth Cook, liner notes, *Welder*.
5 Bufwack and Oermann, *Finding Her Voice*, 480–81.
6 Malone, *Don't Get Above Your Raisin'*, 254.
7 Malone, *Don't Get Above Your Raisin*, 256.
8 Malone, *Don't Get Above Your Raisin*, 258.
9 Bufwack and Oermann, *Finding Her Voice*, 490.
10 Diane Pecknold discusses the 1960s transition during which country's always engaged, once rural-now urban audience came to be viewed as something of a marketable mass: "Country music listeners had themselves become a commodity, and their identity as consumers threatened to overwhelm their identity as an audience" (*Selling Sound*, 167).
11 Peterson, *Creating Country Music*, 150–54.
12 Fillingim, "Oft Made to Wonder," 49.
13 Sizer, *Gospel Hymns and Social Religion*, 30.

Chapter 8: Abigail Washburn

1 Heilbut, *Gospel Sound*, xv.
2 Cantwell, *When We Were Good*, 325–26.
3 Casebolt and Niekro, "Some UUs Are More U than U," 235.
4 Washburn's present-day perspectives, particularly her view of human beings as profoundly flexible and continually reshaped by all manner of relationships, seem to draw some on Riker's thought. Witness this brief excerpt from one of his books: "We are webs—networks of inter-related needs, emotions, capacities, and character traits—and are inextricably interwoven with the networks of society, culture, and nature" (*Human Excellence and an Ecological Conception of the Psyche*, 150).

Conclusion

1 John Morthland, liner notes, Lucinda Williams, *Happy Woman Blues*.

Bibliography

Alden, Grant. "Buddy Miller: A Disquisition on the Centrality of Love and Faith in the Music of Buddy Miller and the Several Other Reasons He Is Artist of the Decade. And Stuff." *No Depression*, May-June 2008.

———. "Everyday Sunshine: Elizabeth Cook Isn't (Yet) a Country Star, But She's on the Right Path." *No Depression*, May–June 2007.

Barker, Hugh, and Yuval Taylor. *Faking It: The Quest for Authenticity in Popular Music*. New York: Norton, 2007.

Barnett, Lashonda Katrice, ed. *I Got Thunder: Black Women Songwriters on Their Craft*. New York: Thunder's Mouth, 2007.

Braddock, Bobby. *Down in Orburndale: A Songwriter's Youth in Old Florida*. Baton Rouge: Louisiana State University Press, 2007.

Bufwack, Mary A., and Robert K. Oermann. *Finding Her Voice: Women in Country Music 1800–2000*. Nashville: Country Music Foundation Press and Vanderbilt University Press, 2003.

Bynum, Caroline Walker. *Fragmentation and Redemption: Essays on Gender and the Human Body in Medieval Religion*. New York: Zone, 1991.

Cantwell, Robert. *When We Were Good: The Folk Revival.* Cambridge, Mass.: Harvard University Press, 1996.

Casebolt, James, and Tiffany Niekro. "Some UUs Are More U Than U: Theological Self-Descriptors Chosen by Unitarian Universalists." *Review of Religious Research* 46 (2005): 235–42.

Casmier, Stephen J., and Donald H. Matthews. "Why Scatting Is Like Speaking in Tongues: Post-Modern Reflections on Jazz, Pentecostalism and 'Africomysticism.'" *Literature and Theology* 13 (1999): 166–76.

Church, H. Carlyle, Jr. "The Accommodation and Liberation of Women in the Church of God in Christ." *Journal of Religious Thought* 52/53, no. 2/1 (1996): 77–90.

Cohen, Jason. "Shocking: One of Texas' Most Famous Folkies Finds a New Record Label—And Faith." *Texas Monthly*, November 26, 1996.

Cone, James H. *The Spirituals and the Blues.* New York: Seabury Press, 1972.

Cox, Harvey. *Fire from Heaven: The Rise of Pentecostal Spirituality and the Reshaping of Religion in the Twenty-First Century.* Reading, Mass.: Addison-Wesley, 1995.

Dark, David. *Everyday Apocalypse: The Sacred Revealed in Radiohead, The Simpsons, and Other Pop Culture Icons.* Grand Rapids: Brazos, 2002.

Davis, Angela Y. *Blues Legacies and Black Feminism: Gertrude "Ma" Rainey, Bessie Smith, and Billie Holiday.* New York: Pantheon, 1998.

Dickens, Hazel, and Bill C. Malone. *Working Girl Blues: The Life & Music of Hazel Dickens.* Urbana: University of Illinois Press, 2008.

Ellison, Curtis W. "Keeping Faith: Evangelical Performance in Country Music." In *Reading Country Music: Steel Guitars, Opry Stars, and Honky-Tonk Bars*, edited by Cecilia Tichi, 121–52. Durham, N.C.: Duke University Press, 1998.

Epstein, Heidi. *Melting the Venusberg: A Feminist Theology of Music.* New York: Continuum, 2004.

Farley, Wendy. *The Wounding and Healing of Desire: Weaving Heaven and Earth.* Louisville, Ky.: Westminster John Knox, 2005.

Fillingim, David. "Oft Made to Wonder: Southern Gospel Music as Theodicy." In *More Than Precious Memories: The Rhetoric of Southern Gospel Music*, edited by Michael P. Graves and David Fillingim, 43–56. Macon, Ga.: Mercer University Press, 2004.

———. *Redneck Liberation: Country Music as Theology*. Macon, Ga.: Mercer University Press, 2003.

Floyd-Thomas, Stacey M. *Mining the Motherlode: Methods in Womanist Ethics*. Cleveland, Ohio: Pilgrim Press, 2006.

Frank, Thomas. "Pop Music in the Shadow of Irony." *Harper's Magazine*, March 1998.

Frey, Darcy. "Lucinda Williams Is in Pain." *New York Times Magazine*, September 14, 1997.

Friskics-Warren, Bill. *I'll Take You There: Pop Music and the Urge for Transcendence*. New York: Continuum, 2005.

Gilmour, Michael J. "Radios in Religious Studies Departments: Preliminary Reflections on the Study of Religion in Popular Music." In *Call Me the Seeker: Listening to Religion in Popular Music*, edited by Michael J. Gilmour, vii–x. New York: Continuum, 2005.

Goff, James R. *Close Harmony: A History of Southern Gospel*. Chapel Hill: University of North Carolina Press, 2002.

Greig, Charlotte. "Female Identity and the Woman Songwriter." In *Sexing the Groove: Popular Music and Gender*, edited by Sheila Whiteley, 168–77. London: Routledge, 1997.

Guralnick, Peter. *Feel Like Going Home: Portraits in Blues and Rock 'n' Roll*. New York: Back Bay, 1999.

———. *Sweet Soul Music, Rhythm and Blues and the Southern Dream of Freedom*. Boston: Back Bay, 1999.

Heilbut, Anthony. *The Gospel Sound: Good News and Bad Times*. Rev. ed. New York: Limelight, 2002.

Hight, Jewly. "The Monochromatic Christian Music Industry." Unpublished paper, Vanderbilt University Divinity School, 2007.

Isasi-Díaz, Ada María. *Mujerista Theology*. Maryknoll, N.Y.: Orbis, 1997.

Jones, Arthur C. *Wade in the Water: The Wisdom of the Spirituals*. Eugene, Ore.: Wipf & Stock, 2003.

Jones, Lisa C. "Are Whites Taking Gospel Music?" *Ebony*, July 1995.

Kaufman, Gordon D. *Theology For a Nuclear Age*. Manchester, UK: Manchester University Press, 1985.

L'Engle, Madeleine. *Walking on Water: Reflections on Faith and Art*. 1980. Reprint, New York: North Point Press, 1995.

Malone, Bill C. *Country Music U.S.A.* Rev. ed. Austin: University of Texas Press, 1985.

———. *Don't Get Above Your Raisin': Country Music and the Southern Working Class*. Urbana: University of Illinois Press, 2002.

Malone, Bill C., and David Stricklin. *Southern Music/American Music*. Lexington: University Press of Kentucky, 2003.

Marcus, Greil. *Mystery Train: Images of America in Rock 'n' Roll Music*. New York: E.P. Dutton, 1976.

———. *The Old, Weird America: The World of Bob Dylan's Basement Tapes*. New York: Picador USA, 1997.

Mazor, Barry. *Meeting Jimmie Rodgers: How America's Original Roots Music Hero Changed the Pop Sounds of a Century*. Oxford: Oxford University Press, 2009.

McClure, John S. "The Theosymbolic Code." In *The Four Codes of Preaching: Rhetorical Strategies*, 93–135. Louisville, Ky.: Westminster John Knox, 2003.

McCusker, Kristine M., and Diane Pecknold, eds. *A Boy Named Sue: Gender and Country Music*. Jackson: University of Mississippi Press, 2004.

McFague, Sallie. *Models of God: Theology for an Ecological, Nuclear Age*. Philadelphia: Fortress, 1987.

Miller, Karl Hagstrom. *Segregating Sound: Inventing Folk and Pop Music in the Age of Jim Crow*. Durham, N.C.: Duke University Press, 2010.

Ochs, Meredith. "Sweet Relief: An Interview with Victoria Williams." *Salon.com*, January 14, 1998. http://www.salon.com/music/int/1998/01/14int.html (accessed September 27, 2009).

O'Connor, Flannery. "A Good Man Is Hard to Find." In *Flannery O'Connor: Collected Works*, 137–53. New York: Library of America, 1988.

———. "Some Aspects of the Grotesque in Southern Fiction." In

Mystery and Manners: Occasional Prose. Edited by Sally and Robert Fitzgerald, 36–50. 1969. Reprint, New York: Noonday Press, 1997.

————. "Wise Blood." In *Flannery O'Connor: Collected Works*, 1–131. New York: Library of America, 1988.

Patoski, Joe Nick. *Willie Nelson: An Epic Life.* New York: Back Bay, 2008.

Pecknold, Diane. "Selling Out or Buying In? Alt.Country's Cultural Politics of Commercialism." In *Old Roots New Routes: The Cultural Politics of Alt.Country Music*, edited by Pamela Fox and Barbara Ching, 28–50. Ann Arbor: University of Michigan Press, 2008.

————. *The Selling Sound: The Rise of the Country Music Industry.* Durham, N.C.: Duke University Press, 2007.

Peterson, Richard A. *Creating Country Music: Fabricating Authenticity.* Chicago: University of Chicago Press, 1997.

Petroff, Elizabeth. "Medieval Women Visionaries: Seven Stages to Power." *Frontiers: A Journal of Women Studies* 3 (1978): 34–45.

Petrusich, Amanda. *It Still Moves: Lost Songs, Lost Highways and the Search for the Next American Music.* New York: Faber & Faber, 2008.

Powell, Mark Alan. *Encyclopedia of Contemporary Christian Music.* Peabody, Mass.: Hendrickson, 2002.

Riker, John. *Human Excellence and an Ecological Conception of the Psyche.* Albany: State University of New York Press, 1991.

Russell, Tony. *Blacks, Whites and Blues.* New York: Stein & Day, 1970.

Sample, Tex. *White Soul: Country Music, the Church and Working Americans.* Nashville: Abingdon, 1996.

Schlansky, Evan. "Lucinda Williams: On Record, Extended and Uncut." *American Songwriter*, October 29, 2008. http://www.americansongwriter.com/2008/10/lucinda-williams-on-record-extended-and-uncut/ (accessed July 3, 2010).

Sizer, Sandra S. *Gospel Hymns and Social Religion: The Rhetoric of Nineteenth-Century Revivalism.* Philadelphia: Temple University, 1978.

Spencer, Jon Michael. *Protest and Praise: Sacred Music of Black Religion*. Minneapolis: Fortress, 1990.

Swora, Maria Gabrielle. "The Rhetoric of Transformation in the Healing of Alcoholism: The Twelve Steps of Alcoholics Anonymous." *Mental Health, Religion & Culture* 7 (2004): 187–209.

Wald, Gayle F. *Shout, Sister, Shout! The Untold Story of Rock-and-Roll Trailblazer Sister Rosetta Tharpe*. Boston: Beacon, 2007.

Welch, Sharon D. "Virtuosity." In *Sweet Dreams in America: Making Ethics and Spirituality Work*, 1–26. New York: Routledge, 1999.

Welty, Eudora. *One Writer's Beginnings*. New York: Warner, 1984.

Werner, Craig. *A Change Is Gonna Come: Music, Race & the Soul of America*. New York: Plume, 1999.

Williams, Miller. "Notes in a Minister's Hymnbook." In *Halfway from Hoxie: New & Selected Poems*, 15–16. Baton Rouge: Louisiana State University, 1977.

Williams, Victoria. *Happy Come Home*. VHS. Filmed by Chris Hegedus and D. A. Pennebaker. New York: Pennebaker Associates & Rough Trade, 1987.

Wolfe, Charles K., and James E. Akenson, eds. *The Women of Country Music: A Reader*. Lexington: University Press of Kentucky, 2003.

General Index

Index of Songs

✳ ✳ ✳